COLLECTING CHRONICLES,
MAINTAINING TRADITION,
AND
PRESERVING
ACTS OF DISCIPLES

The Historical Series of the Reformed Church in America
No. 105

COLLECTING CHRONICLES, MAINTAINING TRADITION, AND PRESERVING ACTS OF DISCIPLES

Essays in Honor of Russell L. Gasero

James Hart Brumm, ed.

Reformed Church Press
Grand Rapids, Michigan

© 2022 Reformed Church Press
All rights reserved

ISBN: 978-1-950572-26-7

Library of Congress Control Number: 2022936451

For Maria Gasero,

who has faithfully accompanied her husband
and countless boxes of manuscripts around the country
for God and Christ's Church

The Historical Series of the Reformed Church in America

The series was inaugurated in 1968 by the General Synod of the Reformed Church in America acting through the Commission on History to communicate the church's heritage and collective memory and to reflect on our identity and mission, encouraging historical scholarship which informs both church and academy.

www.rca.org/series

General Editor
James Hart Brumm, MDiv, MPhil
   New Brunswick Theological Seminary

Managing Editor
Matthew Gasero
   Digital Archivist, Reformed Church in America

Production Editor
Russell L. Gasero
   Archivist Emeritus, Reformed Church in America
   Wit & Intellect Publishing LLC

Cover Design
Wit & Intellect Publishing LLC

General Editor Emeritus
Donald J. Bruggink, PhD, DD
   Van Raalte Institute, Hope College

Commission on History
   Corstain DeVos, MDiv, Churchville, PA
   Lynn Japinga, PhD, Hope College
   Daniel Meeeter, PhD, New Paltz, NY
   Steven Pierce, DMin, Grand Rapids, MI
   Doug Shepler, MDiv, New Brunswick, NJ
   David Zomer, MDiv, Kalamazoo, MI

Contents

	Preface	ix
	James Hart Brumm	
	Contributors	xiii
	Sponsors	xvii
	Foreward	
	Steven D. Pierce	xix
1	And God Remembered: Some Theology for the Archives	
	Daniel Meeter	1
2	Wondrous Growth: A Sermon on Matthew 13:31-32 for the First Reformed Church of New Brunswick, New Jersey	
	Hartmut Kramer-Mills	9
3	The First Professorial Certificates in the Reformed Church in America	
	John W. Coakley	25
4	A Case Study in Archival Use: The Writing of a Prologue to a History of the Dutch American Historical Commission	
	Donald J. Bruggink	33
5	Uncovering and Interpreting the Hidden Stories: The Reverend James Murphy	
	Renée S. House	47
6	Ecclesiastical Membership of Reformed Church Ministers	
	Matthew J. van Maastricht	69
7	Kings and Consistories and Charters, Oh My!: A Case Study in Keeping and Reading Historical Documents	
	James Hart Brumm	85

8	Prophetic Teachers: Reflections on the Office of the General Synod Professor in the Reformed Church in America	
	Micah L. McCreary	99
9	When the Bonds Break: Reflections on the History of Divorce in the RCA	
	Lynn Japinga	113
10	"[T]he Everlasting Gospel should be preached to them in their own language": The First Transition from Dutch to English in the Dutch Reformed Congregations of North America	
	Dirk Mouw	135
11	Saving the Stories of RCA Women: A Tribute to Russell Gasero	
	Mary L. Kansfield	151
12	Found in the Archives: Notes from Friends	171
	Publications of the Historical Series	175
	Scripture Index	195
	Subject Index	197

Preface

James Hart Brumm

In another part of my life, I teach people about worship. One of the things that I often teach my worship students—something I learned from Howard Hageman—is that, since liturgy comes from two Greek words that mean "public" and "working," or, literally, "what the people do," there is no such thing as a "non-liturgical" church. Once people get together, even if all they do is sit silently, as some Quakers might do, they are living out a liturgy.

By that same kind of logic, I submit that there is no such thing as an organization without an archives'. The word "archives," according to the *Cambridge Dictionary*, means "a place where historical records are kept."[1] Once people within an organization have passed their first note or stuck their first receipt in a drawer, that organization has an archives'. Once Jonas Michaelius, freshly arrived in New Amsterdam in April of 1628, signed for the key to whatever rooms were being provided for his family, the Reformed Protestant Dutch Church in the City of

---

[1] "Archives" in *Cambridge Dictionary* online. https://dictionary.cambridge.org/us/dictionary/english/archive. Accessed 23 August 2021.

New York—and, by extension, the Reformed Church in America—had an archives'.

Now, any of us who have kept receipts in a drawer to be organized later or shoved letters one after another into a file, promising ourselves we'd organize them someday, knows there is a huge difference between an archives' and a well-run and useful archives. The Archives of the Reformed Church in America spent years shoved into sundry corners of church offices and, no doubt, under the beds of synod and coetus clerks before finally passing into the care of the Collegiate Church in New York, because the RCA had no office space of its own. With the construction of Gardner A. Sage Library at New Brunswick Theological Seminary in 1875, the denominational archives came to the Seminary, and specifically to a fireproof closet in Sage. Members of the Library staff and the Seminary faculty looked after the Archives as best they could, along with looking after the school's own archives and, eventually, the Bussing Museum of missionary objects. Unfortunately, when well-meaning but busy people look out for something like that in their spare time, it is often not well-kept.

Fortunately, in 1978, the Commission on History made a successful argument that professional archival maintenance was required. Even more fortunately, Russell Gasero, a child of the RCA and a talented archivist, answered the call to serve as the first person in that role. He took on this task when good intentions, benign neglect, and entropy had a head start of three-and-a-half centuries. Over the next four decades, he diligently and professionally organized all of those collected records and collected more, from every corner of the denomination, from denominational offices and foreign missions. He built relationships with global scholars and local consistories, with other archivists and women's guilds, preserving records and recording stories, making these miles of records into an easily accessible resource that promotes sacred and secular needs of the entire church. Along the way, as one of the staff members who kept showing up, year after year, as others came and went, he also became the living memory of the RCA, the one who knew what had happened because he was there, or how to find out what had happened because he cataloged the documents.

At the same time, Russ inspired a couple of generations of scholars, pastors, and storytellers that the story of the RCA was something worth studying and sharing. He helped us be better at sharing those stories and helped us imagine new ways to tell them. Reflecting theologically and waxing whimsically, he would refer to the place he worked as "The Office of Chronicle Collection, Tradition Maintenance, and Preservation of the Acts of Disciples"—and that's where we get the title of this book. Together with the Commission on History, he gave the church tools to understand its past to better grow into its future.

This festschrift includes essays by many of those scholars and storytellers whom Russ has inspired, enlightened, and just plain welcomed over the years. The first two reflect theologically on memory and what knowing our history can help us do. The next five show different things we can learn and share by paying careful attention to the records we save, not as quaint historical curiosities, but as keys to understanding the present and future. The final four essays were all studies made possible by the RCA Archives and records that Russ has made accessible. These collected stories, by women and men of various ages and backgrounds, living in various places in North America, deal with local church transformation, the relationship of pastors and congregations, property management, church order, theological education, divorce, human sexuality, the place of women, demographic shifts, racism, sexism, and fear of change. There are also some memories and reminiscences from people who have been literally and metaphorically welcomed into the Archives over the years.

Many thanks are due the sponsors and supporters of this work, including the Commission on History—it is never easy working on a secret volume in the *Historical Series*, and many of us have learned it is difficult to do any research at all during the recent pandemic. Many thanks to Cathy Proctor, Vice President for Advancement at New Brunswick Theological Seminary, for engineering the fundraising scheme to help support this work. Last, but not least, special kudos to Matthew Gasero and the RCA Archives, for everything he has done to facilitate this effort and so many others in the *Historical Series*.

Neither this book nor even a volume matching the breadth and depth of the holdings in the RCA Archives could properly express the respect, affection, and gratitude so many of us have for the first professional archivist of the RCA: our colleague and friend, Russell. We can only hope that this volume in his honor can add to the scholarship and understanding of the church as a sign of the many ways he has already done so and likely will in the future.

Soli Deo Gloria!
James Hart Brumm
August, 2021

Contributors

Donald J. Bruggink is a Senior Research Fellow at the Van Raalte Institute at Hope College in Holland, Michigan, James A.H. Cornell Professor, Emeritus, of Historical Theology at Western Theological Seminary in Holland, Michigan, a General Synod Professor, Emeritus, of the Reformed Church in America, and General Editor, Emeritus, of the *Historical Series of the Reformed Church in America*, where he shepherded the first ninety-five volumes of the *Series* to publication. An expert on religious architecture as well as church history, he co-authored, with Carl H. Droppers, *Christ and Architecture: Building Presbyterian/Reformed Churches* (Eerdmans, 1965).

James Hart Brumm is the Director of the Reformed Church Center and the Theological Writing Center at New Brunswick Theological Seminary in New Brunswick, New Jersey, and General Editor of this *Series*. He is the author and editor of volumes on Reformed Church History, multiple liturgical resources, and approximately 350 hymns.

John W. Coakley is L. Russell Feakes Memorial Professor of Church History, Emeritus, at New Brunswick Theological Seminary and a General Synod Professor Emeritus of the Reformed Church in America. He is the author of multiple articles, essays, and book reviews, and the editor or author of six books, including *New Brunswick Theological Seminary: An Illustrated History, 1784-2014* (Eerdmans, 2014).

Renée S. House is pastor and teacher of Old Dutch Reformed Church in Kingston, New York, and a former General Synod Professor of the Reformed Church in America. She has a Ph.D. in Christian Education from Princeton Theological Seminary in Princeton, New Jersey, and is the author and editor of various books, articles, and essays.

Lynn Japinga is Professor of Religion at Hope College and the author of *Loyalty and Loss: The Reformed Church in America, 1945-1994* (Eerdmans, 2013). She holds a Ph.D. in history from Union Theological Seminary in New York.

Mary Kansfield is an independent scholar. She is the author of *An American Understanding of English Education: A Manual for American Visitors to England* (Pickwick Publications, 1992). She is also the author of *Letters to Hazel: Ministry within the Woman's Board of Foreign Missions of the Reformed Church in America* (Eerdmans, 2004) and a committed advocate for preserving the stories and history of RCA women.

Hartmut Kramer-Mills is the current pastor of the Spotswood Reformed Church in Spotswood, New Jersey. He taught church history at Erfurt College, now Erfurt University, in Germany and served congregations in Germany and the United States. He received his Th.D. from Greifswald University in Germany and is married to Susan Kramer-Mills. They have two grown children, Lillian and Allison.

Micah L. McCreary is President and John Henry Livingston Professor of Theology at New Brunswick Theological Seminary. He received his Ph.D. in Psychology from Virginia Commonwealth University and is the author of numerous articles, essays, and books.

Daniel Meeter served five congregations in the Reformed Church in America and taught part-time at New Brunswick Theological Seminary. He earned his Ph.D. from Drew University. His wife, Rev. Melody Takken

Meeter, worked at the Reformed Church Archives during 1978 and 1979. He and Melody live in New Paltz, New York, where they help the local pastors and churches.

Dirk Mouw is a historian of early America, specializing in Dutch religion and culture in the pre-Revolutionary period, and a historical translator. Mouw earned his Ph.D. at the University of Iowa and is a fellow of the Reformed Church Center at New Brunswick Theological Seminary and of the New Netherland Institute.

Steven D. Pierce is Senior Minister of Central Reformed Church, Grand Rapids, Michigan, and moderator of the Commission on History of the Reformed Church in America. He holds a D. Min. from Western Theological Seminary.

Matthew J. van Maastricht is the pastor of the Altamont Reformed Church in Altamont, New York, an adjunct instructor and Fellow of the Reformed Church Center at New Brunswick Theological Seminary, and a Ph. D. candidate at the Vrije Universiteit Amsterdam.

Sponsors

In over four decades of ministry to the RCA, Russell Gasero has made many friends and earned the respect of people from all over the church and beyond. Many of those people have supported the cost of this volume as sponsors, and we gratefully recognize them here.

Eddy Alemán
David Alexander
Benjamin Alicea
David R. Armstrong
Laurel Auchampaugh
Michael S. Bos
David Brechter
James Brownson
Kathleen and James Hart Brumm
Sally Ann Castle
Alan Delozier

Phil and Stephanie Doeschot
Dutch Cousins of Kentucky
Stephen Eckert
Leah Ennis
Joanne Fernandez
Laura Giacobbe
Robert L. Gram
George and Juel Grevenstuk
Robert J. Hoeksema
Elizabeth Johnson and Peter Paulsen
David Jones

Earl and Nella Kennedy
Rui Kohiyama
Bruce G. Laverman
Carolyn Leonard
Ronald D. Lokhorst
Patrick Milas
Nelson R. Murphy
Michelle Novak
Mark and Pamela Pater-Ennis
Deborah M. Pierce
Okke Postma
Cathy Proctor
Roland and Una Ratmeyer
Reformed Church in America Archives

Tomoe Scanlan
Lynne Stenberg
Robin Suydam
Cora Taitt
Philip Tanis
Christina Tazelaar
Norman Tellier
Douglas Van Aartsen
Albert Vander Meer
Harold S. Vogelaar
Rett Zabriskie
David W. Zomer

Foreword

Steven D. Pierce

When I think of Russell Louis Gasero, so many thoughts dance across my mind. He's gentle, unassuming, easy-going, and fun-loving. As a committed husband and loving father, his priorities haven't changed. He's a strategic thinker, a commended academic, a well-known researcher, and has partnered with countless scholars, pastors, missionaries, and archivists from across the United States and around the world. He is a friend to many and has mentored many aspiring researchers, all of whom have marveled at his brilliance and visionary leadership. But above all, his dedication and loyalty to Christ through the ministry and mission of the Reformed Church in America will go unmatched for years to come.

Here are a few things you should know about Russ...

His roots in the Reformed Church run deep. Russ grew up in the Steinway Reformed Church in Queens, New York, and, in 1973, he received a Bachelor of Arts degree from Hope College in Holland, Michigan. He worked in the Archives of the United Nations in New

York City for five years, doing distinguished work in one of the world's elite archival programs. In 1977, the Commission on History, seeking to preserve the records of the Reformed Church in America, received the approval of the General Synod, our highest assembly, to begin a professionally managed archival program and then proceeded to recruit and hire Russ to be its first archivist.

In the ensuing forty-two years, Russ built the Archives from a collection of documents kept in closets at the New Brunswick Theological Seminary's Gardner A. Sage Library into a comprehensive, fully accessible collection of documents, video media, and other artifacts, including over one-half mile of paper records stored in New Brunswick, New Jersey, and Grand Rapids, Michigan, collecting and preserving the acts of apostles who make up the Reformed Church in America. While serving as archivist, he earned a Master's degree from the Graduate School of Education at Rutgers University and had continuously partnered with denominational staff, classes, synods, and consistories to faithfully preserve and catalog their records, saving the Reformed Church in America and its agencies hundreds of thousands of dollars in legal expenses—and even saving the acronym "RCA" for us— through timely accession of needed records that were anywhere from months to centuries-old, and saving congregations untold thousands of dollars through such storage.

As a visionary leader, Russ partnered with RCA colleges to create internship opportunities, partnered with denominational staff members to create volunteer service opportunities, and visited scores of congregations and church groups, expanding the awareness of the whole church in the preservation of its history. Distinguishing himself in the membership and leadership of professional groups and historical associations, including the Society of American Archivists, the Mid-Atlantic Regional Archives Conference, the American Association for State and Local History, and the Dutch Cousins, Russ has helped to secure a bright future for professional archival work in the Reformed Church in America and all of North America.

Russ served the Commission on History not only as consultant but as staff and as production editor for *The Historical Series of the Reformed Church in America*, helping make possible over one hundred volumes in that series which enlighten and edify the entire church and scholars far beyond us. He also worked with the faculty and administration of New Brunswick Theological Seminary to create a partnership with the Reformed Church Center, whereby scholarship is expanded, local congregations and classes are supported in their work, and a ten-year grant program has been established that is helping the Archives expand its work, digitizing records to make them more easily accessible well into the future.

No one in the history of the Reformed Church in America has attended more consecutive General Synods than Russ. Often, he drove countless items across the country to these meetings not only for the Office of Historical Services and *The Historical Series of the Reformed Church in America* but also for other programs and agencies of the church. His wife, Maria, joined him for many of these trips and would pitch in as volunteer labor. *Thank you, Maria!*

Russ was a supportive presence to his staff colleagues for decades and became the living institutional memory of the Reformed Church in America, the one person we could all count on to keep us honest. On January 29, 2021, the Commission on History, in a spirit of thanksgiving and celebration, declared Russell L. Gasero to be archivist emeritus of the Reformed Church in America. It was the least we could do for someone who gave us his very best, at all times and in all circumstances—both good and bad.

Festschrift is a term borrowed from the German language that can mean "celebration writing." It's fitting that a collection of essays in Russ's honor should be made available. For what's left to do but celebrate a man gifted with limitless insight and who has given us so much and expected so little in return? Nothing...*except to read this book!*

Congratulations, Russ!

Steven D. Pierce

CHAPTER 1

And God Remembered: Some Theology for the Archives

Daniel Meeter

Remembering

"And God remembered Noah" (Genesis 8:1). That short sentence is the dramatic center of the Flood story and the hinge on which the story turns from judgment to renewal. Of course, the image of "God remembering" rubs against our doctrine of God's omniscience—that God knows everything all the time anyway. So we could chalk the image up to anthropomorphism, but then every last word in all of theology is ultimately anthropomorphic. Or we could give room to the image and let it speak. When "God remembers," that means more than a static omniscience. It means that God engages our history and experience with attention and intention. It means the good news of God turning to us and entering our lives and moving and going with us. It means that God is not an "unmoved mover."

Just as God remembered Noah, so "God remembered Abraham," and delivered Lot from the overthrow of Sodom (Genesis 19:29). "God remembered Rachel" and opened her womb (Genesis 30:25). "God remembered his covenant with Abraham, Isaac, and Jacob" when God heard the groaning of the Children of Israel in Egypt (Exodus 2:24). In each case, God's remembering is not just God recalling the past. It is not mere reminiscing—it is purposeful. God's remembering is about the past, but it's for the future. God's remembering is the bridge from God's actions in the past to God's actions in the future.

God is free to act however God wants to in our time and space. Indeed, God is absolutely free, and the future is absolutely open to God. Only God is absolutely free. Yet God has shared some measure of God's unique freedom with the world that God made. In biblical religion, the future is not inevitable, and the future is not compelled by the past. There is no Fate nor Karma, nor is time circular. The world is given a freedom that the other ancient religions did not imagine. In biblical religion, it is only under the bondage and delusion of human sin that the past controls the future, and salvation's purpose is to set us free from that so that we might share in the freedom of God.

But while God is absolutely free, it's also true that God exercises that absolute freedom in faithfulness. God self-limits God's choices by being true and faithful to God's gracious commitments in the past. When the Flood had receded, and God set the bow in the clouds, God said to Noah, "I will remember my covenant" (Genesis 9:15). This shows us that the image of "God remembering" is an image of the unity of God's faithfulness and God's freedom.

In biblical religion, God's remembering is the ground of our future hope. The doctrine of eternal life, for example, which gradually develops from faint glimmers to a powerful promise, is grounded not on Hellenistic ideas of the native immortality of the soul but on the Hebrew vision that God remembers us beyond our deaths. Even the thief on the cross bears witness to this when he says, "Jesus, remember me when you come into your kingdom"—which kingdom will have to be on the other side of their deaths. This version of life beyond death is illustrated in the raising of Lazarus, which is clearly a resurrection of the body rather than the immortality of the soul, when Our Lord calls him back by name. Lazarus, even while dead, is made able, by that call, to recognize the voice of the Lord and obey it. The resurrection is manifestly a "re-calling," a bringing of the past back into present life for freedom and faithfulness.

We Remember

As God remembers, we remember too. Because we are in God's image and are given some measure of God's freedom, we are also called to be faithful. We are called to be God's covenantal partners, and thus to remember as well. We are reminded to remember by means of the physical signs of the developing covenants—the tree in the Garden, the rainbow, circumcision, the Tabernacle—and thus to believe and act accordingly as we journey with God through our mutual history in the world.

Furthermore, our remembering is more than a "re-minding," more than reliving the past in our minds. It is also "re-calling" the past and calling it to life again in the present. We do this, for example, in the "anamnesis" of the Lord's Supper, when, in obedience to Our Lord's command, we remember him. Our remembering him does not just leave him in the past for our reminiscing or reminding, but it serves the Lord Jesus, who, in covenantal partnership with us, and through our sharing of the Holy Spirit, makes himself fully present in the words and actions—the covenantal signs—by which we remember him.

The physical signs of the covenant are not the only reminders of our mutual remembering with God. There is also the book, the scroll, the written document, which eventually became the chief sign of God's covenant with Israel. This was a unique and remarkable development within the field of world religions that a written document, modeled on the suzerainty treaties of the time and in the language of the people should be elevated to such status at the center of the cult.

The written document was a natural and necessary development in God's way with Israel. The words and actions of God's free faithfulness were written down in order to be passed along and remembered by successive generations. This has generated the peculiar character of Israelite religion as a religion of the Book. The Torah, the Book of the Law, was the covenantal sign that outlasted all the other physical signs to become the great and enduring sign of the covenant. And in every synagogue today, the most sacred space is actually a kind of sacred archive, containing written documents—Torah scrolls, which in Jewish worship are virtually sacramental. The written document is not just the means to remember the past for the present and the future—it actually brings the historic faithfulness of God into the present so that the community might be both free and faithful for the future.

The Written Record

In the popular imagination, the Law of God was first written on stone tablets by the finger of God. But actually, according to the Book of Exodus, it was first written out by Moses himself and on parchment, not stone. The story is told in chapter 24, which is as central to the Bible as it is poorly known, despite Our Lord's remembering it at the Last Supper and its being the *ur*-source of Christian worship. In the story, Moses takes a scroll and writes out from memory what God had dictated to him on the mountain. The next day he reads this out to the congregation. The people agree to it, sacrifices are made, the people are sprinkled (with blood), and the covenant with Israel is ratified and then celebrated by means of a meal with God upon the mountain—the first Lord's Supper. This covenant is the keystone covenant with Israel; it is *the* "old testament" that gives the Hebrews Scriptures its familiar Christian name.

Thereafter, as the relationship between God and Israel developed, the scroll was expanded into the larger Torah, the Pentateuch, the Books of Moses. The scroll was expanded in both directions, as it were, forwards and backward. Its forward expansion is obvious enough in the later chapters of Exodus, plus the books of Leviticus, Numbers, and Deuteronomy. It was expanded backward with chapters 1 through 19 of Exodus, plus Genesis, which were conceived as "remembering" from the perspective of Mount Sinai.

We Christians tend to read the Book of Genesis from the opposite perspective of its intention as if its greatest concern is Creation and the Fall; this is especially true of the Kuyperian tradition, with its "Creation-Fall-Redemption ground-motif." But of course, Genesis has more to say about Joseph and his brothers than about Creation and Fall, which makes sense if we read it looking backward, that is, from the perspective of Mount Sinai, of Israel just having made covenant with God. It was written, or redacted, or edited—take your pick—in order to answer the relevant questions at Sinai: "Where are you taking us? How did we get to Egypt? Who was Joseph? Why are we twelve tribes? Who are Jacob, Isaac, and Abraham? Who is this "Yahweh" God? What about the rest of the world?" As the remembering reaches further back, the stories get more abstract, until the boundary poem of Genesis 1, which celebrates a worldview in sharp contrast to that of Egypt, or Canaan, or Babylon—take your pick.

The Book of Genesis is the core archive of Israel, which is why it contains genealogies. It is the written record of the past that needs to be remembered in an active way for covenantal living into the future. By means of the record, Israel could remember that God remembers. Of course, other ancient peoples had their archives, which typically were the records of the exploits of their rulers. But how different is the archive of Israel, with its purpose to make present in every new generation the historic faithfulness and freedom of the God who makes a way with them through time as history develops?

Reading the Record as Worship

It is not a given in world religion that the scriptures are read out loud in worship—that Christians and Muslims read their scriptures as an act of worship is a gift of the Jews (although it is a poor act of worship when, in some churches, the only scripture that is read out loud are the verses selected by the preacher for his fodder). From Exodus 24 to Nehemiah 8, whenever the Torah was read out loud, the people responded liturgically, apparently instinctively, and sometimes with profound emotion and conviction, as in Nehemiah.

There are significant differences in how Jews, Christians, and Muslims read out scripture as an act of worship. For Muslims, the Holy Quran is sung out, preferably from memory, in order to express how it presents itself—as direct angelic speech, unsullied by human interaction in its composition or interpretation—and thus it may only ever be in the original Arabic of its angelic dictation. For Jews, the Torah is also sung in Hebrew as the defining conversation between God and Israel, but it is always read from the scroll, which expresses that it is a covenant. The reading functions also like a sacrament in that God and Israel meet each other in the reading, and in that meeting, Israel finds itself again as much as it finds God.

Unlike the recitation of the Holy Quran, the conversation of the Torah has a variety of genres within it. It has lengthy stories that develop characters in all their warts and failures as much as their successes. It has genealogies, census records, floor plans, dress codes, food rules, land-use laws, calendar rules, and sanitary procedures. All of these convey the investment of God in the real history of Israel. And, because this history continues forward into time, the liturgical reading is augmented by readings from the Prophets and then by rabbinic commentary in the vernacular to give the sense of the Torah, as depicted in Nehemiah 8. The interpretation of the reading becomes itself an act of worship.

So it is not coincidental that literacy should be of such relative importance to Jews, Christian, and Muslims, as full participation in the religion requires it—not just to gather the information and doctrines of the religion, but fully to participate in worship. Reading is in itself spiritual. Reading ancient records is an act of worship, and so is interpreting those records. The result is that, for Christians, reading and interpreting ancient records, including genealogies and floor plans, is something manifestly spiritual.

Missionary Correspondence

We know from several sources that the early church maintained the Jewish liturgical practice of reading the Torah and the Prophets in their worship. From the First Apology of Justin Martyr, we know that the church also began to read in the same way the "memoirs of the Apostles," that is, what we now call the New Testament. These "memoirs" became scripture not only because of their content and authorship but also because of their use that they were deemed worthy of reading in worship—the liturgical foundation of the authority of scripture is underestimated by Protestants. The effect of this, speaking anachronistically, was to raise two archival genres to the level of scripture: missionary correspondence, and to a lesser degree, congregational records.

We know about the founding of the congregation in Antioch, we know the names of its pastoral team, and we can surmise its four ethnic groups. We know about the founding of the church in Philippi, where it met, and the names of many of its members. We know about the founding and location and leadership and issues of the church in Corinth. We have letters from the missionary leaders to a whole number of their congregations. We have three letters to the missionary pastors, Timothy and Titus. The New Testament is a small church archive that has been elevated to scripture. To read the letters of missionaries is a biblical thing, to contemplate them is spiritual in character, and even to interpret them can be an act of worship.

Here we see one great distinction between Christianity and its sisters of Judaism and Islam as a consequence of the doctrine of the Holy Spirit. Our two Ecumenical Creeds remind us that upon the Ascension of Our Lord, the work of the Holy Spirit begins in the world, and the uniqueness and once-for-all-ness of the Lord Jesus are balanced by the manifold variety and constant creativity of the Holy Spirit in the ongoing history of the world. The Creeds remind us that the first work of the Spirit is the Holy Catholic Church, although the Spirit is never confined to the Church. The Holy Spirit gives form to churchly expressions in every culture and language, and from this work of the Spirit comes the critical importance of missionary correspondence and congregational records for the church.

This summer, I read Gerald De Jong's magnificent history of the Amoy mission, *The Reformed Church in China, 1842-1951*.[1] It was not only informative but spiritually inspiring and uplifting. The author interpreted the records of the mission as well as the correspondence of the missionaries, both official and personal, to reveal the real interaction of the Holy Spirit in human culture and experience, both among the missionaries and the people that they served. And, just as with the Torah, the story includes not only real persons with their successes, failures, and arguments, but also floor plans, food practices, sanitation, and clothing. The correspondence is found, of course, in the Archives, and the witness of these documents to the history of the Holy Spirit in the world makes the archives a sacred place.

Judges and Kings

Many Christians have difficulty understanding the biblical books of Judges and First and Second Kings. Why are these sordid histories in the Bible? Why did Israel include them among the class of scripture they called the Prophets? How are they the Word of God? We have an easier time with Joshua and First and Second Samuel, which tell more positive stories. We could say much about this, but the short answer is that the rebellion and disobedience of Israel is a full part of its honest conversation with God. But even in these sad and troubling stories, the grace of God is always the answer to God's righteous judgment. The value of these difficult stories is in their complex and sophisticated witness to the covenantal freedom and faithfulness of God, and although, in Israel, the books of the Prophets do not have the same status as Torah, they, too are used as scripture in the synagogue.

We know from the stories themselves that they are based on earlier written records: "The rest of the deeds of Hezekiah . . . are they not written in the Book of the Chronicles of the Kings of Judah?" (2 Kings 20:20). But these stories as they are retold in the Prophets could rise to the status of scripture because they are interpreted in their telling, and the prism of their interpretation is the covenant. That is how, in these stories of real tribes, real characters, and real communities, we can even find ourselves today.

The Reformed Church Archives contains great treasures of missionary correspondence and congregational records, and thus the

---

[1] Volume 22 in *The Historical Series of the Reformed Church in America* (Grand Rapids, MI: Eerdmans, 1992).

permanently secured memories of real persons and real communities. But an archive is more than a simple repository. An archive is also the staff that preserves and presents it, the visitors who use it, and the scholars who publish and interpret its riches. An archive is not bare records but also an interpretive community. Denominational archives make it possible for a denomination to know itself, not for mere reminiscence, but to remember, in all the rich sense of remembering, how God in both judgment and grace has journeyed with that denomination through its history in real-time.

Remembrance, Communion, and Hope

I became acquainted with the Archives of the Reformed Church in America during my years as a seminary student in the 1970s, when Russ Gasero began his remarkable career with his amazing talent for remembering. I came to the archives to learn remembrance—the active kind of remembering that I described above. I also came to them, increasingly, for communion. I began to find my own story in the accounts of others before me. I began to share in the stories of pastors and congregations, and I began to sense myself in communion with those who had gone on before me. And, ultimately, I came in hope, despite so many stories of frustration and closings and decline, because the story in a church archives is not just about human beings and their institutions, but more about the Holy Spirit who makes a way with us through history in freedom and faithfulness. That this free and faithful God remembers every pastor, every congregation, every missionary, every Sunday School teacher, every committee, every set of Consistory minutes, and even every dusty old sanctuary, and that God remembers them past their endings and our deaths, well, that is what gives me hope.

CHAPTER 2

Wondrous Growth: A Sermon on Matthew 13:31-32 for First Reformed Church of New Brunswick, New Jersey, July 30, 2017

Hartmut Kramer-Mills

Introduction

The following sermon marked my farewell from First Reformed Church after seventeen years of ministry. It had been an unusual time. The church campus included three buildings and a cemetery. The sanctuary was designed to accommodate 1,100 persons[1], but the seating capacity had been reduced to 600 after a devastating fire by arson in 1971.[2] The church's active membership fluctuated between eighty-six in 2001 and fifty-two in 2016. During the same timeframe, the average worship attendance dropped from fifty-four worshippers to twenty-four.[3]

[1] J. David Muyskens, *The Town Clock Church: History of the First Reformed Church New Brunswick, NJ* (New Brunswick, New Jersey: Published by the Consistory), 26.
[2] Muyskens, 121f. In 2000, parts of the historic archives of the church were still water and fire damaged in the basement of the education building. Russ Gasero was instrumental in guiding our Archive Team at the time so that the material could be preserved, cataloged, and then moved to the archives of the denomination.
[3] RCA Consistorial Report, Church Statistical Data, The Reformed Church in America, http://crf.rca.org/public/stats/3913/3887/210?new-starts=0, accessed September 14, 2020.

Despite its size, the congregation of First Reformed Church was very active. After much discussion in church groups and committees, members of the Women's Guild submitted an overture to the Consistory late in 2005, requesting that the church declare itself "welcoming and inclusive...regardless of our differences in understanding particular texts of the Bible" and to amend the Bylaws of the church as follows:

> Candidates for the ordained offices of the church (Deacons, Elders, Pastors) will not be discriminated against on the basis of gender, sexual orientation, age, ethnicity, or physical disability.[4]

Following a congregational meeting on the subject on November 20, 2005, the Consistory unanimously adopted the overture on December 20, 2005. After a deadline for concerns had passed without any being raised, the Consistory proceeded on January 17, 2006, with a second reading of the proposed changes to the Bylaws. With this, First Reformed Church became the first open and affirming congregation in the Classis of New Brunswick.

Other exciting ministries flourished. One of them was the interfaith work of the church. An early highlight was the dramatic reading of the Parable of the Rings from G.E. Lessing's drama *Nathan the Wise*[5] on June 2, 2002. It was conducted with members of Etz Chaim Monroe Township Jewish Center.[6]

Years of intentional interfaith relations with other houses of worship in the city of New Brunswick and the surrounding areas followed. The *Open Doors, Open Mind Program* of the United Methodist Church brought much activity to New Brunswick.[7] It introduced us to the city's largest synagogue, the Anshe Emeth Memorial Temple with Rabbi Bennett Miller, and a Muslim group from Turkey associated with an organization called Interfaith Dialogue Center, now Peace Islands Institute. During winter 2008–2009, twelve church members participated in a trip of nine days to Turkey. Our Turkish partners hosted the trip. It included visits in schools and hospitals, encounters with private families, a chamber of commerce, and visits to places

---

[4] Hartmut Kramer-Mills, Letter to The Reverend Classis of New Brunswick regarding the Consistory of First Reformed Church on Homosexuality, January 20, 2006.

[5] (Berlin, Germany: G.E. Lessing, 1779).

[6] Hartmut Kramer-Mills, From the Pastor's Desk, in The Times, Newsletter of First Reformed Church, May 2002, 1 and 7.

[7] Hartmut Kramer-Mills, Open Doors, Open Minds, in Nuts About It! The Chronicle of the People of God at First Reformed Church, December 2006, 6.

important in the history of Christianity, the Hagia Sophia, Ephesus, and the House of Mary there.[8]

Other signature activities of the small congregation followed. It continued hosting the city's Rotating Homeless Men's Shelter for two weeks every year during the winter months, staffing every night with a team of volunteers.[9] Between 2008 and 2011, the church hosted, in conjunction with the city's community kitchen Elijah's Promise and the Robert Wood Johnson University Hospital Community Health Promotion Program, a family food program in its fellowship hall. It was geared primarily toward immigrants from Central and South America. It soon fed up to sixty people.[10] The church also continued a Lunchtime Recital series that was already in place before my wife and I arrived in 2000. Each concert offered a program of chamber music followed by a free lunch hosted by a team of the church. The series was still in place in 2017.[11] And we had a very active Dutch Dancing Group.[12]

However, the life of the congregation was burdened by the historic building substance of its campus. Its maintenance was a major reason for the annual budget deficit. In addition to this, the building maintenance tied up much volunteer energy that was then lost for other forms of ministry.

Faced with these challenges, the Consistory first pursued and completed a comprehensive historic preservation project with a volume of 1.1 million dollars. A little over half of this amount came in two state grants administered by the New Jersey Historic Trust. The other part had to be covered by the church. Some came from its reserves, but

[8] Sandra Boyles, Turkey Trip – "A Hope for the Future", in Nuts about It!, February 2009, 11; Hartmut Kramer-Mills, Turkey Travelogue, in ibid., 6, as well as in the following newsletters, March 2009, 6, and May 2009, 8.

[9] See Muyskens, 143, for the beginning of the shelter in the late 1980s. The church still participated in hosting the shelter after the conclusion of my pastorate. For a late reflection on this work, see Hartmut Kramer-Mills, From Pastor's Desk, in FRC Newsletter, February 2017, 1f.

[10] Susan Kramer Mills, "House of Manna," in Nuts about It! The Chronicle of the People of God at First Reformed Church, An Open and Affirming Congregation, October 2008, 4.

[11] Benjamin Berman, "Music Notes," in Newsletter of FRC, May 2017, 2, and Hartmut Kramer-Mills, "Lunchtime Recitals as Community Event," in Newsletter of FRC, May 2017, 3. The Series was funded in part by the Middlesex County Board of Chosen Freeholders, the Middlesex County Cultural & Heritage Commission, with assistance through a grant provided by the NJ State Council on the Arts/Department of State.

[12] For a reflection on a trip of the group to Cape May where we performed at a community event, see Hartmut Kramer-Mills, "Dutch Dancers in Cape May," in Newsletter of the First Reformed Church in New Brunswick, May 2013, 2.

the larger amount had to be fundraised. For a time, the Consistory organized two fundraising teams, one for individual donors and fundraisers and one for corporate giving. The historic preservation project was completed in 2011.[13] Westfield Architects of Haddonfield, New Jersey, under the wonderful leadership of Margaret Westfield, made this possible. Numerous volunteer groups from the church, other churches within the Classis of New Brunswick, and the surrounding community were an indispensable part of this.

Parallel to the restoration of the buildings and continuing afterward, the Consistory organized a sequence of vision meetings, first on a committee level and then involving the wider congregation in the form of congregational meetings.[14] In 2009, the Consistory received permission from the Classis of New Brunswick to pursue a feasibility study to reconfigure the church's sanctuary. The goal was to create a worship space more appropriate in size to the congregation's current

---

[13] One of the bigger side projects parallel to the main body of work was the painting of the façade of the Sexton's House by student volunteers from Rutgers University, who spent many Saturdays doing this. Another side project was the removal of the large oil tank that had served the education building and the church for decades. The removal was in large part covered by a state grant.

[14] The interplay between the congregational meetings and their advisory resolutions and the meetings of the Consistory with its binding decisions was complex in these years. We pastors monitored this with the help of a review chart that was regularly updated. This document became a part of a comprehensive presentation by us pastors and other church delegates at a meeting of the Administrative Council of the Classis of New Brunswick on February 24, 2014.

needs and to devote the remainder of the space to a ministry yet to be defined. Kruhly Architects of Philadelphia was contracted to provide the study. It was presented at a congregational meeting on February 21, 2010. It showed the possibility of constructing between eight and eleven single-room apartments for permanent supportive housing in parts of the sanctuary space. This was shared at a congregational meeting on May 2, 2010.[15]

Recognizing the severity of future decisions, the Consistory then organized a sequence of additional congregational meetings to ascertain the congregation's will. The next congregational meeting followed already on February 28, 2010. It focused on establishing a community development corporation so that the church would have an organizational means to materialize the envisioned reconfiguration. The congregation endorsed the founding of its 501 (c) (3) Community Development Corporation in the third meeting on May 2, 2010. In the fourth meeting, on June 27, 2010, the Consistory and its vision team informed the congregation that the new corporation had been registered with the State of New Jersey as Town Clock Community Development Corporation (TCCDC). The congregation also learned about meetings with state and municipal representatives who encouraged the project. On October 31, 2010, TCCDC presented its selection of

---

[15] Susan Kramer-Mills, Interior Design of the Sanctuary, in *Nuts about It*, May 2010, 3. See also her subsequent reports for the Building Vision Group in the same newsletter, June and July 2010.

possible architects and service providers to the congregation. The last congregational meeting of the year was held on December 12. TCCDC announced the distribution of a questionnaire to all church members regarding a choice between two possible reconfiguration designs. The Consistory discussed the preferred design in a meeting on February 13, 2011. A week later, on February 27, 2011, a congregational meeting received the good news that Architect Jeff Venezia of Design Ideas in New Brunswick had been contracted for the project. Another week later, on March 7, our denomination's General Secretary, Rev. Wesley Granberg-Michaelson, sent a letter to the church after Laura DeVries had visited the church in mid-February as a representative of the General Synod Office. The letter stated,

> Your newest vision, to convert a portion of your worship space to low-income housing for at-risk women and children is an inspiring vision and one I want to encourage you in.[16]

Many more meetings of the congregation and the Consistory followed these beginnings. On December 31, 2014, the officials started the demolition of the sanctuary interior. Already three months earlier, in October 2014, we had reached one of the most difficult junctures of

---

[16] Wesley Granberg-Michaelson, Letter to Rev. Susan and Rev. Hartmut Kramer-Mills and brothers and sisters at First Reformed Church, March 7, 2011, in Minutes of the Consistory, the Spiritual Leaders of the First Reformed Church in New Brunswick, April 19, 2011, 7:30PM.

the demolition phase. It became clear that we could save much-needed funding if church members could remove the church pews instead of a demolition company. But the task proved to be emotionally too difficult. A group from the neighboring Suydam Street Reformed Church was kind enough to do the job for us.[17]

Already in December 2012, the pastoral relationship with my wife, Rev. Susan Kramer-Mills, was dissolved. Together, we had served First Reformed Church in a co-pastorate since the fall of 2000. Since 2004, Susan has also been the Executive Minister of the Classis of New Brunswick. Stepping down from the pastorate at First Reformed Church allowed her to develop her role as the executive director of TCCDC. The successful reconfiguration of the sanctuary became TCCDC's first project, Dina's Dwellings. It comprises ten apartments of permanent supportive housing for victims of domestic violence, women, and children. We celebrated the grand opening on February 11, 2016.[18]

In early 2017, we had led Dina's Dwellings and the congregation in its reconfigured worship space for one year—enough time to work out any of the difficulties of the start-up time. After this, I felt called to another pastorate. The sermon below was my farewell sermon to First

[17] Hartmut Kramer-Mills, "The Pews Are Gone but not the Church!" in *Newsletter* of FRC, November 2014, 6.
[18] Sherri Novack, "TCCDC Ribbon Cutting," in *Newsletter* of FRC, March 2016, 6.

16 COLLECTING CHRONICLES

Reformed Church after seventeen years of ministry there. The sanctuary was filled with the congregation and many members of the community, city hall, and the surrounding houses of worship, including members of Anshe Memorial Temple and the Turkish-American Peace Islands Institute.

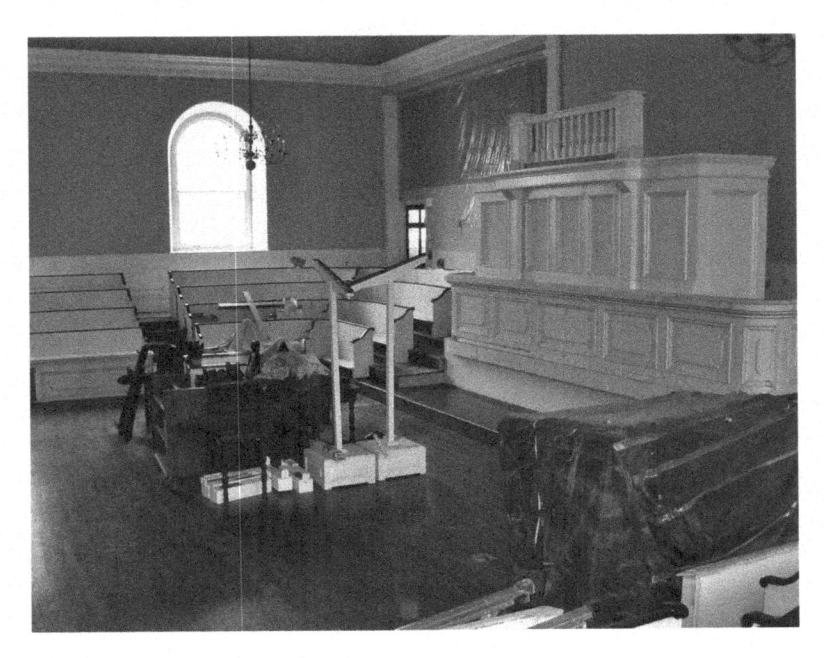

Mustard seed in Israel, March 1, 2016
Photo: Hartmut Kramer-Mills

Sermon

It is really interesting to what degree the text selections of the Lectionary are oftentimes so timely and of an actuality that has been simply amazing on more than one occasion.

Today, for this farewell sermon, the Lectionary presents us with a parable. Like a week ago, it is one of the Kingdom parables of our Lord. But it is much shorter than last week's, and in this sense, in sync with the main image it employs, the Mustard Seed.

Two short verses for a tiny seed! And yet, this is so memorable a parable because it was here that the Lord, in the words of the great American scholar Ben Witherington, created this fundamental "...contrast between small beginnings and a huge conclusion."[19]

---

[19] Ben Witherington, III, *Matthew*, Smyth & Helwys Bible Commentary 19, (Macon, Georgia: Smyth & Helwys 2006), 269.

Since we are in a year of Matthew, I will read the parable from this Gospel, chapter 10:31-32. This is on page fourteen in the church Bibles. Listen now for the Word of God in and among the Words of the Savior!

> The Lord put before them another parable: "The kingdom of heaven is like a mustard seed that someone took and sowed in his field; it is the smallest of all the seeds, but when it has grown it is the greatest of shrubs and becomes a tree, so that the birds of the air come and make nests in its branches."
>
> *Pastor*   This is the Word of the Lord.
> *People*   Thanks be to God!

What John Calvin wrote in 1553 about the so-called Kingdom Parables of the Lord is still a really good theological summary today. Calvin's words give us immediate access to the pastoral significance of all these Kingdom parables. In his Commentary on the Synoptic Gospels, Calvin wrote:

> By these parables Christ encourages his disciples not to be offended and turn back on account of the mean beginnings of the Gospel. We see how haughtily profane men despise the Gospel, and even turn it into ridicule, because the ministers by whom it is preached are men of slender reputation and of low rank; because it is not instantly received with applause by the whole world; and because the few disciples whom it does obtain are, for the most part, men of no weight or consideration, and belong to the common people. This leads weak minds to despair of its success, which they are apt to estimate from the manner of its commencement. On the contrary, the Lord opens his reign with a feeble and despicable commencement, for the express purpose, that his power may be more fully illustrated by its unexpected progress.[20]

I had to read the *entire* paragraph to you because it is so beautifully stated here what is so easy to forget in the loud environment of Central Jersey: that, in the pursuit of salvation, God oftentimes favors the *smaller* and *lower* voices, the humble beginnings; the "feeble" and even "despicable," as John Calvin put it.

But I want to caution: As encouraging as the Parable of the Mustard Seed is, it is not a parable about the Church. Therefore, this lovely,

---

[20] John Calvin, *Commentary on Matthew, Mark, Luke*, vol. 2, The AGES Digital Library Commentary (Albany, Oregon: CD-ROM AGES Software Version 1.0, 1997), 92.

short parable does not immediately entail a promise for our future as an institution. Rather, the parable tells of the Kingdom of God—the dominion of God that, according to the witness of our Lord, was beginning to unfold from the moment he was born.

The Church, of course, has always been an important tool of God in the unfolding of the Kingdom. But a tool is not identical with the desired outcome for which it is employed. It would be silly if a good carpenter like Julius[21] looked at his scroll saw and said, "My, you are already so beautiful. I will no longer use you to cut wood but rather put you on a cubby counter to look at you." Compared with God's Kingdom, the Church is but a tool—just as the scroll saw compared to some of the woodwork that Julius creates.

But this is also where the comparison stops. The scroll saw is a fairly reliable tool, and the outcome of its use fairly predictable—at least in the hands of a good carpenter who does not cut him or herself too often.

The Church, by contrast, has not always been *as reliable* as a good scroll saw might be. And I am not even speaking of the great evils like

- the Holy Inquisition,
- the Crusades,
- the role of Protestantism in Western colonialism and later imperialism,
- or even Dr. Samuel How's unfortunate address to General Synod in 1855 here in this pulpit on the subject of "Slaveholding not Sinful." How much easier is it to remember instead the visit of Bishop Desmond Tutu in 1984 here at First Reformed when he preached in this pulpit!

The sins of the worldwide church are undeniable. But let's face it:. Problems arise just as much, or even more often, at far less significant levels. Too often, we church folks resemble the first apostles whom the Lord called in the Galilee. They oftentimes had a lot of things on their minds, so, often enough, they were not able to follow what he was saying or live up to their calling. They suffered from

- doubting,
- lack of faith,

---

[21] Since leading a church with historic buildings has sometimes similarities to the work of a support group for a historic tall ship, there is always a need for good carpenters. Mr. Julius Fekete served in this function at First Reformed Church from 2000 to his death in 2018.

- and sufficient anxiety to even betray and deny the Lord in times of crisis.

The *last* of these first apostles was perhaps one of the worst: Paul, a former persecutor of Christ. Then stricken with blindness, he was entrusted with spreading God's Kingdom further than ever before.

And yet, despite the disciples' many problems, the Christian message of God's unconditional incarnation-love is today more universally known than *ever* before in the history of the Church. And some of this has to do with the mustard seed and its special qualities. It spreads and spreads and spreads—even if the tools for its distribution are not always the best.

...

Its uncanny ability to spread even under adverse circumstances has earned the mustard plant the title "noxious." For sure, the mustard seed must also have some limited useful qualities. But according to Dr. Witherington, the mustard plant was first considered in Israel, I quote, "a noxious bush that gobbles up space and will overrun other things in the garden."[22]

Witherington even refers to a Mishnah tractate, a part of the Jewish oral law that contains the warning to *never plant* a mustard seed in the garden.[23] Witherington, therefore, asks whether the Lord was perhaps *ironic* when he chose the example of the mustard seed.

Well, in contrast to first-century Galileans, we are *not* peasant farmers. We can afford to view things in a more relaxed way. "Noxious" is perhaps a wee-bit too stiff a word when we consider the actual beauty of the plant. To prove my point, there is a picture in the bulletins. But its beauty shall not deceive us regarding the unstoppable character of this plant. And we should ask ourselves where we may have experienced some of this: The Kingdom of God as an *unstoppable* force, and yet originating from very low and unexpected beginnings. Do we know something about this?

On discussing the Parable of the Mustard Seed, our Bible class earlier this month compiled several examples:

- In 2000, when Susan and I assumed the pastorate here, the three historic churches of this neighborhood—Christ Episcopal and the United Methodist Church in addition to us—had, with the exception of Susan, all foreign-born ministers. Were there

---

[22] Witherington, 268.
[23] Witherington, 268.

no American-born pastors available? There were questions even prior to my installation whether a foreigner could really understand the culture of an American church family. My colleagues across the street faced similar questions. The governing bodies of these three churches were very courageous back then—as they are now!

- Another humble beginning brought up during the Bible class was the confirmation of Walter Boyles: A non-verbal young man with Autism confessing his faith to the Elders by singing the Doxology that his team had taught him during many months of hard work. Could it have been humbler? And yet, those of us who attended the Confirmation service in 2008 are aware of what this meant.
- Someone else mentioned the capital grant we received from the State of New Jersey at a pivotal point in time when it made all the difference in whether we could continue to care for our buildings or not. The grant was highly competitive, and we did not even have a treasurer for the application! But we had Stef Beemsterboer with his hard accent, newly arrived with his wife Erie and their children from the Netherlands, a computer scientist with a savant talent but at the time not an experienced treasurer in the non-profit world. And yet, I hope that all of us who worked with Stef would agree that, somehow, there was God's guidance behind all of this—beginning with the fact that Stef and his family were from the Mother Country and ending with the observation that Stef and Erie became really good friends to many of us. But to the outside world, it was just another humble beginning.
- The same with Dina's Dwellings. I don't need to go into details here; the story is still unfolding. But for a church sometimes teetering on the abyss, it is rather remarkable how God used our congregation to address a serious problem of particular homelessness and gave us, in the course of it, an appropriately sized, fully renovated, and air-conditioned sanctuary.

The Bible class reviewed a few more of our humble beginnings, like our 2008 church trip to Turkey. But I would like to stop here because the more we continue this route, the more we may commit the already mentioned mistake of mixing up the tool with the result for which it was employed. The church is not the kingdom of God, even if it reflects some of the dynamics of that Kingdom.

...

So what do we do on a day like this? We are celebrating not only the humble beginnings but also what God has made of them beyond the institutional realm of the Church.

And in looking at all of this, we remember the mustard seed. And we wonder, perhaps, how that seed could spread so far despite everything we may have, oftentimes inadvertently, put in its way.

We pastors, the Consistory, our committees, we all have our flaws and shortcomings. Ask us to design a horse, and we will come up with a camel instead! Some would say we were a most unlikely crew to have sailed this tall ship together. And yet, we did! And it was great—not because of the things we did, but because God's mustard-seed force employed these things for purposes beyond our reach.

You can say this is looking forward and looking back. When we look forward, we look towards the final coming of Christ and the salvation of the world to come. And when we look back, we see the cloud of witnesses that have gone before us here at First Reformed Church, family names that are still remembered here, and who have left many tombstones in our graveyard:

- Abeel,
- Ackerman,
- Hardenbergh,
- Van Bunschooten,
- Scudder,
- Condict,
- Livingston,
- Ludlow,
- Heyer,
- Nevius,
- Outcalt,
- Provost,
- Shiffner,
- Suydam,
- Van Arsdalen,
- Voorhees,

to name, almost randomly, just a few of the many, many ancestors in the faith who have served as members of this church family before us.

The list reflects my work with the cemetery, as well as the families for which I have most often received genealogical inquiries in the years past. As such, this list is, of course, unfair. It contains only the names of the popular families and not the names of

- the slaves,
- the freed,
- the single mother of Victorian times or in the 1950s,
- many, many children—the catalog of the library of our Sunday School was once a printed book,
- people with different sexual orientations,
- conscientious objectors,
- and not anyone with an ethnic background different from the mainstream in this place.

You can see a lot of historical work is calling to be done!

And still, looking back at these families that were once so pivotal in this church and in this town, I would say that their heritage obliges—not by itself, as if only the privileged would count, but as evidence that the full cloud of witnesses in this place is waiting to be discovered still!

With these presuppositions in place, it is indeed something precious when God brought us together and made us a part of the communion of this particular fellowship here. May God continue to help you as the church family here to be kind to the legacy of all who have gone before you!

But even more amazing than the only half-discovered historic heritage of this church is the continuing experience of this church family that God has not stopped calling you into employment for the Kingdom! In the often-repeated words of the late Dr. Waanders, in the light of these things, today we can only return thanks to God. And that's what we do, with a flower of the mustard plant in our hands.

Amen.

CHAPTER 3

The First Professorial Certificates in the Reformed Church in America

John W. Coakley

Prefatory note: I offer the following description, text, and translation of an archival document in honor of my friend and colleague, Russell Gasero, who has been rightly called, in print, an "archivist extraordinaire"[1] and whose work has literally made possible much of the history-writing that has been done within the Reformed Church in America in the last several decades, and not a little such writing beyond it. JWC

The archives of the Collegiate Church of New York contain a collection of papers of the Rev. Dr. John Henry Livingston (1746-1825), who was one of its ministers from 1770 to 1810. Among those papers are manuscripts of sermons that Livingston preached at the Collegiate Church and elsewhere, some unbound and some sewn together in booklets. The collection also includes fragmentary lecture notes and miscellaneous other documents pertaining to his role as the first person to occupy the office of "Professor" in the Reformed Church in America

---

[1] Dedication, in Leon van den Broeke, Hans Krabbendam, and Dirk Mouw, eds., *Transatlantic Pieties: Dutch Clergy in Colonial America*, (Grand Rapids: Eerdmans, 2012), v.

(or as it was then, the Reformed Protestant Dutch Church), from 1784 to 1825—the last fifteen of those years being spent at New Brunswick Theological Seminary, of which he was the first faculty member—teaching theology to candidates for ministry. Apparently, members of Livingston's family had held these documents for most of the century after his death; two of his granddaughters, Jane Murray Livingston Crosby (1830-1911), and her sister, Henrietta Ulrica Livingston (1831-1916), donated them to the Collegiate Church in 1910.[2]

The short Latin text that I have transcribed and translated below appears in item number twenty-four of that collection, which is a sewn booklet that originally contained about fifty-four leaves, of which some forty-five have been cut from the middle, leaving six on one side of the gap and three on the other. Each group of leaves stands as though it constituted the opening pages of the booklet, and by inverting it, the reader can begin from either end. The six leaves on one side contain brief and very miscellaneous notes on various historical figures, the history of printing, the cities of China, the building of Solomon's temple, etc. The three leaves on the other side contain our text, which is of a different character.

The text, entitled *"Formula Testimoniorum* [Form for Testimonies]," carefully worded and written out in Livingston's neat hand, consists of templates or models for what we would think of, at first glance anyway, as letters of recommendation that a teacher would write on behalf of students. Here there are, it appears, three of these models. In each one, Livingston commends the hypothetical student in entirely positive terms, but with varying emphasis, and perhaps, when read in sequence, a certain progression of praise: the first student is serious, diligent, and promising; the second has been similarly studious but is also distinguished for the piety that complements his learning; the third is also diligent and pious, but in addition displays erudition. Each of the first two models is interrupted midway by a series of long dashes, no doubt to suggest where expressions more specifically tailored to a given student could be added once the model was put to use. There is, curiously, no such interruption in the third model, in which, at any rate, the hypothetical student's attainments are described in more detail.

---

[2] *Year Book of the (Collegiate) Reformed Protestant Dutch Church of the City of New York* 6/2(1911), 429. The sisters were daughters of John Henry Livingston's son Henry Alexander Livingston (1776-1849) by his second wife Frederica Charlotte Sayers (1797-1870).

What would have been the occasion for producing "testimonies" based on these models? There is a clear answer. Already in October, 1784, in electing Livingston as Professor, the General Synod declared that.

> "from this Professor, students of Theology shall be required to bring a certificate [to the ordaining body, which at this point could be either a classis or the Synod itself] whenever they desire to be admitted to the preparatory examination, for which certificate, as a suitable *honorarium*, the students shall present the Professor at least five pounds."[3]

Then eight years later: in 1792, the "Articles Explanatory of the Government and Discipline of the Reformed Dutch Church in the United States," which the Synod adopted as part the church's Constitution, and of which Livingston was one of the drafters, are more specific about what the certificate is to include, stipulating that in order to be examined, the prospective candidate for ordination must present, in addition to a college diploma and evidence of church membership,

> [a] Testimonial under the hand and seal of a Professor of Theology declaring such Student to have studied Theology with him (or with some person expressly authorised for that purpose by the General Synod), for the space of at least two years; and recommending said Student as well qualified for becoming a Candidate in the holy Ministry.[4]

Livingston's model testimonials respond specifically, on the candidates' behalf, to this requirement as the "Articles Explanatory" articulated it, although, given the earlier action of the Synod, Livingston may have made use of them as far back as 1786, when his first students would have reached the two-year mark. In any event, the fact that he refers not just to the hypothetical students, but also to the hypothetical recommender, as "N.N."—inserting a blank, in other words, for the name to be added—shows that he envisioned a generalized use for these

---

[3] *Acts and Proceedings of the General Synod of the Reformed Protestant Dutch Church in North America* (New York: Board of Publication, R.P.D.C., 1859), 1:125. Livingston was otherwise not compensated for his service, until coming to New Brunswick in 1810. John W. Coakley, "John Henry Livingston (1746-1825): Interpreter of the Dutch Reformed Tradition in the Early American Republic," in *Transatlantic Pieties* [see note 1], 307-12.

[4] *The Constitution of the Reformed Dutch Church in the United States of America* (New York: William Durelle, 1793), 304.

models; he was assuming that other students besides his own would, in the future anyway, need such testimonials.

A word is in order finally about the legacy of these testimonials in the Reformed Church in America. Their main and lasting legacy is their function to qualify candidates for their ordination exams, but they fairly quickly lost the character of a teacher's personal recommendation. After the formal organization in 1812 of New Brunswick Theological Seminary, where the office of Professor was given a permanent home, the testimonial quickly became a "certificate" of the student's successful completion of the school's curriculum. It was still signed by the Professor(s), and was known as the "Professorial Certificate," but from an early date, its granting was approved upon motion of the Board of Superintendents annually before commencement, after the members of the Board had witnessed the students' final examinations as the Professors conducted them.[5] The issuing of the Certificate had thus become, as one might say, an institutional act rather than a personal one. The same has been true at the other Reformed Church in America (RCA) seminary, Western Theological Seminary in Holland, Michigan, founded in 1866, where the tradition is for its Board to approve the granting of the Certificate upon recommendation by the faculty, though not for faculty members to personally sign the documents. At New Brunswick, the Certificate also was for many years the closest thing to a diploma that the school offered to all its students, for it was not until 1926 that all graduates received a degree; Western Seminary, however, conferred degrees from an early date through its connection to Hope College.[6]

The Certificate has continued to evolve beyond its close connection with the denominational office of Professor. At the two RCA seminaries, though the faculties approve the granting of the Certificate, many of their members are not now holders of the office of Professor. Furthermore, in 1985, the "Theological Education Agency"—later reorganized and renamed the Ministerial Formation Coordinating Agency"—was formed as an accrediting body for RCA students studying at non-RCA seminaries, with its own authority to grant the Certificate. Accordingly, no longer being closely connected

---

[5] *Acts and Proceedings*, 1812, 433.
[6] John W. Coakley, *New Brunswick Theological Seminary: An Illustrated History, 1784-2014* (Grand Rapids: Eerdmans, 2014), 59-60. For the details given here of the practice of granting the Certificate at Western Theological Seminary I thank Dr. Dennis Voskuil, President Emeritus of that institution.

to the office of Professor (though holders of the office are included in its agency's certification committees), the Professorial Certificate was renamed the "Certificate of Fitness for Ministry,"[7] and that is the name it goes by now, even when granted by the seminaries.

Text
Testimoniorum formula

[1]
Triennium est, ex quo sub mea cura versatus est ornatissimus Juvenis N.N. quo quidem temporis spatio, uti omnibus bonis fidem fecit, momentumque pondusque muneris ecclesiastici, cui olim obeundo se mancipavit, haud perfunctorie a se intelligi, ita nihil reliquum fecit, ut iis artibus imbueretur, quibus imbutos esse Theologorum animos oportet. _____ _____

_____
ad haec commendavit se modestia et morum comitate. Quae cum ita sint, non potui quin bene merenti ejus rei testimonium exhiberem, Deum venerans ut studiis et conatibus ejus etiam in sequens tempus sic praesse velit, quo cedant ad proferendas terminos regni sospitatoris nostri, et multorum aeternam salutem. Dabam [....]

[2]

    L:B:S.

    N: N: S.S. Th: D: & prof.

Per quam eximius Dominus N.N. S.S. Theol. Studiosus biennuim sub mea cura theologiae dogmaticae et elencticae studiis summa cum modestia et adtentione incubuit, et in examinibus signa suorum progressuum, quos fecit haud mediocres edidit luculenta. Scientiam quam sibi comparavit, excoluit pietate : tantum enim abfuit, ut sola pictura veritatum salutarium suum animum occulosque pasceret, ut etiam in succum et sanguinem eas converteret suum. _____

_____ _____ _____ _____

Supremum quod veneramur numen faxit, ut in examine, non ita multo post adeundo, omnium suffragiorum albo calculo comprobatus, in messem suam multo uberrimam, tanquam operarius haud erubescendus, emissus, Americano orbi lumen praeferat, ad nominis sui gloriam et multorum salutem.

---

[7] See *Acts and Proceedings*, 1987, 183.

[3]

      L.S.

Quo major plerumque eorum est numerus, qui non nisi levissimam sanctiori disciplinae dant operam, de verae etiam pietatis studio parum solliciti, eo certe majori in pretio habendi, propensioriqiue studio commendandi sunt, quotquot ex pio animi proposito, muneri sacro semet consecrant, totiusque vitae tenore certissimam Ecclesiae aedificationem pollicentur. Hanc certe laudem ornatissimus vir Juvenis N.N. reportabit, qui quamdiu studiis Theologicis incubuit omnes ex optatissimi Christianae Theologiae cultoris numeros abunde implevit. A natura instructus, ingenio facile, acri judicio ac tenaci memoria, id egit hactenus, ut eximias hasce dotes continuo, tum aliarum scientiarum, tum inprimis sanctissimi theologiae, cultu, perficeret.

Mihi certe, revelatae religionis dogmata exponenti, industrium attentumque praestitit auditorem. Ea vero, tum in examinibus, tum saepissime in congressibus privatis, deposuit specimina, ut satis superque constiterit, ipsum luculentos admodum et egregios in re theologica fecisse progressus. Cumque praeterea, quam acquisivit eruditionis copiam, morum probitate, modestia, comitate et minime fucata erga Deum pietate, ornaverit. Quo nomine et pro meritis, eum omnibus bonis etiam atque etiam commendo. ceterum S.O.M. supplex veneror, ut spiritus sui immine perpetim ipsi adesse, ac spem, haud leviter de eo conceptam, natam jubere velit! Dabam [...]

Translation

[1]

Three years ago, the very distinguished youth N.N. was given over to my care, during which time, as he had vowed to do by all that is good, he has devoted himself to understanding, in no superficial way, the importance, and weight of the ecclesiastical office to which he then dedicated himself, such that now he has no more to do to become instructed in the skills that the minds of theologians require.

To these he has devoted himself with propriety and a gentleness of manner. And they are such that I cannot but give testimony to what he has so well earned, entreating God that by his zeal and efforts in the time to come he shall be willing to press on, as they lead to the destination of the kingdom of our Defender, and the eternal salvation of many. I give...

[2]
N. N., Doctor of Sacred Theology and Professor, greets the kind reader. The very excellent Master N.N., student of sacred theology, has been under my care for two years. He has been proper and attentive in the study of dogmatic and elenctic theology, and in examinations has produced splendid evidence of his progress, which has been by no means indifferent. By his piety he has improved upon the knowledge that he has acquired: for that knowledge by itself could not have provided his mind and his sight with a prospect of the saving truth that would transform his very life-blood. _____
_____ _____ _____ _____

The Supreme Deity whom we worship, confirming all his judgments with a white stone [Rev. 2:17] in the time of trial not long after receiving his inheritance, caused his harvest to be abundant. Just so, [this] workman by no means ashamed [cf. 2 Tim. 2:15], being sent out, offers light to the American world, to the glory of His name and the salvation of many.

[3]
To the Reader, Greetings.

Though there are many more persons who pay only the slightest attention to sacred disciplines and have little care for the study of true piety, the ones who are more to be valued, and to be commended for their zealous inclination, are those [few] who by a pious resolve in their souls consecrate themselves to their holy office, and who through the whole course of their lives offer the surest promise of building up the church. Such praise the very distinguished young man N.N. will certainly elicit. For while engaged in theological studies, he has abundantly fulfilled all the highest expectations for a cultivator of Christian theology. Being naturally equipped with an agreeable disposition, a sharp judgment and a tenacious memory he has attended continually to the fulfilling of these excellent talents by the cultivation both of other fields of knowledge and, chiefly, of sacred theology. I certify him to be diligent and attentive, and an excellent student of the exposition of the teachings of revealed religion. For both in examinations, and in frequent private meetings, he has given enough and more than enough evidence of the splendid and exceptional progress he has made in theology. Furthermore, whatever abundance of erudition he has acquired he will honor with uprightness of character, propriety, kindness and an unblemished piety before God, in whose name and for whose merits I commend him in all good things again and again. Furthermore, as a suppliant, I entreat the supreme Preserver of the world to will his spirit to be perpetually near to him, and to excite that hope which he has inspired in no superficial way, to come to fruition. I give [...]

CHAPTER 4

Case Study in Archival Use: The Writing of a Prologue to a History of the Dutch American Historical Commission

Donald J. Bruggink

As the oldest surviving member of the Dutch American Historical Commission, I was appointed to write its history. Desiring to make it a respectable history and not simply a memoir it was necessary to consult the Joint Archives of Holland and those of Heritage Hall of Calvin University to check on the accuracy of my memory at ninety-one years of age. It soon became apparent that the word "simply" as used above was extremely appropriate. Without the archives, or rather, where the archives said nothing about instances where "facts" in my memory seemed to be indelibly etched, I was faced with the problem of historical integrity. Those instances have been duly noted. In other instances, crucial materials to the origins of the Dutch American Historical Commission (DAHC) were without author or date. In these cases, some archival detective work in subsequent files made it possible to construct the evidence.

The prologue to the formation of the DAHC is a story of rollicking good intrigue, especially if the reader allows her/his own speculation to fill in remaining gaps: e.g., Does the Lord really tell researchers to get off the bus in the sight of a house where a treasure trove of archival-worthy papers is to be found? Or ... ? More pointedly, the prologue raises the question as to what was the precipitating factor in bringing five institutions harboring some suspicion and residual animus together to form this organization?

As a case study, it will be my methodology to present the prologue in its present draft and to delineate my trials, tribulations, and successes in the use of the above archives in italics.

Prologue

What were the precipitating events that led to the founding of the DAHC? Formal meetings began to be held under the title of "A Cooperative Colonial Origins Project" in the autumn of 1963, with minutes for an *ad hoc* committee meeting on November 21. Its stated objectives were "to bring together historical materials ... which relate to the heritage upon which our institutions are founded." *So far, so good, the above were in the Joint Archive of Holland (JAH)*. But what happened in 1963 to bring these institutions, Reformed and Christian Reformed, together in a common project? *And it is here the archives are without some crucial but "remembered" details.*

The disparate but connected, intertwined events involved the purchase and gift of the Van Raalte house, the demolition of the Van Raalte house, the Van Raalte papers, and a University of Chicago doctoral student writing on the sources of secession.

The background for the above drama was the William B. Eerdmans Publishing Company, which has always been a combination business and philanthropic enterprise. *The philanthropic part is a matter of memory of books published for friends, but also for many of the ninety-six titles for which I was responsible as General Editor of the Historical Series of the Reformed Church in America (RCA)—but archival evidence for that would have taken the narrative re the DAHC well off the track.* Initially serving the Dutch community in the Midwest, Eerdmans grew from bookstore to publisher. As it prospered, it also took risks in publishing works that were deemed "needed" even in an unproven market. These ranged from publishing books written by personal friends to such risks as the translation of Kittel's nine-volume *Theological Dictionary of the New Testament* (abandoned by Harper and Rowe) and later the *Theological Dictionary of the Old Testament*.[1]

---

[1] Larry ten Harmsel with Reinder Van Til, *An Eerdmans Century 1911-2011* (Grand Rapids, Michigan: Eerdmans, 2011), 101-3.

The Van Raalte Homestead

As the company prospered, the philanthropic instincts of William B. Eerdmans, Sr., expanded from serving the Dutch community with print to the preservation of its physical heritage. Prof. Albert Hyma of the University of Michigan had published two books with Eerdmans and urged him to purchase the home of the founder of Holland, Michigan, Rev. Albertus C. Van Raalte.

Eerdmans did so and, to "restore and renovate it in good condition," spent $40,000.[2] The intention was that this stately brick house would "provide a connection to the earliest experience of Dutch Calvinist immigrants in Michigan, [and] would serve as a repository for important documents and [become] a research and study center."[3]

When news of the Eerdmans purchase of the Van Raalte property hit the Holland Evening Sentinel of February 13, 1947, it was filled with grand ideas for the property: "A boulevard is expected to be built from M-21 [Chicago Drive] to the foot of 10th Street, and a statue of Holland's founder would be placed at the Van Raalte homestead."[4] Unfortunately, the grand plan for an academic historical foundation with trustees of note failed to materialize. Eerdmans noted that he had tried to find a "historian/curator" to lead the foundation but had failed. On September 23, 1947, in both the *Holland Evening Sentinel* and *the Grand Rapids Press*, the announcement was made that William B. Eerdmans, Sr., was donating the Van Raalte homestead to Hope College. The gift was marked by a festive occasion at the Peninsular Club (Grand Rapids' most prestigious venue), where Eerdmans presented the deed to the property to President Irwin Lubbers. The only explanation given

---

[2] Ten Harmsel and Van Til, 101. In view of subsequent descriptions of the house it is possible that this figure included the purchase price, especially when one considers that this sum is equal to $467,063 in contemporary value. US Inflation Calculator, accessed November 28, 2020, http://www.usinflationcalculator.org. Here it would have been nice to have some archival evidence rather than a *"it is possible."*

[3] Ten Harmsel and Van Til , 111.

[4] Elton J. Bruins, *Albertus and Christina, The Van Raalte Family, Home and Roots* (Grand Rapids, Michigan: Eerdmans, 2004), 41-42. Elements of this have taken place in the form of a street extending from Chicago Drive south past the Van Andel Soccer stadium where the Van Raalte house once stood. Jacob E. Nyenhuis *et alii*, *Hope College at 150: Anchored in Faith, Educating for Leadership and Service in a Global Society* (Holland, Michigan: Van Raalte Press, 2019), end papers. A handsome bronze statue of Van Raalte has been placed, albeit in Centennial Park. Jacob E. Nyenhuis and Jeanne M. Jacobson, *A Dream Fulfilled: The Van Raalte Statue in Centennial Park* (Holland, Michigan: Hope College, 1997).

was that "the homestead and grounds should stay with Hope College."[5] As part of the front-page story, Eerdmans was quoted as saying, "Hope College may use the property in any way it chooses."[6]

In the student newspaper, *The Anchor*, on October 16, 1947, there was an announcement of the gift and a description of the house by two coeds, "Judy and I" *[Was "I" an editor? The JAH did have a copy of that Anchor, but there were several young women serving on its staff with no way of knowing if one of them had accompanied Judy on this adventure.]* who "got into the locked house through a tunnel" which connected the barn to the house. They explored all three floors and found very little furniture but "documents written by Van Raalte himself."[7] Bruins observed that "Their ready access to the house gives the first clue as to why Hope College had increasing trouble with...vandals.... From the beginning of its ownership, Hope College failed to take sufficient steps to protect the property and to prevent deterioration and vandalism of this historic house."[8] The *Hope College Alumni Magazine* of January 1948 devoted all of page ten to Eerdmans's gift of the Van Raalte property. Included in the article was its possible use as a guest house and that "No doubt the land will provide a fine location for a college athletic field, thus allowing for building expansion on the present campus site."[9] At no time during 1947 or 1948 was there any mention of this gift in the Minutes of the Board of Trustees or the Minutes of its Executive Committee.[10]

The Van Raalte Papers

Holland celebrated its centennial in 1947, and for the occasion, Professor Albert Hyma was to write a biography of the city's founder, Albertus C. Van Raalte, to be published by Eerdmans. To that end, Hyma needed access to Van Raalte's papers, some 5,000 of which he purchased from Dick Van Raalte for $1,100 ($14,689 in contemporary value[11]) sometime in the fall of 1946.[12] Hyma subsequently offered

[5] Bruins, 43.
[6] Bruins, 43, quoting the *Grand Rapids Press*.
[7] Bruins, 43-44.
[8] Bruins, 44.
[9] Bruins, 44.
[10] Hope College Collection (HCC), Board of Trustees (BOT), box 4, 1945-55, Joint Archives of Holland (JAH).
[11] US Inflation Calculator, accessed November 28, 2020, http://www.usinflationcalculator.org.
[12] Bruins, chapter 3, "The Van Raalte Papers" tells this tale of intrigue in great detail, and while herein frequently cited, only brushes the surface of the drama, 53-62.

the papers to William B. Eerdmans Sr., which were purchased for an undisclosed price.[13] The intention was that the historic Van Raalte homestead would also be an academic center containing the Van Raalte papers for the study of the history of Holland and its founder.

Hyma is described by ten Harmsel as "something of a genius about gathering papers connected to Van Raalte. For example, on one occasion, he claimed that a voice from the Lord told him to get off the bus and knock on the door of a house near the bus stop. And there he discovered a trove of previously unknown letters from Van Raalte."[14] (The reader is left to speculate about the source of this trove, which like the rest of the Van Raalte papers were sold to Eerdmans.)

Act II, The Intervening Decade

For Hope College, the fifties were momentous, with burgeoning enrollment and the perpetual shortage of dormitories. While Eerdmans's generous gift of the Van Raalte House was heralded as an important event, the immediate usefulness of the house with so many other pressing needs was a matter of question.

In 1958, Willard C. (Bill) Wichers, who played an extremely important role in college affairs, took action which would leverage any decision regarding the Van Raalte house. Wichers was Director of the Midwest Division of the Netherland Information Service, a member of the Hope College Board of Trustees, chair of the Michigan Historical Commission, and director of the Netherlands Museum. From those aggregate positions, he was well placed to solicit the informed opinion regarding the Van Raalte house from "Warren L. Rindge, a member of the Michigan Society of the Architects Committee for the Preservation of Historic Buildings."[15] Having inspected the house, Rindge advised Wichers: "'It is my opinion, that while the building is sound structurally, it is devoid of anything approaching architectural distinction. From the standpoint of design, I do not feel that there is anything either inside or out, that would warrant the extensive rehabilitation necessary that would restore it to use.'"[16] Based on this professional opinion, the official response of the Michigan Historical Commission was even more damning:

---

[13] Bruins, 58-59.
[14] Ten Harmsel and Van Til, 112.
[15] Bruins, 47.
[16] Bruins, 47-48, n. 51-52.

> WHEREAS the report of these individuals [including Rindge] indicate that the house lacks architectural distinction, that the original Van Raalte furnishings could not be placed in the house, and that the restoration of the house, as well as its maintenance and operation as a museum or historical building, would be extremely expensive...be it RESOLVED that the Michigan Historical Society advises Hope College that the restoration of the Van Raalte house would not be a prudent expenditure of funds.[17]
> March 19, 1958

Whether or not that was the response Wichers desired, it certainly played well with those who wished to use the property for an athletic field. *It is tempting, but perhaps unrealistic for obvious reasons, to wish that the archives held evidence as to the source of the idea to approach Rindge, and with what expectation there was for the response.*

One might wish the archives contained evidence as to whether Eerdmans had known of the response of the Michigan Historical Commission. A letter by William B. Eerdmans, Sr., to President Lubbers on May 26, 1958, indicates that Eerdmans recognized the probable consequences of the deterioration of the house:

> You promised me, Dr. Lubbers, that the house would be restored, and that it would be put to good use; partly as a museum and partly as a residence for visiting dignitaries... Well, Dr. Lubbers, we all know what has happened during these past ten years. The house has been absolutely neglected, and has been made the object of vandalism, as Mr. P. J. Rissseeuw writes in the Dutch daily, TROUW, April 2, 1958, "It is a painful experience to stand in Holland, Michigan, before the totally neglected house. There is a tremendous difference between this wreck and the loving care bestowed at Pella upon the perfectly restored home of Rev. Scholte."[18]

Lubbers waited to reply until June 30, 1958, after a Board Meeting, at which he reported that a committee had been formed to discuss the Van Raalte property.[19] Lubbers further went on to recite the difficulties

---

[17] Bruins, 48.
[18] Bruins, 48. I believe the Scholte home was continuously occupied by a member or descendant of the Scholte family. During my undergraduate years at Central College I was a guide there during Pella's Tulip Time.
[19] Bruins, 48.

of the college in preserving the house. Acerbating the security of the structure was the fact that it lay outside the boundaries of the city of Holland, and was therefore without its police protection. Despite efforts to protect the property, it had been subject to vandalism inside and out. Also included in his letter was the resolution of the Michigan Historical Society. On September 23 of the same year, Lubbers again wrote to Eerdmans that the committee was hard at work to find a solution to the problem, but "the building is now in such complete ruin that rebuilding seems altogether out of the question."[20]

There was, however, very intentional activity surrounding the Van Raalte property. At the Board of Trustees meeting of May 28 and 29, 1959, it was noted that two parcels of land adjacent to the Van Raalte home would cost in the vicinity of $50,000, which added to the seven acres of the Van Raalte property would bring the total acreage of the site to twenty-five acres. Authority was given to the Executive Committee to purchase this property.[21]

At the Regular Meeting of the Board of Trustees on June 2-3, 1960, the administration presented its plan for meeting the needs of Hope's athletic program. Stage one was an engineering survey of land adjacent to the Van Raalte property to ascertain the expense involved in clearing and leveling the approximately twenty-five acres of wooded, uneven land. The sum of $3,000 for the firm of Daverman to do this work was referred to the Building Committee with power to act. Stage two involved the acquisition of this land and "... a sum of $100,000 has been designated for this purpose ... and a pledge of $50,000 toward it has been received." Stage 3 involved the "development of this property for use in all fields of athletics."[22]

---

[20] Bruins, 49.
[21] Hope College Collection (HCC), Board of Trustees (BOT), box 5 (1959-62), June 2-3, 1960, 8, Joint Archives of Holland (JAH). This was the first meeting at which I served as a trustee, representing the Particular Synod of New York. My next was a special meeting on December 18, 1959, hosted by member Titus Hager at the Peninsular Club in Grand Rapids for the purpose of approving a government bond of one million dollars ($8,948,041 in today's currency) for the purpose of building new dormitories.
[22] HCC, BOT, 6. The clearest understanding of the land involved is best seen on the end papers at the rear of Nyenhuis, *Hope College at 150*. The Van Raalte house stood approximately where the Van Andel Soccer Stadium stands. It should be noted that it was usually the "property" that was stated, the future of the house remaining unsaid. If my construction of events based on the archives rather than my memory is correct, then it was at this meeting (June 2-3, 1960) that President Lubbers indicated that the Van Raalte house would take the expenditure of a million dollars to restore to its original glory. It would also be in the way of the

Presumably, Wm. B. Eerdmans Sr. would at least take some comfort that at a meeting of the Hope College Board of Trustees Executive Committee Meeting on June 2, 1961, "On motion by Lubbers, supported by Dykstra, it was voted to name the property on Fairbanks Avenue the 'A. C. Van Raalte Campus.'"[23] At the same meeting, the following expenditures concerning the A. C. Van Raalte Campus were passed unanimously: 1) $43,319 to the DeForest Excavating Co.; 2) $16,298 for construction of a running track; 3) purchase of the house and land adjoining the Van Raalte Campus on the southwest be referred to the Long Range Planning Committee.[24]

The Long Range Planning Committee of the Board of Trustees met on October 7, 1961, where "Mr. R. Visscher, Business Manager of Hope College reported that the Van Raalte home, which was given to Hope College and is located on the Van Raalte Campus, was razed due to the hazard created for neighborhood children. This report was received for information."[25]

Professor Albert Hyma had purchased some 5,000 items of the Van Raalte papers in 1946, ostensibly to write his centennial history of Holland. These had subsequently been sold to William B. Eerdmans for an undisclosed price sometime before June of 1948. Fortunately, these Van Raalte papers and others purchased from Hyma, with pride, resided in the "Van Raalte Room" at Eerdmans offices at 255 Jefferson Avenue.[26]

It was a decade later, in 1958, that William B. Eerdmans, Sr., had written in high dudgeon to President Irwin Lubbers concerning the neglect, deterioration, and vandalism to the Van Raalte house, which

---

proposed athletic complex. As a result, an informal vote to demolish the house was taken—informal because that vote is not recorded in the Board Minutes. Only trustee Willard Wichers and myself voted against it, an especially painful vote for both of us: for Wichers, considering his role with the Michigan Historical Society; for me, as a first time, very young trustee who was also a first cousin once-removed of President Irwin Lubbers. *Prior to consulting the archives, it was my memory that it was at a Board of Trustees meeting in June of 1961 that this vote was taken. As such it caused Elton Bruins to enter this incorrect date into his meticulously documented history—he was careful to attribute the date to me on page 49, footnote 58. When consulting the archives for this history I found that the annual June meeting of the Board in 1961 was held on October 6 and 7. That informal vote could not have been taken at this meeting because by that time, as indicated in the minutes of October 7, 1961 of the Long Range Planning Committee, the Van Raalte house had already been torn down.*

[23] HCC, BOT, 6 April 1961, 4
[24] HCC, BOT, 2 June 1961, 4.
[25] HCC, BOT, 7 October 1961.
[26] Bruins, 59, n. 24.

Eerdmans had generously given to Hope College. Now, in 1961, his worst fears had been realized with the demolition of the Van Raalte house by Hope College. The dream of restoring the Van Raalte house into a center for historical research, to be graced by the Van Raalte papers, had irrevocably been destroyed.

The end of that dream also raised the question of the assured preservation of the Van Raalte papers at a responsible institution. The dereliction of Hope College regarding the Van Raalte house convinced Eerdmans that Hope would not be a responsible custodian of his valuable collection of papers. The University of Michigan would have been eager to have the collection for its archives.[27] However, with Eerdmans's Dutch heritage and Reformed religious commitment, it might be assumed that the collection would remain among the Dutch in Western Michigan, and specifically at Calvin College.

But if there was any doubt, a serendipitous event certainly sealed their ultimate home. William Spoelhof, president of Calvin College, was driving through Holland on Chicago Drive (Route 31), facing the Van Raalte house two blocks away on the day of demolition. Seeing the destruction in progress, Spoelhof drove to the site, secured permission from workers, and retrieved a desk, loose papers, some bricks, and two windowpanes.[28]

> At this point, WBE was understandably furious with Hope College. He arranged to give his entire collection of Van Raalte papers and documents to Calvin College, with the proviso that they would never be given to Hope. Around the same time, [1962] WBE also made the $10,000 gift [$86,221 in contemporary dollars[29]] that began the Calvin Foundation (now the Meeter Study Center) for the encouragement of Calvinistic scholarship.[30]

The two windowpanes Spoelhof retrieved from the Van Raalte house are now installed in Calvin's archives.

Gerrit ten Zythoff

It is at this point that the research of Rev. Gerrit J. ten Zythoff provides the precipitating factor for what was to become the DAHC.

---

[27] Bruins, 58, 60.
[28] Ten Harmsel and Van Til, 112.
[29] US Inflation Calculator, accessed November 28, 2020, http://www.usinflationcalculator.org.
[30] Ten Harmsel and Van Til, 113. Bruins, 59: Eerdmans "gave the papers to Calvin College in early 1962."

Born in the Netherlands in 1922, he served in the resistance during World War II, was arrested, and during his confinement, his health was seriously compromised. He emigrated to Canada where he served a United Church of Canada in Plainfield, Ontario, 1951-52; Brockville Community Church, Ontario, 1952-54; and Hope Reformed, Vancouver, British Columbia, 1954-59.[31] It was during this period that he received an STM at Union College, BC, and became a Trustee of Hope College.

The years 1961-62 and 1963-64 found ten Zythoff teaching at Western Theological Seminary, having completed his MA at the University of Chicago in 1961. The completion of the master's degree immediately found ten Zythoff enrolled in the doctoral program. The subject of his doctoral thesis was the sources of the secession of 1834 from the Nederlands Hervormdkerk. Since Van Raalte was a part of that secession, and since he continued to have correspondence with leaders of the secession, it would have been a serious omission not to have consulted the Van Raalte papers for relevant material. However, the explicit stipulation by Eerdmans that the papers "never be given to Hope," followed by the munificent gift of $10,000, probably left Calvin officials in something of a quandary. Should a minister of the Reformed Church in America, and a member of the Board of Trustees of Hope College who was teaching at Western Theological Seminary, be allowed access to the Van Raalte papers? Would this be offensive to their generous benefactor, William B. Eerdmans, Sr.? The college hesitated.

It is my recollection that initially, it was this "hesitation" that barred ten Zythoff from access to Calvin's Van Raalte papers and that it was the process of making them available that precipitated the founding of what was to become the DAHC.[32] Once again, note that it is "my recollection" that provides the basis for my hypothesis. Unfortunately, there is no archival evidence that explicitly states that this was the case. However, the archival evidence in the founding documents repeatedly states that the purpose of the group is to make their archival collections

---

[31] Russell L. Gasero, ed., *Historical Directory of the Reformed Church in America 1628-2000* (Grand Rapids, MI: Eerdmans, 2000), 390.

[32] It was in 1962 that I returned to Western Theological Seminary as a sabbatical replacement in systematic theology for Dr. M. Eugene Osterhaven. I found Gerrit to be a most engaging friend, with an always cheerful enthusiasm, an able scholar, and committed Christian. His successful doctoral thesis found publication as *Sources of Secession: The Netherlands Hervormde Kerk on the Eve of the Dutch Immigration to the Midwest*, number 17 in *The Historical Series of the Reformed Church in America* (Grand Rapids, Michigan: Eerdmans, 1987), xxii-180.

available to all scholars. That archival evidence is made with sufficient frequency that it may well be considered adequate support for my hypotheses.

Chapter One: The Beginning of the Dutch American Historical Commission

It was at this point that Willard (Bill) Wichers became involved. A participant in all things Dutch, Bill was a natural advocate for the ebullient Gerrit Jan ten Zythoff. Being very cognizant of the debacle attendant upon the destruction of the Van Raalte house, as well as lingering feelings of hostility between the RCA and Christian Reformed Church (CRC), Wichers realized that the approach to the issue would involve academic reciprocity. Accordingly, he sought the assistance of Dr. Lester de Koster, director of the Calvin College library. Together they enlisted other sympathetic academics from their seminaries and colleges to begin discussions of an ecumenical organization that would make the historical resources of the represented institutions available to all scholars for academic research.

There is an institutional variant to the above which nonetheless has a similar ending. In an *undated, unsigned* document entitled "The Dutch-American Historical Commission," containing reference to action taken in 1966 (page 3), is the following:

> The Commission took its origins from a pilot project committee report prepared by the Pilot Study Committee on Oral History and Colonial Origins Documentation which was formed at Calvin College and Seminary in 1963. The Committee soon recognized that a cooperative effort combining both the Reformed Church and the Christian Reformed Church would be a more advantageous vehicle for the collection of Dutch-American historical documents....Thus, the Committee chairman contacted Mr. Willard Wichers, Director of the Netherlands Information Service who in that capacity represents no church, thus giving our organization a representative having no official ecclesiastical interest. Wichers contacted interested parties at Hope College and Western Theological Seminary, and together we soon began formulating a working agreement...."[33]

---

[33] Donald J. Bruggink (DJB), Dutch American Historical Commission (DAHC) W89-1019, 1963-1977, JAH. *Here it would appear that the quoted material was resourced from the memory of someone at Calvin, for the document is undated and unsigned. However, the document as a whole included information which would have required a date sometime in 1967 or 1968. The memory of that writer in no way contradicts the ten Zythoff hypothesis.*

The first record of this group was dated October 3, 1963, and was designated "A Working Agreement For A Cooperative Colonial Origins Project."[34] *Unfortunately, the attendees are not listed.* On November 12 *(again, the participants are not listed)*, there was a "Revised working agreement" of the above which was considered at an *"Ad hoc* Committee of the Cooperative Colonial Origins Project" on November 21, 1963. It was attended by Herbert Brinks, Lester de Koster, Gordon Sykman, Henry Ippel of Calvin, John R. May of Hope, Gerrit ten Zythoff of Western Seminary, and Willard Wichers of the Netherlands Museum. The agreement of November 21, based on the meeting of October 3, was accepted, with minor adjustments to the above.[35]

The above three-page document was signed by H. Ippel. Building on earlier work, "It is **reasserted** that the purpose of the project is to share the holdings and acquisitions of the participants." The academic needs of Gerrit ten Zythoff can be seen to be implied in this the reasserted "purpose of the project" which immediately addresses that problem.[36]

In the section on Objectives in the above project, the need for making collected documents available is immediately addressed: to "bring together historical materials, by collection, copying, and exchange, which relate to the heritage upon which our institutions are founded...[and] to facilitate the sharing of the holdings and acquisitions of the participants, [and] the establishment of a Master Check List has high priority."[37]

The second page of the document contains its Ground Rules in which it is again emphasized that "All participants will exchange leads and share their acquisitions."

The document concludes with a description of the *modus operandi*, again pointing out that "since this is a cooperative venture, the diverse activities will be well-coordinated." It further stated that "It is agreed that each participant, through its administration, will give formal (written) approval of this working agreement."[38]

The use of the name "Dutch-American Historical Commission" corresponds with the first record I have of that name. It occurs in a letter dated February 22, 1966, from George Cook (representing the Netherlands Museum) to Herbert Brinks about a missed meeting of the "Dutch American Historical Commission."

[34] Elton J. Bruins (EJB), DAHC A88-0019, 1963-1979, 21 11 1963, 1. JAH.
[35] EJB, DAHC, 1.
[36] EJB, DAHC, 1.
[37] EJB, DAHC, 1.
[38] EJB, DAHC, 2.

After this decisive meeting on November 21 of 1963, there is an absence of minutes until 1967.

There is evidence of continued meetings, e.g., an onion-skinned agenda of a meeting on November 19, 1965, in my handwriting, albeit I am not listed in attendance. Notably, both Wichers and ten Zythof are in attendance. In another year, I find myself copied in a letter dated February 22, 1966. At the subsequent meeting of March 4, 1966, the draft of a document to be used in fundraising again noted more accessibility was desired, "making available to scholars the combined collection for historical investigation and publication." For 1967, Herbert Brinks produced a summary of minutes for the meetings of April 21 and November 17, in which the favorable reception of the Guide to the archival holdings of the institutions are published, thus bringing to fruition the accessibility of documents as initiated by the doctoral research needs of Gerrit ten Zythoff.

CHAPTER 5

Uncovering and Interpreting the Hidden Stories: The Reverend James Murphy

Renée S. House

The Reverend James Murphy was ordained to ministry in the Reformed Protestant Dutch Church on October 19, 1814, by the Classis of Ulster in New York. He began his ministry serving three Reformed Churches in the Mid-Hudson Valley and ended his ministry pastoring several congregations further north in the Mohawk Valley region of the state. Salient information about his past came to light early this century when a researcher found a twenty-page, handwritten manuscript in the Historic Huguenot Street Library. This manuscript, called "The Memorial," was prepared by Mrs. Ann DeWitt Bevier and Mrs. Rachel Westbrook, members of one of Rev. Murphy's congregations, and submitted to the Particular Synod of Albany. In "The Memorial," the women detailed their prior efforts to see that Rev. Murphy was properly disciplined for deceiving his congregations, and they urged the Particular Synod to take action. In support of their case, they appended several important documents that might otherwise have been missing from this complicated story.[1]

---

[1] The researcher, Susan Stessin-Cohn, was Director of Education at Historic

It is, at present, an unfinished story. I do not know how Rev. Murphy's ministry unfolded in the Mohawk Valley churches he served. Portions of the written record no longer exist, and what is available cannot ever tell all there is to know. As with all historical research, the facts I have been able to uncover require interpretation aided by an understanding of the social, historical, and religious contexts within which the story of Rev. Murphy, his congregations, and ministerial colleagues takes place. In the end, as with all interpretation, I can only speculate on certain matters, such as the feelings and motivations of the persons who wrote this story with their lives. What is revealed in this micro-history provides an informative case study in the intersections of gender, race, slavery, and social and ecclesiastical power.

Early Life and Young Adulthood of Rev. Murphy

James Murphy was born in Dutchess County, New York, in 1788.[2] The exact month and day of his birth are not known. He emerges within the documentary history of the Reformed Protestant Dutch Church while he is a student at New Brunswick Theological Seminary, under the care of the Classis of New Brunswick. Seminary records document his matriculation and the fact that he received loans from the Seminary's Board of Superintendents who noted that "Mr. Murphy was already in arrears for boarding...much in want of clothing, and liable to considerable expenses before the conclusion of the Session."[3] The Minutes of the Board also show that he did not have the means to repay these loans while he was a student or in the years immediately following.[4]

Huguenot Street when she discovered a manuscript titled "The Memorial of Ann Bevier and Rachel Westbrook, members of the Reformed Protestant Dutch Church of Rochester," which was submitted "To the Reverend Particular Synod of Albany—to be convened at Albany on the 18th of August [1823]." Appended to the manuscript are several documents that support the facts of the case. The Historic Huguenot Street Library and Archive, New Paltz, New York. https://cdm16694.contentdm.oclc.org/digital/collection/hhs/id/523/rec/3. Hereinafter cited as "The Memorial."

[2] Charles Corwin, *A Manual of the Reformed Church in America (Formerly Reformed Protestant Dutch Church), 1628-1922*, 5th ed., rev. (New York: Board of Publication & Bible School work of the Reformed Church in America, 1922), 169.

[3] "Minutes of the Board of Superintendents, New Brunswick Theological Seminary," vol. 1 (September, 1813). Hereinafter cited as "Minutes of the Board."

[4] "Minutes of the Board," vol. 1 (September, 1814), 22-23; (October, 1815) 32. A letter was sent to Mr. Murphy requesting him to repay a portion of the $300.00 he was loaned, but he did not respond.

To date, I have not been able to find a record of his baptism or church membership during his youth, so it is not clear how he came to study at the church's seminary and prepare for ministry in the Reformed Church. In order to pursue seminary studies, Murphy would have been required to show "a diploma, or certificate of his having passed through a regular course of studies in some College or respectable Academy [and] a certificate of his having been a member in full communion of the Reformed church, at least two years."[5] It is possible that he received a diploma from Queen's College, now Rutgers University, an institution of the Reformed Protestant Dutch Church, and that while a student at the College, he became a member of the Reformed Church. He completed his theological studies in 1814, was successfully examined by the Classis of New Brunswick,[6] and in the same year accepted a call to serve three congregations in New York's Mid-Hudson Valley—Rochester, Warwarsing, and Clove.[7] These churches were situated in Dutch farming communities southwest of what is now Kingston, where the first Reformed Church in the Valley was formally organized in 1659.

It appears that Rev. Murphy was, from the outset, successful in his ministry. Charles Corwin describes Murphy's entire ministry with these words: "He enjoyed in a high degree the respect and esteem of his fellow-citizens, on account of his learning, his meekness, and his assiduity as a Christian teacher" and that "[he] was a preacher of superior abilities and a pastor of approved fidelity."[8] Although we recognize that there is a certain hagiographical character to Corwin's accounts of the Church's ministers, we also accept that there is a measure of truth in what he writes. As will be shown, there is ample documentary evidence that Rev. Murphy was esteemed and greatly appreciated for his preaching and pastoral care by the great majority

---

[5] "Explanatory Articles, 1792," Article III, in Edward Tanjore Corwin, *A Digest of Constitutional and Synodical Legislation of the Reformed Church in America* (New York: Board of Publication of the Reformed Church in America, 1906), Article X. These "Articles" constitute the first indigenous church order of the Reformed Protestant Dutch Church, in America. https://archive.org/details/digestofconstitu00corwiala/page/x/mode/2up. Hereinafter cited as "Explanatory Articles, 1792."

[6] "Minutes of the Classis of New Brunswick," vol. 2 (June 1-2, 1814), 86-87. Hereinafter cited as "Classis of New Brunswick."

[7] "Classis of New Brunswick," vol. 2 (October 2, 1814), 98.

[8] Edward T. Corwin, *A Manual of the Reformed Church in America*, second edition revised (New York, NY: Board of Publications of the Reformed Church in America, 1869), 169.

of members in the first three congregations he served. In 1840 he was elected president of the church's General Synod,[9] and ten years later his book, *The Bible and Geology Consistent*, was published.[10]

The Case Against Reverend Murphy Begins to Unfold

In 1822, nearly nine years into his ministry, a few members of the Rochester Church, Ann Bevier and Rachel Westbrook chief among them, undertook a serious inquiry into reports concerning Rev. Murphy's parentage. Shortly after he began to serve in 1814, Rev. Murphy penned a letter to someone named Cornelius expressing great grief that his mother had just died and been buried in Schenectady beside his father, as she had requested.[11] In the letter, he described his final moments with his mother during which she "bade me adieu, with her last strength pressed my hand, her last affection was a smile of tenderness..."[12] This letter suggests that, when Rev. Murphy arrived in the Mid-Hudson Valley, members of his new congregations quite naturally began to inquire about where he was born and raised, and the current whereabouts of his family. Given what begins to come to light in 1822, it appears that Rev. Murphy had hoped, with his letter, pre-emptively, to quiet any further questions about his early life—his parents were dead, and it appeared that he was the only surviving member of his family.[13]

Unfortunately for him, this would not be the end of the matter. By September of 1822, it was rumored that his mother was still alive. John J. Hardenbergh, an Elder at the Rochester Church, and Elisha Ostrander, a member there, were requested by Judge Derrick Westbrook, another member, to bring this fact to the attention of the Rochester

---

[9] *Acts and Proceedings of the General Synod*, 1840. Hereinafter referred to as *MGS*.
[10] Cited in "Is the Science of Geology True?," *The Presbyterian Quarterly Review* (vol. 1), 1852, p. 83.
[11] "The Memorial," Letter from James Murphy to Cornelius, November 14, 1814, appended item "A."
[12] "The Memorial," appended item "A."
[13] The "Letter" itself as included with "The Memorial" does not provide the last name of the addressee, Cornelius. The addressee is revealed as Cornelius Elting in another "Letter," appended to "The Memorial" as item "G." Cornelius was born and raised in Hurley, New York, studied at Queens College (now Rutgers University) and New Brunswick Seminary 1812-1816. Genealogical Society of Bergen County, Family Records, https://www.njgsbc.org/files/familyfiles/p396.htm. Given that James Murphy was at the Seminary from 1812-1814, it is likely that he and Cornelius met at this time, since the College and Seminary shared the same building in New Brunswick, NJ.

Consistory.[14] When these reports reached Rev. Murphy, he immediately called meetings of all three of his consistories in which he admitted that his mother was indeed alive, "explained...and acknowledged, that in what he had said [about his mother's death] he had misled the public in this case. He expressed his humility and sorrow for the same and left his case before the consistory."[15]

The Consistory Minutes do not disclose the details of what Rev. Murphy "explained and acknowledged," but we know the details because following these Consistory meetings in 1822, Ann Bevier and Rachel Westbrook, aided by three men from the Church, instigated an investigation into the rumors.[16] What they discovered was that Rev. Murphy had fabricated the story of his mother's death deliberately to hide the fact that he was born to a slave woman belonging to David Johnston. Definite proof came from Johnston's son John, who confirmed in writing on March 1, 1823, that James Murphy "was born in my late Father's family, his mother named Jane a mulatto and a slave at that time" who was still living and now freed.[17] A second affidavit, prepared by a Dutchess County Justice of the Peace, dated February 28, 1823, indicates that Jane Cox, under oath, confirmed that James Murphy "was born from her body in the town of Washington...."[18] She "signed" this document with an "X."

It is significant that Ann Bevier and Rachel Westbrook undertook their investigation *after* Rev. Murphy had revealed the truth to his consistories, and they had formally responded to his confession with sympathy and forgiveness. The minutes of all three consistories record their response in exactly the same words:

> The consistory having taken all the circumstances into consideration resolved that while they most sincerely lament the occurrence, yet as it is a case involving very unusual considerations, the consistory feel that much delicacy and tenderness [is]

---

[14] "Letter from John J. Hardenbergh to Elisha Ostrander, 9th Sept. 1822," included in the "Minutes of the Classis of Ulster" (May 6, 1823), [vol. 1], 416.

[15] "Minutes of the Rochester Consistory, September 15, 1822;""Minutes of the Warwarsing Consistory, September 12, 1822;" Minutes of the Clove Consistory, September 24, 1822," included in the "Minutes of the Classis of Ulster" (May 6, 1823), [vol. 1], 419-420.

[16] They were joined in this by three male members of the Rochester Church, Louis Bevier (possibly the brother-in-law of Ann Bevier), Elisha Ostrander, and Judge Derrick Westbrook. "The Memorial," Letter from the complainants to the Classis of Ulster, appended as item G.

[17] "The Memorial," document appended as item B.

[18] "The Memorial," document appended as item C.

due to our afflicted Pastor and so many extenuating reasons offer themselves that they feel willing to overlook the offence and to restore a fallen brother in the spirit of weakness: praying that the Lord in his infinite Grace and Mercy may uphold him and make him useful in the Church of the Redeemer."[19]

After nine years with Rev. Murphy, the consistories appreciated his ministry among them, and clearly understood why their pastor would have hidden his parentage from them—it was a risk Murphy was unwilling to take given the fact that slavery was still practiced in New York; members of the Rochester Consistory and congregation still owned slaves; and attitudes toward African Americans, both slave and free, were mixed. As members of the Rochester Church, Ann and Rachel were fully aware of the consistories' decision to treat Rev. Murphy with compassion and grace. With a few male members of the Rochester Church, they believed that he should be disciplined for his deception and brought their case to the Classis of Ulster, the Particular Synod of Albany, and the General Synod. Below we will detail their efforts and consider the larger reality of slavery and race within which this story situates. But first, we learn more about David Johnston, James Murphy's owner, and Ann DeWitt Bevier, his most determined critic.

David Johnston—Owner of Jane Cox and Her Son James

The Son of a mulatto slave woman, James Murphy was born into the household of David Johnston. Ann Bevier and Rachel Westbrook were not interested in knowing who Rev. Murphy's father might have been, and to this day, it is not known. However, the fact that he was able to pass as white suggests that his father may have been Caucasian. In an article published in 2013, journalist Lynn Woods asserts that David Johnston was in fact James' father but did not cite a specific source for this information.[20] It may be reasonable speculation—we know that white slave masters had sexual relations with their female slaves—but it remains unproven without more concrete evidence.

---

[19] "Minutes of the Classis of Ulster," which include minutes of the Consistories of Rochester (Sept. 15, 1822); of Warwarsing (Sept. 12, 1822); Clove (Sept. 24, 1822).

[20] Lynn Woods, "A Pastor's Double Life Unearthed," hudsonvalleyone.com/2013/05/05/the-mystery-of-james-murphy, accessed August 12, 2020. Woods' article draws on the research of Susan Stessin-Cohn, who, it appears has concluded that David Johnston is James' father, but there is no specific source cited for this conclusion.

It does appear that James, although the son of a slave and therefore himself sharing her status in the Johnston household, received special attention during his formative years, having been thoroughly educated and fully prepared for seminary studies by the time he was in his early twenties. This is especially notable given that his mother Jane was unable to write even her own name, using an "X" instead. Further evidence of special regard for both James and his mother appears in the will of David Johnston, which provides for the manumission of "my said negro man James" following Johnston's death, and the manumission of "my said negro wench Jane" following the death of his wife, Magdalene.[21] At the time, Johnston owned multiple slaves, but only this mother and son were slated for emancipation in his will. This special treatment suggests the possibility that David Johnston, or perhaps another male member of his immediate family, had a particularly intimate connection to Jane and James.

David Johnston was the grandson of Dr. John Johnston, a Scottish immigrant who served as Mayor of New York City from 1714–1718.[22] His maternal grandfather was Chief Justice David Jamison, who was Secretary of State and Attorney-General of the Colony of New York, and one of the "Nine Partners" who, in 1697, bought 145,000 acres of prime land in Dutchess County. David was born in 1724 to John Johnston, Jr., and Elizabeth Jamison Johnston. As a young man, he became a significant wine importer and merchant in New York City and was also elected to the State's General Assembly. Having been born into wealth and being himself a successful merchant, Johnston owned a mansion in the east village of the City and a country residence in Perth Amboy. He inherited a share of the "Nine Partners" property belonging to his mother. He moved to the family estate following the Revolutionary War, which included an Episcopal chapel, with his wife Magdalen Walton Johnston and their nine children. In 1788, when Johnston was sixty-four, infant James Murphy entered this household, which in the 1800 Census for the Dutchess County included a total of fifteen slaves.[23]

---

[21] "Will of David Johnston," New York Heritage Digital Collections, Historic Huguenot Street, "African American Presence in the Hudson Valley, https://cdm16694.contentdm.oclc.org/digital/collection/hhs/id/752/rec/1.

[22] https://househistree.com/people/david-johnston.

[23] Hudson River Valley Heritage, "The Missing Chapter: Untold Stories of the African American Presence in the Mid-Hudson Valley. https://www.hrvh.org/exhibit/aa07/education/hh/Cast_of_Characters.pdf.

Upon the death of David Johnston in 1809, James Murphy was emancipated at the age of 21. He may have left the Johnston estate soon after to begin his undergraduate studies, then entered the Dutch Reformed Seminary in 1811, completed his ministry preparation in 1814, and took a call to serve in Ulster County, New York. It remains a mystery how this young man, a former slave, came to be a Dutch Reformed minister.

Mrs. Ann DeWitt Bevier

By the time Rev. Murphy became the minister of the Rochester Church, Ann was widowed. Her husband, Philip Bevier, had served as a captain in New York's Continental Army during the American Revolution and was a wealthy man, having inherited a large family estate in Rochester (Ulster County), as well as other properties, some of which were obtained through land grants for his service in the War.[24] A prominent man in the community, Philip also served in the New York State Assembly and was an Ulster County Judge.[25] Upon his death in 1802, Ann became the legal head of the family's extensive agricultural business, a brick kiln, rental property, and investments in financial instruments, "supervising a staff of both slave and free labor, and raising eight children."[26] According to the 1800 Federal Census for the Town of Rochester, Ulster County, the household of Philip and Ann included eleven slaves.[27]

As the legal owner of the family's large estate and operator of several thriving businesses, Ann had substantial financial means and social standing in the community. Her multiple interactions with other merchants—most of whom would have been male—and her regular exchanges with customers created a wide web of relationships in her life, gave her genuine equality with other businessmen, and, arguably, a social status superior to many in her community. Within two years of her husband's death, Ann built a very large stone house which stood as a visible statement of her wealth and social standing.[28] Not only was Ann a successful businesswoman, but she was also an attentive mother,

---

[24] Sally M. Schultz and Joan Hollister, "The Ledger of Ann DeWitt Bevier (1762-1834), Early American Estate Manager and Mother." *Accounting Historians Journal*, vol 35, no.1 (June, 2008), 140. Hereinafter cited as "The Ledger."
[25] "The Ledger," 140.
[26] "The Ledger," 135.
[27] Federal Census, Town of Rochester, Ulster County New York, 1800. From unpublished research compiled by Wendy Harris.
[28] "The Ledger," 156. The DeWitt Bevier house still stands.

fully invested in the education and future success of her children. All of her seven daughters, having begun their education in a one-room schoolhouse, attended the Litchfield Female Academy in Connecticut, which was founded in 1792 in recognition of the intellectual equality of the sexes.[29]

In 1814, when the newly ordained, twenty-six-year-old Rev. Murphy became Mrs. Ann DeWitt Bevier's minister, she had been operating the family's businesses for roughly twelve years. In view of her wealth, it seems likely that she was a significant contributor to the Rochester Church's income and, on this basis, would have experienced herself as an important stakeholder whose opinions would have mattered to the Consistory.

When the truth of Rev. Murphy's parentage came to light, and the Consistory forgave him, Ann was a prosperous woman approaching her mid-60s. Her closest partners in pursuing the case against Rev. Murphy were Rachel Hoornbeck Westbrook, who was about half Ann's age,[30] and Judge Derrick Westbrook, Ann's personal attorney,[31] and an Ulster County judge. Judge Westbrook—the person who was actually present at the larger assemblies of the Dutch Reformed Church, both as a complainant in the conflict and counsel to Ann and Rachel—died before the matter was resolved.

The Case Against Reverend Murphy Unfolds

When the consistories of the churches Rev. Murphy served refused to reconsider their decision to forgive Rev. Murphy for his deception, Ann Bevier, Rachel Westbrook, and others who dissented from the decision brought charges against Rev. Murphy and a complaint against the Rochester Consistory to the Classis of Ulster. When their efforts at the classis level failed, Ann and Rachel prepared their lengthy "Memorial" to appeal their case to the Particular Synod of Albany. In it, they described themselves as "two helpless and defenceless [sic] females [who] shrink not from the painful duty of prosecuting [the] painful concern" that Rev. Murphy and those who support him have

---

[29] "The Ledger," 159. For more information about the Academy see https://connecticuthistory.org/sarah-pierces-litchfield-female-academy/.

[30] "Find a Grave," Jacob Hoornbeck, https://www.findagrave.com/memorial/19714760/jacob-hoornbeck/. Rachel was married to Wessel Westbrook who is most likely related to Judge Westbrook.

[31] "The Ledger," 144. His first name is spelled "Derick" in Rochester Church correspondence. He is called "Judge Westbrook" in "The Memorial."

relaxed the "doctrine of dissimilation and misrepresentation" to the peril of themselves and others.[32]

What follows is a chronological summary of Ann Bevier's and Rachel Westbrook's "Memorial," in which events along with their experiences and feelings are conveyed. They have preserved a slice of history in which we witness the persistence of two white women in the first quarter of the nineteenth century who were without formal power in the Church's assemblies but repeatedly tried to make their case against an African American minister who had transcended the limits of his race and former life as a slave.

They began their "Memorial" averring that Rev. Murphy "well knew—from his manifold and various acts to conceal it...[that] the opprobrium that must follow the discovery of the nature and complexion of [his] parentage...[would fall] not upon himself alone, but also upon his own people." For the memorialists "his own people" refers to those in his congregations. They were forced to submit to the public disgrace, "the infamy," of his being African American and the son of a slave woman.[33] Their explicit charge against him was that he deliberately engaged in "Falsehood and Deception," but it is clear that part of their upset is that they felt they had been disgraced by their minister's race and former status as a slave.

To make matters worse, Ann and Rachel perceived that in the moment he should have been behaving contritely and apologetically for lying and shaming the congregation, Rev. Murphy, having been forgiven by his consistories, "put on the bold front of Bravado" and did all that he could to gain the upper hand in the situation by 1) gathering 1,700 and 2,000 signatures from members of his congregations who were "satisfied with him as a neighbor, a man, a gentleman, and a clergyman [and] believed his ministry had been and still was beneficial to them;"[34] 2) attempting to bribe one of the male Church members to deliver a letter to his mother Jane in exchange for some cash and his support in the next election of consistory officers; and, 3) immediately preaching a sermon in which he appealed "to the sympathies of his people by declaring that his enemies" were seeking to harm his family, thereby, in the memorialist's judgment, polluting the sanctuary and perverting the word of God.[35] This arrogance on Rev. Murphy's part

---

[32] "The Memorial," 12.
[33] "The Memorial," 1.
[34] "The Memorial," 3.
[35] "The Memorial," 3.

seems to have fueled the flames of their discontent, as did the fact that others who supported him tried to do away with the "imputation of African mixture in his pedigree" by claiming that he was actually "the illegitimate child of a woman highly connected in life" and was given to Jane to hide the "clandestine" love in which he was begotten.[36]

Convinced that the Rochester Consistory had not properly investigated the circumstances of Rev. Murphy's birth nor had they responded adequately to his deception, thus causing "doubt, anxiety and dissatisfaction" in the congregation about his character,"[37] Ann Bevier, Rachel Westbrook, and Judge Westbrook filed charges against their minister and a complaint against the Consistory with the Ulster Classis. This filing prompted the Consistory to request, in writing, that Judge Westbrook refrain from further involvement with those who "excite disorder and confusion in the church of our common Lord at whose birth peace was sung and at whose death peace was bequeathed," and meet with them.[38] When Westbrook did not desist, refused to meet, and "treated the Consistory with contempt and manifested the most open insubordination," on March 18, 1823, they suspended him from "the use of the sacrament of the Lord Supper until [sic] he shall give evidence of repentance for his conduct...."[39] Throughout the entire conflict, the Consistory disciplined none of the other complainants. Perhaps the Consistory had hoped that Judge Westbrook—a prominent man in the community, a respected member of the Church with whom the Consistory had "often taken sweet council"[40]—would be willing and able to dissuade his client and the others involved from taking further action. But he was not willing and stayed involved until he died, prior to the resolution of the matter.[41]

The charges and the complaint were on the agenda of the May 1823 meeting of the Classis. The Classis had in evidence letters from

---

[36] "The Memorial," 4.
[37] " The Memorial," 3; also, Minutes of the Ulster Classis, vol. 1 (May 6, 1823).
[38] "Letter from the Consistory of Rochester to Derick Westbrook," March 18, 1823. Included as exhibit D in "The Memorial." https://cdm16694.contentdm.oclc.org/digital/collection/hhs/id/538.
[39] "The Memorial," exhibit E. Second letter from the Consistory of Rochester to Derick Westbrook.
[40] "The Memorial," exhibit D.
[41] On August 30, 1823, the Consistory lifted the suspension and restored Derrick Westbrook's standing in the Church, with the prayer that as a result of the discipline he would "experience the preventing and leading grace of God." "[3rd] Letter from the Consistory of Rochester to Derick Westbrook," August 30, 1823. Included as exhibit H in "The Memorial."

the great consistories all three of Rev. Murphy's churches stating that he had been faithful in his ministry and has added, "many hopeful converts to the church of our dear Redeemer."[42] At the time, Rev. Murphy was President of the Classis and apparently did not recuse himself from the discussion.[43] The Classis resolved that the allegations against Rev. Murphy were "not constitutionally before this Classis" and ruled that the Rochester Consistory had acted properly in its response to Rev. Murphy's situation.[44]

The complainants appealed the Classis's decision to the Particular Synod of Albany, where the Committee of Overtures concluded that their charge and complaint were "of a malicious character and contained nothing which called for the interposition of that Synod..."[45] Judge Westbrook appealed the Particular Synod's decision, on the spot, but the Synod voted to reject the appeal as having no grounds.[46] The verdict of the Particular Synod of Albany was then appealed to the June 1823 meeting of the General Synod, which concluded that the matter had been regularly before the Consistory, Classis, and Particular Synod and that a "suitable discipline" had already been administered, and therefore would not be further considered by the General Synod.[47]

Having failed in the Dutch Reformed Church's broader assemblies, in December of 1823 or January of 1824, the complainants requested Rev. Murphy to call a meeting of his consistories, which he refused to do.[48] They then asked that he, as President of Classis, call a special meeting, which he also refused to do. Subsequently, four ministers and two elders requested a special meeting of Classis, which Rev. Murphy evaded. At another special meeting of the Ulster Classis to conduct other business, the situation with Rev. Murphy was brought to the body's attention, and he was ordered to call a meeting of the Rochester Consistory, which he did. However, having settled the matter in September of 1822, the Consistory refused to hear any testimony from the complainants as "malicious, [and] unchristian..."

---

[42] Minutes of the Ulster Classis, vol. 1 (May 6, 1823). Letters from Rochester (April 17, 1823); Warwarsing (April 7, 1823); Clove (April 8, 1823) all providing testimony in essentially the same words.
[43] "The Memorial, 3; Minutes of the Ulster Classis, vol. 1 (May 6, 1823).
[44] Minutes of the Ulster Classis, vol. 1 (May 6, 1823)
[45] "The Memorial," 7.
[46] "The Memorial," 7.
[47] The Memorial," 8.
[48] "The Memorial," 8. All that follows in this paragraph is from the same source and page.

Rev. Murphy added that they had "no more right to appeal than his horse."[49]

Apparently indefatigable in their cause, in February of 1824—a year and five months after Rev. Murphy's three consistories had forgiven him—the complainants presented a memorial to the Ulster Classis meeting, in which they claimed that the Rochester Consistory's conduct had served "to confirm others in their evil principles and throw open the doors of confusion and disorganization."[50] The memorialists also insisted that unless the Classis intervened for their relief, "several members of respectability and good Christian standing will be shut out from the gates of Zion."[51] Working with a committee of the Classis seeking resolution in the matter, the complainants themselves presented a proposal for a way forward which asked that the Consistory of Rochester dismiss Ann Bevier, Derrick Westbrook, and Rachel Westbrook with written testimonials indicating that they were in good and regular standing in the Church, and, release all complainants from their financial pledges as long as Rev. Murphy remained the minister at Rochester.[52] Further, they requested that the Consistory certify: 1) that Rev. Murphy did write the November 1814 letter falsely describing his mother's death; and, 2) that the two legal documents pertaining to his maternity did contain the truth, and then allow these certifications to be reported in the Minutes of Classis. They agreed that if all of these requests were met, Ann, Rachel, and Derrick would withdraw "any and all charges" previously submitted to any of the Church's assemblies. Finally, they asked that the consistories of the three churches served by Rev. Murphy would expunge from their minutes anything that might tend "to criminate"[sic] them.[53] It appears that their proposal was not accepted or enacted by the Classis or consistories.

Three months later, at the May 1824 Classis meeting, the case was visited again. Finally, the complainants' concerns were taken up by the Classis, and the specific charges against Rev. Murphy (which we no longer have a record of), were clearly proven.[54] In response, Rev.

[49] "The Memorial," 8.
[50] "The Memorial," exhibit F, https://cdm16694.contentdm.oclc.org/digital/collection/hhs/id/540.
[51] "The Memorial," appended exhibit F.
[52] "The Memorial," appended exhibit G, https://cdm16694.contentdm.oclc.org/digital/collection/hhs/id/541.
[53] "The Memorial," appended exhibit G, https://cdm16694.contentdm.oclc.org/digital/collection/hhs/id/542.
[54] "The Memorial," 9.

Murphy proposed that he "surrender his license to preach the gospel and his ministerial credentials" on condition that nothing concerning the controversy be published by the complainants and all records pertaining to it be placed in the archives of the Church at Montgomery.[55] The Classis agreed not to publish anything concerning the case "except in self-defense" and, they received Rev. Murphy's license to preach, thus effectively revoking his ministerial credentials.

But the matter did not end there. At the regular meeting of the Particular Synod of Albany, on May 19, 1824, a committee which had reviewed the minutes of the Ulster Classis as related to the controversy concerning Rev. Murphy judged that 1) the Classis could not suppress any of its minutes for any reason; and, 2) that the "reception of the licensure of a minister charged with a notorious offence" was not applicable in the case of Rev. Murphy, and that the Classis should "proceed to exercise that discipline upon [him], which is prescribed in the constitution towards offending members, and which his case deserves."[56] Essentially, the Particular Synod overturned the Classis' discipline that was imposed on Rev. Murphy, judging that what he had done to conceal his parentage ought not to be judged as a "notorious offence," and directing Classis to exercise appropriate discipline—rebuke, admonishment, or suspension from the Lord's Table.[57]

Subsequent to the ruling of the Particular Synod, Rev. Murphy's license to preach was restored to him by the Classis in June 1824.[58] The complainants made one final appeal for the Classis to discipline Rev. Murphy rather than leave it to the consistories, but the Classis ruled that it did not have jurisdiction in the case and refused to entertain any further appeals.[59] Classis ended the whole matter by asking the Consistories of Wawarsing, Rochester, and Clove to furnish Ann and Rachel with copies of all records related to the controversy, but, given that Rev. Murphy was President of all these assemblies, he refused.

For nearly two years, the conflict between Rev. James Murphy and the Rochester Consistory and a handful of members in that Church continued, fueled chiefly by the energies of Ann Bevier, Rachel Westbrook, and Judge Derrick Westbrook. In the end, their core concern was not satisfactorily resolved—Rev. Murphy was not properly

---

[55] "The Memorial," 10.
[56] *The Acts and Proceedings of the Particular Synod of Albany, May 19, 1824*, (Albany: Printed at the Office of the Daily Advertiser, 1824), 7.
[57] "Explanatory Articles, 1792," Article XXXII.
[58] "The Memorial," 10.
[59] "The Memorial," 11.

disciplined. By the time Ann and Rachel submitted their "Memorial" to the Particular Synod of Albany, Judge Westbrook had died, and they were left on their own, "two helpless and defenceless females" to prosecute their case.[60] They were convinced that the true facts of the case had been withheld from the members of Rev. Murphy's congregations and that Consistory and Classis had been complicit in erecting a "privileged order" in which "a Minister can shield himself behind his consistory and that the Classis who alone are his peers cannot call him to account without the regular presentation of that consistory..."[61] They were certain that such a "privileged order" in which ministers are shielded and decisions are made "independent of the people" would "finally be brought down by an utter aversion from securing to any minister [sic] the annual payment of his salary."[62] They implored the "Christian Brethren" in the Particular Synod to overturn the decisions of the Classis and consistories in order to secure the moral obligation to refrain from falsehood and deception and to secure the Ministry of the Word in its high standing.[63]

With their closing remarks, it becomes clear that these two women were trying to find some kind of foothold in an ecclesiastical system in which only males held formal power. They did not have the right to vote or hold office in the church or in civil government, which meant they had no direct voice in these male assemblies. They were calling for ecclesiastical bodies that listened to the will of all the congregants and pleaded for a church order in which there were genuine checks and balances.

Before further analyzing this lengthy conflict, it is necessary to place this story within the larger context of slavery in New York state and Ulster County during this period.

Overview of Slavery in New York State and the Mid-Hudson Valley in the Seventeenth to Nineteenth Centuries.

We must begin in the colonial period. In 1628, the Dutch banned slavery within their own country, but the ban "did not bar Dutch companies and citizens from participating in the slave trade" or from

---

[60] "The Memorial," 12.
[61] "The Memorial," 12.
[62] "The Memorial," 12.
[63] "The Memorial," 7.

owning slaves if they lived in Dutch colonies or protectorates.[64] The Dutch West India Company, which colonized New Amsterdam, New Jersey, and areas of the Hudson Valley in the early seventeenth century, was engaged in the slave trade, and both ministers and members of the Protestant Dutch Reformed Church owned slaves.[65] The first African slaves arrived in New Amsterdam about 1626 and, by the middle of the eighteenth century, Africans "constituted about fifteen percent of the population of New York," and Dutch farmers in the Hudson Valley were "among the most extensive users of slave labor...."[66]

According to historian Gerald De Jong, the attitudes of early Dutch Reformed ministers in the American colonies toward slavery were shaped by the Dutch theologians with whom they studied in the Netherlands before coming to serve here. There were Dutch theologians who believed and taught that the slave trade and the holding of slaves were sinful, but the majority "did not object strongly to Negro slavery."[67] One of the most important treatises in support of slavery was written by Rev. Jacobus Elias Joannes Capitein, a former African slave, who studied at the University of Leiden, was ordained to ministry in the Dutch Reformed Church in the Netherlands around 1730 and was employed by the Dutch West India Company as a missionary to native Ghanaians.[68] Capitein argued that slave masters should treat their slaves kindly, but that owning slaves was not itself against Christianity since Scripture shows that what is essential is "spiritual freedom from sin and not bodily freedom from slavery."[69] African slaves should be converted to Christianity, not *physically* emancipated. It is not difficult to see how this theology would have appealed to both Dutch Reformed heads of the Dutch West India Company and to ministers in the Americas in the eighteenth and nineteenth centuries who found in it support for the practice of slavery.

In the period following the Revolutionary War and independence from British rule, for many New Yorkers, "slavery increasingly seemed incompatible with popular ideas about freedom, economic growth,

---

[64] David Kofi Amponsah, "Christian Slavery, Colonialism, and Violence: The Life and Writings of an African Ex Slave, 1717-1747," *Journal of Africana Religions*, Vol. 1, No. 4 (2013), 431-457. Hereinafter cited as Amponsah, "Christian Slavery."
[65] Gerald Francis De Jong, "The Dutch Reformed Church and Negro Slavery in Colonial America," *Church History*, Vol. 40, No. 4 (Dec., 1971), 423-436.
[66] De Jong, 423-424.
[67] De Jong, 424-425.
[68] See further Amponsah, "Christian Slavery."
[69] De Jong, "The Dutch Reformed Church," 425.

regional identity, social justice, and race" and discussions about slavery and race were increasingly apropos to discussions of citizenship and participation in the newly forming nation.[70] The idea of citizenship, which emerged after U.S. independence, embraced three essentials: the right to vote, competence to earn one's own living and be independent of public or charitable financial support, and the ability to participate in political debate and cultural discussions.

Following the Revolutionary War, in which many blacks—free and slave—participated, there was growing unrest among those who remained enslaved. The incidence of slaves running away from their owners was on the increase, as were efforts on the part of abolitionists, such as those in the New York Manumission Society, to bring an end to the institution of slavery.[71] Whites who owned and operated large farms in the Mid-Hudson Valley were especially dependent on the labor of slaves who also worked in the grain mills, iron manufacturing, and river commerce, and therefore opposed emancipation and frustrated the efforts of the state's legislature to enact state-wide abolition laws.[72]

In the years before emancipation became law, the treatment of slaves varied by municipalities and by owners. Wendy Harris and Arnold Pickman document that, in the seventeenth and eighteenth century, males slaves enjoyed a degree of legal standing in the courts of Kingston, New York; some had monies of their own which were used, in one case, to pay for the building of Dutch Reformed Church in Warwarsing, and, in another case, for the purchase of a small tract of land shortly following emancipation.[73] Some owners bequeathed large tracts of land to their former slaves.[74] When James Murphy was born in 1788, emancipation was a private matter between owner and slave, and, as we know, he was emancipated in 1809 when his owner David Johnston died. During the years Murphy was growing up, slave owners were required to teach the enslaved children in their households to read the Holy Scriptures by the time they were twenty-one.[75] Some had their slaves baptized and included in the membership of their

---

[70] David Gellman, *Emancipating New York: The Politics of Slavery and Freedom, 1777-1827* (Baton Rouge, La.: Louisiana State University Press, ©2006), 5-6.
[71] David Gellman, 8-9.
[72] David Gellman, 20.
[73] Harris and Pickman, 1-3.
[74] Harris and Pickman, 3.
[75] "The Missing Chapter" https://www.hrvh.org/exhibit/aa07/education/curriculum/Key_Points_Of_The_Gradual_Emancipation_Acts.pdf.

Dutch Reformed Churches.[76] Others did not because they feared that baptism, which was a sign and seal of a person's freedom in Christ, would prompt slaves to expect *physical* emancipation.[77]

In 1788, the year that Murphy was born, the General Synod of the Dutch Reformed Church resolved "that slaves should be accepted in the church and that they did not need the consent of their masters or mistresses."[78] By 1792 the Church had adopted its own church order which addressed the inclusion of slaves and "black people":

> In the Church there is no difference between bond and free, but all are one in Christ. Whenever therefore, slaves or black people shall be baptised [sic]or become members in full communion of the Church, they shall be admitted to equal privileges with all other members of the same standing; and their infant children shall be entitled to baptism, and in every respect be treated with the same attention that the children of white or free parents are in the Church. Any Minister who, upon any pretence [sic], shall refuse to admit slaves or their children to the privileges to which they are entitled, shall, upon complaint being exhibited and proved, be severely reprimanded by the Classis to which he belongs.[79]

Despite the Church's explicit requirements concerning full communion and equal privileges for African Americans, historian Andrea Mosterman notes a decline in their presence in the Church from the seventeenth to the eighteenth century.[80] The causes of this decline are complex, but among them, she cites evidence that white congregants objected to the inclusion of African Americans on the grounds that they were "of a species very different from us—witness their nauseous sweat, complexion, and manners."[81] This is one example of the reality that, by the late 1700s, racist attitudes were already entrenched— whites perceived themselves as superior to blacks and did not hesitate

---

[76] The membership records of the "Old Dutch Church" in Kingston, New York, where I serve, show the reception of nine adult African slaves into membership from 1730-1802.

[77] Andrea C. Mosterman, *Sharing Spaces in a New World Environment: African-Dutch Contributions to North American Culture, 1626-1826*, Ph.D Dissertation (Boston University Graduate School of Arts and Sciences, 2012), 169.

[78] Mosterman, 169.

[79] "Explanatory Articles, 1792," Article LIX.

[80] Mosterman, 169.

[81] Mosterman, 162-3. Letter from Peter Lowe letter to an unidentified friend, 1788, cited in fn. 578.

to declare their worldview openly. They resisted the inclusion and equal regard of African Americans in the Church as something that would bring disgrace to them and would be a threat to what they perceived was a God-ordained inequality that should be maintained in both Church and society.[82]

The New York state legislature finally passed its "Act for the Gradual Abolition of Slavery."[83] This Act required that "any child born to a slave woman after July 4, 1799, was deemed free, but that child would have to serve their mother's master until the age of 28, if a male, and the age of 25, if a female."[84] Another Act was passed in 1817, which provided that *all* slaves, regardless of birthdate, were to be freed by before or on July 4, 1827.

During the years that Rev. Murphy was serving the Rochester Church, 1814-1825, several members of his congregation and consistory owned multiple slaves,[85] including Philip and Ann Bevier. Rev. Murphy himself owned four slaves.[86] The 1830 census for the Town of Warwarsing—where one of Rev. Murphy's churches was located—included a new category for "freed colored persons," most of whom were still living in the homes of their former enslavers. The same census shows that ten former enslaved men had established their own households.[87] The transition to the full emancipation of all slaves was underway, and racist attitudes were also already entrenched in the culture and in the church.

Analysis of the Conflict Between Rev. Murphy and His Opponents

As we have seen, Rev. Murphy's consistories—made up entirely of white males— received his confession and forgave his deception in

---

[82] Mosterman, 161-165.
[83] For a much more detailed discussion of slavery in Ulster County see, Wendy E. Harris and Arnold Pickman, "A Forgotten History: The Story of Slavery in Ulster County and the Town of Wawarsing," https://www.cragsmoorhistoricalsociety.com/slavery-film. Hereinafter cited as Harris and Pickman.
[84] "The Missing Chapter: Untold Stories of the African American Presence in the Hudson Valley." https://www.hrvh.org/exhibit/aa07/education/curriculum/Key_Points_Of_The_Gradual_Emancipation_Acts.pdf.
[85] "1800 Census, Town of Rochester, New York." Unpublished notes compiled by researcher Wendy Harris.
[86] "The Missing Chapter," https://www.hrvh.org/exhibit/aa07/education/hh/Cast_of_Characters.pdf.
[87] Wendy E. Harris and Arnold Pickman, "A Forgotten History: The Story of Slavery in Ulster County and the Town of Wawarsing," https://www.cragsmoorhistoricalsociety.com/slavery-film, 6.

September of 1822. They understood his motivations. They had labored with him in the gospel ministry for almost ten years and had come to respect him as a person and a minister, appreciated his ability and effectiveness as their pastor, and supported him unconditionally. For years they had experienced him as white, and the circumstances of his birth and the reality of his racial heritage did not alter their perception of him. This was also the case for most of his congregants and his male colleagues in the Classis and the Particular Synod, who repeatedly affirmed that the process followed by the Consistory was in order and that their response to Rev. Murphy's deception was appropriate.

So how might we understand the ongoing appeals from Ann DeWitt Bevier, Rachel Westbrook, and a handful of others who believed that Rev. Murphy should have been more seriously disciplined? To begin, we can give them the benefit of believing that they were genuinely concerned that their minister should be a moral exemplar and refrain from any kind of deception for any reason. In addition, at least the female authors of "The Memorial" perceived that he had brought public shame and infamy upon the people in his congregations because of his race and former status as a slave.[88] The discovery of Rev. Murphy's full identity had caused them to suffer through no fault of their own, but he offered no apology. Instead, rather than behave humbly and penitently, he aggressively gathered support for himself from others and used the pulpit to present himself as a guiltless victim of enemies in the church.[89]

Although there were white male complainants in the case against Rev. Murphy, it was ultimately two white women who persisted in prosecuting the case against him, and of these two, Ann DeWitt Bevier held the greater social power and standing by virtue of her birth into the prominent and wealthy DeWitt family, her marriage to Philip Bevier, and her ownership and operation of the family's business. I am convinced that it is her voice that predominates in "The Memorial." She was undoubtedly a significant financial contributor to the Rochester Church. She was the owner of as many as fifteen slaves.

Given our current understanding of systemic racism and the operation of white superiority, privilege, and power, there can be no doubt that racism played a substantial role in this conflict. Rev. Murphy had intentionally presented himself as white throughout his seminary studies, his call process, and his ordination to ministry and

---

[88] "The Memorial," 1.
[89] "The Memorial," 2.

had transcended the limits of his birth and social status. Having fully accepted him, Rev. Murphy's fellow office holders in the church and most congregants had also transcended their own bias.

I do not know about Rachel Westbrook's social standing or whether there were slaves in her household. But, for Ann Bevier, the discovery of Rev. Murphy's background would likely have disturbed her worldview and the ordering of her own household in which African slaves necessarily held a lower social status than she. This was all about to change with the legal implementation of full emancipation in 1827, a fact that would have a significant impact on Ann's life and livelihood. She was embedded in the dynamics of both systemic and personal racism, and I am certain that this fueled her energy in pursuing the case against Rev. Murphy.

Beyond this, it is my perception that what drives Ann is a sense of unfairness. Rev. Murphy was able, literally, to "step out of his place." As an American citizen, passing as white, he was entitled to vote. She was not. As a minister, he had power over her. She was not able in the church to transcend the limits of her gender. In "The Memorial," Ann describes herself and Rachel as two "poor and defenceless" women who are trying to be heard in a church system formally controlled by male officeholders. It seemed to Ann Bevier that these officers had created a "privileged order" that allowed Rev. Murphy to "shield himself" from being accountable to all the people he served, both male and female.[90] Yet she had no recourse but to express her concerns to the ministers and elders of this privileged order. In the end, this is a story of how privilege and power operate in church and society and of how we can see some forms of privilege and be blind to others—most notably our own. It is an unfinished story.

[90] "The Memorial," 12.

CHAPTER 6

Ecclesial Membership of Reformed Church Ministers

Mathew J. van Maastricht

It is a privilege to have the opportunity to participate in honoring Russell Gasero. Russ has been a very important person in my life, and this opportunity to honor that, and him, is a gift to me. Russ has been an encourager, a resource, a reflection partner, and a guide in my growth as a historian. I offer, then, a study in historic church polity, a field in which Russ has helped me with various projects as the denominational Archivist. Archives do two related but distinct tasks: the first is that they hold the records of the corporation, which is a very practical matter. The second is that they steward the memory of the church, and for Russ, the memory of the church was not simply to look backward and long for days gone by. Indeed, it is by remembering where we have been, that we can move forward in a sound and informed way. For all that he has taught me, for the opportunities that he had opened up to me, and for his friendship, I owe him a great debt of gratitude. It is a privilege, then, to be able to offer this essay to Russ and to the church.

...

"A Minister of Word and Sacrament who is installed as a pastor of a local church shall be a member of that church by virtue of installation.

A minister not installed as a pastor shall become a member of a local church."[1]

This is a peculiar regulation. Confessing members are members of local churches, and this includes elders and deacons. It is often understood that the minister is a member of the classis alone. As we see from this regulation, however, this is not quite accurate. On the one hand, a minister's membership is held by the classis, and it is to the classis that a minister is amenable.[2] On the other hand, there is a membership(-type?) connection with a local church which is effected automatically when a minister is installed, but which must, in some way, be effected with a minister who is specialized, retired, or not installed as the pastor and teacher of a local church.

This is peculiar because it opens up two possibilities, neither of which are quite proper. The first is that the minister is wholly accountable both to the classis and to the board of elders of the local church in question. Other sections of the order indicate that this is not the case.[3] General Synod Professors, while historically being members of the General Synod, are now members of classes, but are amenable to the General Synod in terms of doctrine. So the Office of Professor is dually accountable; however, the accountability is split between doctrine (General Synod) and life (classis). There is nothing that indicates that this is the case for ministers. The other possibility is that ministers are members of the local church but are not accountable to the board of elders as members are, and so the membership is of a different order. Both possibilities are problematic because they create situations where one serves two masters or where membership is not actually membership.

---

[1] *Book of Church Order of the Reformed Church in America* (Grand Rapids, Michigan: Reformed Church Press, 2019), 1.II.15.6. Hereinafter referred to as *BCO*.

[2] The *Book of Church Order* speaks in several places about the minister being a member of the classis. It is true that elders can sometimes be considered members of the classis, but that is usually a membership of a different sort.

One might say that an elder who is credentialed as a delegate to classis would be a member of the classis, albeit temporarily, amenability does not shift from the local board of elders to the classis. Amenability for commissioned pastors (who are elders commissioned by the classis for limited pastoral service) does temporarily transfer to the classis (*BCO*, 2.I.3.3), but, whereas ministers are expected to serve the church in the ministry of the Word for life, commissioned pastors only serve for a period. Therefore, the simple language of membership does not categorically mean the same thing.

[3] See, among other places, *BCO* 2.I.3.4a and 2.I.3.4c.

This essay will briefly track the development of the relationship between ministers and ecclesiastical bodies in an attempt to gain some insight and clarity about what, exactly, it means for a minister to be a member of a local church. How did this relationship develop? Why is this the case? The hope behind this essay is that it will help contribute to a conversation which, I think, is important to consider as the church moves into a future different from where we have been.

The Early Reformed Church and Ministerial Church Membership

The Dutch synodical acta and church orders between 1571 and 1619 did not explicitly address the question of the membership of the minister.[4] It is possible that, because there were no specific regulations regarding it, that it might be assumed that the minister would be a member of the local church. The question arises, however, whether this was an intentional choice with an ecclesiological foundation, or whether it was largely the contextual reality of a church under pressure which was in the midst of a war for independence. Neither are wrong, but it is important to try to avoid confusing the latter with the former. What is clear, however, is that there was always an asymmetry between the members who are not ministers and the members who are ministers.[5] This asymmetry does not conclusively necessitate classical membership of ministers, but it does indicate an accountability to the broader church.

When the (now) Reformed Church in America adopted its Constitution in 1792, it adopted the Church Order of Dort as the church order and also adopted the Explanatory Articles to help apply the, by then, 173-year-old church order to a context foreign to its original context in 1619, and these Explanatory Articles were declared to be

---

[4] See C. Hooijer, *Oude Kerkordeningen Der Nederlandsche Hervormde Gemeenten (1563-1638)* (Zalt-Bommel: Joh. Noman & Zoon, 1865).

[5] One place in which this can be most clearly seen is if an office-bearer would commit a significant public sin which brings "disgrace and slander" (Acta of the Synod of Emden (1571), Article 33 as in C. Hooijer, *Oude Kerkordeningen,* translation mine) to the church—the parallel to today's "notorious and scandalous"—elders and deacons are to be deposed from office by the consistory. However, ministers are only able to be suspended, and the question of their deposition is left to the classis (Emden (1571), Art. 33; Dordrecht (1578), Art. 100; Middelburg (1581), Art. 64; Gravenhage (1586), Art. 72; Dordrecht (1618/19), Art. 79). While the consistory is not powerless regarding a minister, it is clear that the power that the consistory has over a minister is different from the power that the classis has over the minister.

consistent in spirit with the church order of Dordrecht.[6] A development from the previous orders, the Church Order of Dort allowed churches to delegate a minister, but—and here is the development—if there was more than one minister at a church, they all had the right to be present and vote in classis.[7] This was followed with the Explanatory Articles of 1792 with the independence of the (then) Reformed Protestant Dutch Church, "A Classis consists of all the Ministers, with each an Elder ..."[8] This reality gave all ministers a seat and a vote in the classis. In the Explanatory Articles the regulations of its predecessor church orders regarding ministerial discipline were maintained, noting that the classis is the body which tries the minister, not the consistory, and indeed, "the proceedings of the Consistory in such cases, is at their peril, and is not to be considered as a trial ..."[9] While there are no specific regulations here related to the membership of ministers, one can see how this will eventually transition to a *de jure* classical membership of ministers even though it had long been *de facto*.

Church order regulations regarding the membership of ministers remained relatively static, with no clear regulation governing it, but rather, it seems, practice and tradition. In my research, I have not found a single significant argument from the early days of the Reformed Church that challenged classical membership of ministers. It seems to have always been understood to be the case.[10] A hundred years after the

[6] Explanatory Article LXXIII, in Edward Tanjore Corwin, *Digest of Constitutional and Synodical Legislation of the Reformed Church in America* (New York: Board of Publication of the Reformed Church in America, 1906).

[7] Church Order of the National Synod of Dordrecht, 1618-1619, Art 42 in Hooijer, *Oude Kerkordeningen*. In all of the earlier orders, the church was to delegate a definite number of ministers and elders, usually one of each, and that other ministers and elders were able to be present and vote, but only those delegated could vote. In the order of Dort of 1618/19, the ministers were still delegated by the consistories, but the difference is *all* the ministers have the right to vote. Again, this does not automatically mean classical membership, but it does show a more significant bond between the classis and the ministers, not just the classis and the churches.

[8] Explanatory Article XXXVIII in Corwin.

[9] Explanatory Article LXXII in Corwin.

[10] One prominent example from the early years of the Reformed Church can be illustrative. In 1818, Conrad Ten Eyck, the minister of the Owasco church in upstate New York, was charged with holding heretical doctrines. While the concerns originated within his church, the charge was filed with the Classis of Montgomery, who took original cognizance of the matter (*Acts and Proceedings of the General Synod of the Reformed Dutch Church in North America*, June 1820 [hereinafter referred to as *MGS*], 18.; William O. Van Eyck, *Landmarks of the Reformed Fathers* [Grand Rapids, Michigan: The Reformed Press, 1922], 219). Throughout the

Explanatory Articles, in one of the first commentaries on the church order, David D. Demarest noted, unequivocally, that "[a] minister always...is a member of the Classis."[11]

Ministers as Members of Churches in the Reformed Church in America

Overture from the Classis of Grand River, 1906

The first time that the matter of church membership of ministers came to be a topic of discussion was in 1906, with an overture to the General Synod by the Classis of Grand River, "asking for a statement of General Synod on 'the status of membership of Licenciates and Ministers.'" A special committee was formed to handle this question and report to the next General Synod.[12]

In 1907, this committee returned with an extensive report. They noted that "[t]he petition referred to your committee desires the General Synod to direct 'the ministers of our Church to maintain their membership in some Church or congregation.'"[13] The reason behind this was advice that the General Synod gave in 1824 regarding how to deal with members who seceded. The General Synod noted, "(t)hat it is an established principle in Church Government, that the relation subsisting between a Church and its members, can be dissolved only by death or dismission, or an act of discipline."[14] The argument by the classis was that there was no dismission, and therefore ministers must remain members of the local church; and further, the classis has no authority to handle memberships, and because they cannot receive a member, they cannot hold the memberships of ministers—who were, at one time, among the confessing membership before their ordination to the ministry of the Word. To this, the 1907 Committee noted that, because classes form and disband churches, they have to handle

---

case, the matter was between the General Synod, the Particular Synod of Albany, and the Classis of Montgomery. Indeed, the body to labor with Ten Eyck was not the Consistory at Owasco, but rather the Classis of Montgomery. The operative church order at this time was still the order from Dort with the Explanatory Articles, and, while the minister was not explicitly *de jure* a member of the classis, it is clear that this was the practice, even from the earliest days of the Reformed Church, at least in North America. This is but one example, and there are others.

[11] David D. Demarest, *Notes on the Constitution, R.C.A.* (New Brunswick: J. Heidingsfeld's Press, 1896), 18.
[12] *MGS*, 1906, 490.
[13] *MGS*, 1907, 847.
[14] *MGS*, 1824, 46.

matters related to membership, including receiving and dismissing members. Therefore, the classis is competent to hold members.[15]

The report was an apology for the classical, rather than congregational, membership for ministers. Regarding discipline (which is one of the central aspects of membership), the committee noted that

> In cases of moral delinquency, they [the local board of elders] may chide and rebuke, and if this fails to arrest the evil they can refer the matter to Classis. They cannot discipline their pastor. He is amenable not to the elders of his Church, but to the Classis. But if he is a member of a Church, the elders of the Church of which he is a member have original jurisdiction over him and can discipline him.[16]

The committee concluded,

> Thus all through the Constitution there is recognition of the principle that a minister is not a member of a local church...a pastor is a member of the Church at large, is President of the Consistory of the church he serves, having all the rights and privilege of church-membership, is subject to the inspection of the elders of the church in regard to his doctrine and conversation, but amenable only to the Classis....[17]

There was, however, a curious addendum to the report. The Theological Professors of the New Brunswick seminary unanimously endorsed the report. The Theological Professors at the Western Seminary sent a statement signed by J. W. Beardslee, the President of the Faculty:

> The Minister in our Reformed Church ought to occupy his historical position as a member of the church of which he is a pastor, having all the rights and duties of membership in the church and congregation and a voice in the conduct of all its affairs, while as an office-bearer he is amenable to the Classis.[18]

This report was accepted by the General Synod[19] leaving the minister as a member of the classis alone. Yet the statement by the

---

[15] MGS, 1907, 848.
[16] MGS, 1907, 851
[17] MGS, 1907, 853.
[18] MGS, 1907, 853.
[19] MGS, 1907, 853. This phrase "by virtue of installation" is also particularly interesting, because this is the current wording in the church order.

faculty of the Western Theological Seminary unwittingly describes the peculiar situation. How can one be a member of one body but amenable to another one? Without amenability, how does one truly belong? Or how is one amenable to a body to which they do not belong? These questions, in part, bring the question of the meaning of membership, and these are questions we will consider in the next section of this essay.

Constitutional Revision, 1916

However, despite the action of the General Synod in 1907, just a few years later, the Reformed Church was in the midst of a complete revision to the Constitution, and a section was added:

> The minister by virtue of his installation shall always be a member of the church which he serves; or when without charge, of the church of choice within his classis. The minister as an officer in the church is a member of his Classis and amenable solely thereto.[20]

This is a peculiar regulation, particularly coming so soon after the General Synod adopted an extensive report arguing not only for the constitutionality of ministers being members of the classis, but also the rightness of that and not of congregational membership. This was amended in 1915 to replace the phrase, "by virtue of his installation shall always be" with "as pastor, *ipso facto,* shall be." The Committee noted that the phrasing "seems to legalize a method of obtaining a church membership which the committee did not intend."[21] There is no additional indication as to why this addition was made and, in fact, the committee noted that this section was added "by the unanimous action of the General Synod itself."[22] This was included into the church order of 1916.

But what does this mean? It is difficult to say, since there is no rationale given for its inclusion. What we do have, however, is the commentary of William H.S. Demarest, who served on the Committee on Revision of the Constitution when this change was adopted. There are two main questions here. The first "How does this local church membership happen?", and the second is "What does this local church membership mean?" To this first question, Demarest writes,

---

[20] *MGS*, 1913, 814.
[21] *MGS*, 1915, 522.
[22] *MGS*, 1915, 522.

> As an individual, a confessing Christian [the minister] was a member of a local church; this membership was continued when he became a minister, the church giving him a letter of dismission to the church which he, ordained, first served; when he leaves the pastorate of one church to become the pastor of another he becomes *ipso facto* member of this latter church, the relation to the former ceasing *ipso facto*. ... It would seem perhaps preferable for uniformity's sake that a letter of dismission pass from church to church as it passed from the original church to the church of service. Especially does this suggest itself in the light of the attaching provision that the minister if taking no pastorate, becoming without charge and given the liberty to become a member of some church other than the one he last served, is to take a letter of dismission the same as any other member.[23]

It would seem, then, that the ideal situation would be for the minister to receive two certificates of dismission when accepting a new call, one from the local church and one from the classis. This, however, was never specified, and is not now the practice, and whether this had ever been the practice is a matter for subsequent research. Regarding the second question, that is what it means for a minister to be a member of the local church, Demarest offers clarification on the amenability,

> It will be noted that the minister is amenable to the classis only. He is not subject to discipline by the elders of his church. When at not far past time it was newly provided that the minister should be a member of his local church it was further provided that as an officer he should be amenable solely to the classis. This quite surely meant because an officer; but it was open to misunderstanding, as if as a member he was or might be amenable to the elders. Recent amendment, deleting "as an officer," makes the matter clear.[24]

And thus, it seems clear that the minister is indeed considered to be a member of the local church, but is not amenable to the elders as are all other members of a local church. This kind of asymmetry is not altogether new—we saw this above, as well—but it is possible that it is more problematic, in that it separates membership and discipline in a stronger way than before.

---

[23] William H.S. Demarest, *Notes on the Constitution* (Princeton: Princeton University Press, 1928), 42-43.
[24] William H.S. Demarest, 43.

Constitutional Revision, 1958–59

This regulation remained unchanged for another several decades, until another revision of the Constitution brought attempted changes yet again. The Committee on the Revision of the Constitution was working on another significant alteration to the church order. Among other parts, the Committee proposed changing this section. In 1958, they recommended the removal of the church membership for ministers, leaving ministerial membership in the classis alone. The committee noted,

> This was the case until 1916, when an amendment was adopted making a minister *ipso facto* a member of the church of which he is a pastor. This is quite contrary to accepted practice in Reformed Churches, and we have been unable to discover why the change was made. It has been pointed out, correctly, that a minister can never be a full member of a local church since he is not amenable to the discipline of the Board of Elders, but is responsible solely to the Classis.[25]

This change was included with a number of proposed amendments and was, with the others, passed by the General Synod, to recommend to the classes for approval. The Stated Clerk of the General Synod reported in 1959 that the requisite number of classes approved all of the amendments recommended to them.[26] All that was needed was for the General Synod to make the declarative act incorporating them into the church order. Often this vote by the General Synod is thought to simply be a formality. This, however, is not true, and there are times when the classes approve a constitutional amendment but the subsequent General Synod does not secure its adoption, and this is the case here. The General Synod excepted a number of amendments from the declarative act, and this was one.[27] There is, however, no indication in the Minutes as to the reason why the declarative act was not approved.

Overture from the Classis of Cascades in 1978

The church membership of ministers was brought up yet again as a result of an overture from the Classis of Cascades in 1978, seeking

---

[25] *MGS*, 1958, 139.
[26] *MGS*, 1958, 236-37.
[27] *MGS*, 1958, 148.

to "make a distinction between installed pastors, and ministers of the Word without charge who are members of a congregation," and that ministers without charge "would be amenable to classis, but also, as any other regular member of the congregation, under the spiritual oversight of the elders of the congregation."[28] The advisory committee noted that this brought up questions related to the nature of installed pastors being members of the local church which "became part of the *BCO* in this century." Because of this, the committee recommended, and the General Synod voted, to have the matter studied by the Commission on Theology.[29]

The Commission on Theology reported back to the General Synod of 1980 on the question of ministerial church membership and noted the peculiar existence of ministers, in that they are both members of the classis and solely amenable thereto, and also members of local churches, but not amenable to the local board of elders, noting that this is "of recent date, and represents a departure for traditional Reformed Church polity...."[30] The Commission further affirmed their position that "ministers who retain their ecclesiastical office should continue to be members only of a classis."[31]

In speaking of the membership of ministers in a local church, the Commission noted that,

> The practice has some merit, however, in view of the increasing number of "ministers without charge." A local church membership gives such ministers and their families a church identity and home, a place where they express their Christian faith. In any case, as long as ministers retain ecclesiastical office, they should remain solely amenable to a classis.[32]

The Commission further noted that challenge when a minister not serving as the pastor of a local church is elected to the office of elder or deacon on the consistory of a local church but is not accountable to the board of elders. This, while allowed in the church order, provides a lack of consistency in accountability and authority, and causes

---

[28] *MGS*, 1978, 107.
[29] *MGS*, 1978, 107, 108.
[30] *MGS*, 1980, 116.
[31] *MGS*, 1980, 116. It is interesting that the Commission said, "shall continue to be," because already for over six decades installed ministers were *ipso facto* members of the church they served, and ministers not installed were to join a local church. It is possible the Commission intended: shall continue to be *amenable* only to a classis.
[32] *MGS*, 1980, 116.

challenges to the meaning of membership. Therefore, the Commission noted that this practice "should not be encouraged." The Commission recommended no action on the overture, which the General Synod approved.[33]

Committee on Ecclesiastical Office and Ministry

The General Synod of 1984 established a committee "to undertake a comprehensive study of ecclesiastical office and ministry"[34] and this committee reported back to the General Synod, with an extensive report, in 1988.[35] One of the matters taken up was the question of church membership of ministers. The question remained about ministers who were serving in ministry settings and how they lived out their office and how they were connected to the church. The committee suggested, among other things, that these ministers who serve in non-ecclesiastical settings—e.g. chaplaincy, education, *et cetera*—be appointed by the classis to some ecclesiastical position, as well.[36]

The Commission both affirmed the necessity of the office of minister to the church, and also understood the value of a ministry in the world. In closing the question of church membership of ministers, the Commission concluded

> This committee is of the opinion that the revisions of 1913-1918 did little to clarify the matter of a minister's church membership and created a potential for fuzziness, which has existed ever since. Since under the present *Book of Church Order* every minister of the Word is to be installed in an appropriate form of ministry and, if the committee's recommendation is adopted into the *Book of Church Order*, assigned by classis to active service as classis sees fit, local church participation and involvement is more appropriately a matter of assignment than membership.[37]

The General Synod adopted, "in principle," the elimination of ministerial local church membership, and directed the Commission on Church Order to review and make a recommendation to the next General Synod.[38]

---

[33] *MGS*, 1980, 116.
[34] *MGS*, 1984, 185.
[35] *MGS*, 1988, 261ff.
[36] *MGS*, 1988, 280.
[37] *MGS*, 1988, 280.
[38] *MGS*, 1988, 280.

The next year, the Commission on Church Order agreed that all ministers, including retired and without charge, "should be installed into an appropriate ministry...and thus remain solely amenable to the classis."[39] The presented amendment removed the congregational membership of ministers in favor of, "The minister of the Word installed into an appropriate form of ministry shall be a member of and solely amenable to the classis, and may not be member of a local congregation."[40] The General Synod referred this question back to the Commission for clarification, though there is no indication as to the nature of the clarification needed.

In 1990, the Commission reported again, and their report gives an indication of the nature of the clarification desired in 1989, that "this recommendation was not ever intended to discourage involved participation or imply that the minister is no longer welcome in the local congregation."[41] Further, the Commission noted that "the basic issue is ecclesiastical accountability, which in the Reformed Church in America polity clearly places the ordained minister in the classis."[42] The Commission again offered the same church order amendment which would have clarified the membership of ministers by removing this dual membership nature; this time, the General Synod voted to recommend this change to the classes.[43] The classes, however, did not approve the recommended amendment with sufficient numbers, falling three classes short of the requisite two-thirds in order to pass an amendment.[44]

A final change to this section of the church order came in 2004. The previous year, the Classis of New Brunswick requested the removal of the language of language of *ipso facto* membership, because it provides a dual and asymmetrical membership. In response, the General Synod voted to "instruct the Commission on Church Order to...clarify where a minister of Word and sacrament's membership and accountability are held, while also encouraging non-installed ministers active participation in the life of a local church."[45] In 2004, the

---

[39] *MGS*, 1989, 199.
[40] *MGS*, 1989, 199. The quotation here is what the church order *would read* if the amendment was adopted, rather than the recommendation present in the Minutes of General Synod, which noted additions and deletions.
[41] *MGS*, 1990, 225.
[42] *MGS*, 1990, 225.
[43] *MGS*, 1990, 226.
[44] *MGS*, 1991, 49.
[45] *MGS*, 2003, 224.

Commission noted the asymmetry of accountability when ministers are elected as elders and deacons in the local church.[46] In trying to provide a more symmetrical accountability between elders and deacons and ministers who are elected to the office of elder or deacon, the Commission recommended a rewrite of that section,[47] and sought to provide additional symmetry of accountability for ministers serving a local church as elders or deacons,[48] but further confused the nature of the minister's membership. It is this revision of this regulation that remains in force to this day.

The matter of church membership of ministers in the Reformed Church has, as we have seen, a rather complicated history with contradictory decisions, attempts to change, and all those attempts failing for one reason or another. And in fact, despite attempts to clarify the lines of accountability regarding ministers and their existence within the local church, bringing more symmetry actually brings a more complicated manner of existence which contains multiple lines of accountability with additional contingencies. Historical survey is very important to this question, but it is not a matter just of historical development, but also what this means, and it is to this more theologically oriented consideration that we now turn.

Nature of Membership

This all leads to the question: what does membership in the church mean? As Allan Janssen notes, membership is understood to be around the sacramental table.[49] In fact, historically speaking, there was no order for the reception of new members, there were, however, orders for admission to the table.[50] While the admission to the table has been expanded beyond confessing membership, including baptized children, we can still see this connection in the church order of today.[51]

---

[46] MGS, 2004, 50.
[47] Interestingly enough, in the process, the Commission also recommended deleting the *ipso facto* language, and returning to the previously unintended language of "by virtue of installation" (see above).
[48] MGS, 2004, 50-51. The advice of the Commission on Theology in 1980 that the practice of ministers serving as elder or deacon in the local church should not be encouraged (above) seems not to be considered here.
[49] Allan J. Janssen, *Constitutional Theology*, second edition, number 100 in *The Historical Series of the Reformed Church in America* (Grand Rapids, Michigan: Reformed Church Press, 2019), 9.
[50] Gerrit T. Vander Lugt, ed., *Liturgy and Psalms* (New York: The Board of Education of the Reformed Church in America, 1968), 53-60.
[51] For instance, the Lord's Supper is to be celebrated "if possible, at least once every

In understanding church membership around the sacrament, the idea of classical membership does not make much sense, as the classis is not, at its core, a sacramental body. So, then, the question arises, how can anyone be an ongoing member[52] of a non-sacramental body? Does anyone truly have their baptismal identity as a member of the church in a non-sacramental body?

This question leads to a second and related matter: the link between care and discipline.

Members of local churches are subject to the discipline of their board of elders. Indeed, there is an essential link between pastoral care and discipline,[53] that is, the same entity which provides pastoral care is the same entity charged with discipline. As such, care and discipline are two sides of the same coin, and they must go together. To separate them is to make pastoral care incomplete and to make discipline little more than abstract behavioral regulation. For ministers, who have membership in the classis, "The classis shall be responsible for the pastoral care of each enrolled minister and the minister's immediate family."[54] In this way, it is fitting for ministers to be subject to the discipline of the classis. In this way, the care-discipline link is maintained. However, this is not direct. After all, the minister's immediate family, who are members of churches and not classes, are to receive pastoral care from the classis, but under the discipline of the elders of the local church. Which is not to say that the local elders may not care for the minister's immediate family, but rather, the classis is specifically given this responsibility. For ministers to be under the care of the local elders and the discipline of the classis is to break this care-discipline link and transform the classis from a body which provides

---

three months in every church," (1.I.2.11c.) which is four times per year. At the same time, the board of elders is required to "meet at stated times at least four times a year," (1.I.5.1) and that each meeting the elders are to inquire into the spiritual health of the congregation (1.I.5.3). That both of these are required at least four times a year is not a coincidence; indeed, these are designed to go together, the elders inquiry into the spiritual health of the congregation preceding the celebration of the sacrament. Janssen, 82-8). Similarly, with excommunication, the most significant step in ecclesiastical discipline, which lexically means to remove from communion.

[52] While in 1907 the committee noted that the classis is able to hold members, and does so in executing its responsibilities, the examples cited, namely, forming and disbanding churches, the classis holds these members temporarily rather than a permanent and ongoing manner.

[53] Janssen, 47-48.

[54] BCO, 1.II.15.3

care and discipline to one that solely disciplines. This is a problematic possibility.

In some ways, then, ministers have a divided membership. On the one hand, their ontological membership—their existence as baptized Christians—is located in the local church, a sacramental body, and on the other hand, their juridical membership is with the classical body. While it may seem that there would be some form of amenability to the board of elders, from the first time this regulation was introduced in 1916 all the way into the order until today, it has been clear that ministers are amenable to the classis. Indeed, as Janssen notes, "No officer or member of the church stands under the discipline of two assemblies at the same time."[55]

And so we find ourselves in a rather difficult situation. On the one hand, ministers are members of the classis and amenable alone to their classis. On the other hand, ministers are also members of churches,[56] but are not amenable to the local board of elders. Membership without direct amenability raises the question about whether it is true membership in any meaningful way.[57]

Looking Toward the Future

The limits of this essay do not allow a comprehensive exposition of this question, for this is only a part. But it is important to understand the nature of the current reality and to continue to address this in a historically and theologically informed manner. The minister is a full member of a non-sacramental body and a somewhat lesser member of a sacramental body, but without direct amenability to the body which oversees that sacramental body. Another challenging factor is the asymmetry which has always existed with the minister. Indeed, the place of the minister in the life of the church is unique for both theological and practical reasons. This unique place of the minister must be taken into consideration in this and avoid the siren song of what often seem to be simple solutions.

---

[55] Janssen, 179. This is a historic and longstanding principle. However, with the reorganization of the Office of General Synod Professor in 2011, the question of whether or not this is truly accurate any longer is, I think, an open question.

[56] Though unless they received letters of dismission from all their previous churches, the manner of membership is not entirely clear.

[57] It should be clarified that this does not mean that the minister is unaccountable. Indeed, a matter for discipline can be brought to the classis from someone within the church, so the church is most certainly not left out of it. However, that matter is the judgment of the classis rather than the local board of elders.

The status is both difficult to understand, practically speaking, and ecclesiologically problematic. Considering the nature of the ministry and the minister's relationship to the church, it is of not insignificant ecclesiological and practical value, and questions like these will need to be considered for the church to faithfully and effectively move into the future.

CHAPTER 7

Kings and Consistories and Charters, Oh My! A Case Study in Keeping and Reading Historical Docuemtns

James Hart Brumm

The Reformed Church in America (RCA) General Synod of 1998 heard a report from its Judicial Business Commission in which the Classis of New York appealed a judgment of the Regional Synod of New York.[1] But all of this had started as a dispute between two consistories: Bethany Reformed Church had, for many years, leased space in a building owned by the Collegiate Church in the City of New York. That property was needed by Collegiate for a land swap that would allow the Collegiate Consistory to begin a new ministry in the city; the Bethany Consistory, however, claimed that Collegiate could not do so without permission of the Classis:

> The consistory shall not sell, transfer, lease, mortgage or otherwise alienate or encumber any real property of the church

---

[1] *The Acts and Proceedings* (hereafter referred to as *MGS*) *of the 192nd Regular Session of the General Synod, Reformed Church in America, Convened on the Campuses of Hope College and Western Theological Seminary, Holland, Michigan, June 5-10, 1998* (New York: Reformed Church Press, 1998), 97-105.

on which there stands a building designed for worship or religious instruction, or as a residence for the minister, unless the approval of the classis with jurisdiction over the church has been secured.[2]

There were various details of the dispute, outlined in the General Synod minutes, which really aren't of any interest to this case study. But something comes up that isn't found in the typical twentieth-century judicial business report[3]—despite the historic separation of church and state in the United States, the Collegiate Consistory claimed that civil law overrode ecclesiastical law, and that the civil law was determined by a British royal document, written in the year 1696.[4]

It isn't every day that colonial church history plays a role in a modern church judicial proceeding, but the Collegiate Church is not an everyday congregation. Dating itself from the year 1628, when Dominie Jonas Michaelius arrived in New Amsterdam, part of the Dutch New Netherland colony, to establish the first Dutch Reformed congregation in North America,[5] the congregation is, quite literally, as old as the RCA.[6] Then there is the matter of its "collegiate" status; the Collegiate Church, in 1998, was four congregations in Manhattan sharing a single consistory[7]—and eleven other congregations have shared that status over the last 394 years[8]—held together in a relationship that dates back to John Calvin's Geneva.[9] While there are now other congregations in New York, Collegiate was conceived as the one church for its community, and because of its unique statue, it was,

---

[2] *Book of Church Order (BCO)... 2019 edition* (New York: Reformed Church Press, 2019), 1.I.2, sec. 10.

[3] Although, to be fair, it is also cited in the 1963 report of what was then the Permanent Judicial Committee, but more about that later.

[4] Letter from the Consistory of the Collegiate Reformed Protestant Dutch Church in the City of New York to the Regional Synod of New York, April 9, 1997.

[5] Edward Tanjore Corwin, *Manual of the Reformed Church in America*, fourth edition (New York: Board of Publication of the Reformed Church in America, 1902), 19.

[6] Older, if one measures the age of the denomination from the creation of its own constitution (1792), the formation of the first true General Synod (1800), or the adoption of the name "Reformed Church in America (1869)."

[7] MGS 1996, appendix 1, 116.

[8] Russell Gasero, ed. *Historical Directory of the Reformed Church in America, 1628-2000*, number in *The Historical Series of the Reformed Church in America* (Grand Rapids, Michigan, Eerdmans, 2000),

[9] Calvin created just one consistory for that entire city, with authority over all the congregations. See Will Durant, *The Reformation: A History of European Civilization from Wyclif to Calvin: 1300-1564* (New York: Simon and Schuster, 1957), 472-476.

in 1998, the third largest congregation in the RCA in terms of worship attendance, with the second largest annual income.[10]

It is the age of Collegiate, however, which gives rise to the curiosity we are addressing. When it was started in 1628, it was the only congregation of the New Amsterdam colony, and remained the sole church outside of the fort on Manhattan even after the British took over the colony in 1664, thanks to a provision in the Treaty of Breda: "The Dutch here shall enjoy the liberty of their conscience in Divine Worship and church discipline."[11] Even so, by 1688, the Dutch were already seeking to protect their congregation's legal identity.

> To his Excellency, Thomas Dingan, Governor and Captain-General of his Majesty's province of New York, and Dependencies, etc.
>
> The humble Petition of the Minister, Elders, and Deacons, as being the representatives of the Dutch Reformed congregation within this city: That your Petitioners are informed of his Excellency's inclination that a church should be built outside of the fort and within the city; and your Petitioners, upon due advice and consultation with the chief members of their said church, being willing to concur with his Excellency's inclination, and with all possible expedition to build a new church within said city at the proper costs and charges of your Petitioners, provided it be for their and their successor's own proper use and worship. But since the same cannot be accomplished without a vast and considerable charge, which your Petitioners humbly conceive will not be easily be raised unless the disbursers be secured, that the said new church be built at their proper cost and charges, as above said, be confirmed unto them, their successors and posterity forever:
>
> Your Petitioners therefore humbly pray that your Excellency will be pleased, gratis, to establish and confirm your Petitioners to be a Body Corporate and Ecclesiastical, and thereby qualified persons, and capable in law, to have, hold, and enjoy lands and tenements, as also goods and chattels, under the name and style of "The Minister or Ministers, the Elders and Deacons of the

---

[10] *MGS* 1996, appendix 1, 116.

[11] Edward T. Corwin, ed., *Ecclesiastical Records of the State of New York* (hereafter referred to as *ERNY*), 7 volumes, (Albany: published by the State under the supervision of Hugh Hastings, State Historian, 1901-1916), I, 557-558.

Dutch Reformed Church in New York" which are now or shall hereafter be chosen by them; and your Petitioners will ever pray, etc.

Nomine jussuque omnium,
Henry Selens, Minister, Neo-Eboracensis
April 4, 1688[12]

There is no clear record of whether Governor Dongan ever replied, although a charter was not granted at this point, and the Dutch church finally built a building at Garden Street (now 41-51 Exchange Place) in 1693.[13] By 1695, concern was mounting over plans to start an Anglican congregation in the city; would the presence of England's established church lead to an end of Dutch religious freedom? In April, the Consistory appointed Stephanus Van Cortlandt, Nicholas Bayard, Brant Schuyler, and Jacob Van Cortlandt to address Governor Benjamin Fletcher, who had replaced Thomas Dongan, on the matter of a charter.[14] This led to a formal request from the Consistory on June 19, reminding the Governor that the Dutch had "held, used and enjoyed, the right, privilege and benefit of assembling together for the public worship and service of God, according to the Constitution and Directions of the Reformed Churches in Holland, approved and instituted by the Synod of Dort," and that to that end they had, "at their own proper cost and charge made and erected a public edifice or church, and do likewise hold, possess and enjoy sundry messages and tenements, within the said city of New York, as well as the Manor of Fordham...which with great cost and charges they have obtained." They went on in their petition to remind the Governor of their legal right to do this, and then to "MOST HUMBLY PRAY"—the capitalization was theirs—that the Governor would

> "order his Majesty's grant of a confirmation unto your Excellency's petitioners, of all the premises, and to make them and their successors forever capable to hold and enjoy the same, by Incorporating the members of said Dutch congregation into a Body Politic and Corporate...And as such they may hold and enjoy all the benefits, rights privileges, advantages, both in the free exercise of their religion and divine service and worship,

---

[12] *ERNY*, II, 952-53.
[13] Corwin, *Manual*, 996.
[14] *ERNY*, II, 1116.

according to the Rules aforesaid; and also in holding and enjoying of all other properties, rights and advantages, in as full and ample manner, as are held, used occupied and enjoyed, by any corporation, or body politic and corporate, within his Majesty's realm of England and this Province..."[15]

This petition was effective, and a charter was granted on May 11, 1696. One factor in the effectiveness of this attempt may have been that the king, William III, was himself Dutch, and an heir to William of Orange, who had gained freedom for the Netherlands and established the Reformed Church there.[16] On the other hand, a charter was granted to the Anglicans exactly 360 days later to found Trinity Church, and that charter was so nearly identical to the Dutch charter that Corwin saw fit to print them in parallel columns in the *Ecclesiastical Records of the State of New York*.[17] There was to be neither Dutch nor English favoritism in New York, but, in a sense, two established churches.

The Dutch congregation was given "Perfect Religious Freedom" but only freedom to worship "according to the constitutions and direccons [sic] of the reformed churches in Holland, approved and instituted by the Nationall [sic] Synod of Dort."[18] They are declared to be "a body corporate and politick [sic],"[19] with the same sort of rights as any other English corporation, as enumerated by the charter. The Consistory was given the right to own and purchase real property, to have a seal, to hire staff, to collect money for charitable purposes, to assess members of the congregation for salaries and building repairs, and—since the King had no idea what real estate in lower Manhattan would be worth in a few hundred years—to be free of taxes.[20]

The Consistory was also granted the right to "nominate and appoint such of their Members of the said Church [sic] that shall

---

[15] *ERNY*, II, 1127-28. In case we forget that the original settlers came to New Netherland for economic and not religious benefits, notice the emphasis placed on the amount of money they have sunk into their church and on their desire for not just religious, but also economic and political, self-determination.

[16] Corwin, *Manual*, 66.

[17] *ERNY*, II, 1136-65.

[18] *ERNY*, II, 1142.

[19] *ERNY*, II, 1145.

[20] *ERNY*, II, 1163-64. This would be interpreted by the colonial New York Legislature as an exemption from all property taxes for both Collegiate and Trinity, an exemption that was respected by the New York Religious Corporations Law (*ERNY*, VI, 4072-73).

succeed in the office of Elders and Deacons for the year ensuing,"[21] but it should be noted that this was consistent with the church order established by the Great Synod of Dort.[22] Finally, while rules for the congregation were specified, those rules may change without invalidating the charter, as long as they "be not repugnant to the laws of our Realme [sic] of England, and of this our Province, nor dissonant to the principles of Our protestant religion, but as neere [sic] as may be agreeable to the Laws of Our Kingdom of England, and consonant to the articles of faith and worship of God agreed upon by the aforesaid Synod of Dort."[23] What is clear, however, is that all of the free exercise of religion which the Collegiate Church was given was within the boundaries set by the mother denomination. Since the British monarch and "Defender of the Faith" who granted the charter was himself born and raised within the Dutch Reformed Church, and since the document was a nearly perfect duplicate of the one granted to Trinity—part of the English state church—that is hardly surprising.

It would be the English, not the government of the Netherlands nor the Classis of Amsterdam, who were most upset by the arrangement. In 1698, Lord Bellomont[24] complained—it was part of a series of complaints against his predecessor, Governor Fletcher, to the Lords of Trade in Britain—that the charter "sets up a petty jurisdiction to fly in the face of government,"[25] and, in fact, hinted that the gift of a silver plate made to Fletcher by the Collegiate Consistory, given to thank him for securing the charter,[26] was a bribe. Fletcher was cleared

[21] ERNY, II, 1150.
[22] Article XXII of the Articles of Dort, 1619, as cited in Edward Tanjore Corwin, *A Digest of Constitutional and Synodical Legislation of the Reformed Church in America* (New York: Board of Publication of the Reformed Church in America, 1906), xxviii. The charter calls for annual elections while Article XXII specifies two-year terms with half the number being elected annually, but this seems to be more of an editorial difference.
[23] ERNY, II, 1158.
[24] Richard Coote, first Earl of Bellomont (1636-1701), was a member of the English Parliament, an early supporter of William and Mary, and governor of the colonies of New York, Massachusetts Bay, and New Hampshire from 1695 until his death. He didn't arrive in the colonies until 1698, the year of this complaint, and spent most of his time dealing with the divisive politics that arose in the aftermath of the Leisler Rebellion (1689-1691). "Bio: Richard Coote, Lord Bollomont" accessed 30 December 2020, http://www.markhamchesterfield.com/biographies/cootrich3678_bio.pdf.
[25] ERNY, II, 1274.
[26] Edward Tanjore Corwin, "Calendar of Documents, Collegiate Reformed Dutch Church, 1601-1910" (unpublished manuscript in Gardner A. Sage Library, New Brunswick Theological Seminary), entry dated July 26, 1696.

of that charge two months later, when it was ruled that the gift was too insignificant to be bribery.[27]

The Classis of Amsterdam, on the other hand, seemed pleased at the turn of events, and not in the least concerned. Dominie Selyns, in his annual letter to the Classis, reported:

> My Consistory and I have for a long time labored, and taken much trouble to secure certain privileges for our Reformed Church here. These we have at length obtained in a very satisfactory instrument, which is also confirmed with the King's seal. It is entitled "THE CHARTER OF THE REFORMED PROTESTANT DUTCH CHURCH IN THE CITY OF NEW YORK GRANTED A.D.1696." Its contents are in respect to the power of calling one or more ministers; of choosing elders, deacons, chorister, sexton, etc.; and of keeping Dutch-schools, all in conformity to the Church-Order of the Synod of Dort, Anno, 1619; also, the right to possess a church, a parsonage and other church property on our own, and to hold them in our corporate capacity, without alienation. Also the right to receive legacies of either real or personal property, and other donations, for the benefit of the church, etc. This is a circumstance which promises much advantage to God's church, and quiets the former existing uneasiness.[28]

The Classis responds briefly: "We rejoice over the charter for the Dutch churches, at New York, and which is ratified by the King's seal. We trust that they (it) may enjoy the beneficial fruits thereof."[29] Nothing else is ever received from Amsterdam about the matter.

While the charter is amended in 1753 by the Colonial Legislature, to allow for the sale of the Manor at Fordham in Westchester County while allowing the church there to continue to be protected under the charter's provisions,[30] no other substantial changes are made to the document. During the colonial period, the charter is invoked on occasion to defend the congregation's rights. In 1698, members of the

---

[27] *ERNY*, II, 1283-84.
[28] Henricus Selyns, letter to the Classis of Amsterdam, September 30, 1696, *ERNY*, II, 1171-72.
[29] Correspondence from the Deputies of the Classis of Amsterdam to Henricus Selyns, June 10, 1697, *ERNY*, II, 1183.
[30] *ERNY*, V, 3447-3451. The Colonial Legislature officially affirms the validity of the Collegiate Charter at this time. Such an affirmation is never noted for any other charter except Trinity's.

congregation—along with members of the Dutch church at Kington—who were opposed to calling a second minister to serve in New York tried to have the call invalidated on grounds it was not approved by the royal governor, and Collegiate pointed out that the charter exempted them from such approvals.[31] Interestingly, the French (Huguenot) church in the city concurred with that interpretation,[32] and the government chose not to interfere. When, beginning in 1702, Governor Lord Cornbury tries to insist that all ministers—Dutch and Anglican—be licensed by him,[33] the Collegiate Consistory asks the Amsterdam Classis for relief. Your Rev. Assembly is therefore again most urgently requested to ponder what is essential to the real welfare of the Dutch churches in the Province.[34] Pressure from the Classis on the British government is a factor in Cornbury's recall in 1708.[35]

What is clear in all cases where the Collegiate charter is invoked, in the colonial period up to the mid-nineteenth century—and there is little official mention of it after 1852, when it was a deciding factor in a lawsuit[36]—is that it is seen as a document protecting the rights of the church against the state, not against its parent denomination. In fact, in a letter to the Classis of Amsterdam in December of 1698, Henricus Selyns notes that "although our Church [sic] now stands under the jurisdiction of his Royal Majesty of Great Britain...we...will accept your judgment."[37] Nearly two centuries later, at a celebration of the bicentennial of the charter, Dr. Edward B. Coe, senior pastor of the Collegiate Church, calls the charter significant because it "once and for all...established an effective barrier against the civil establishment of religion in America."[38] The charter is not seen as a canon law document at all, but as a steppingstone to the United States Constitution.

Just as the Amsterdam Classis had taken little official notice of the Collegiate charter except to note with pleasure that it protected the church from civil molestation, the new denomination which was

[31] *ERNY*, II, 1273.
[32] *ERNY*, II, 1267.
[33] Answer of the Governor to a petition from the Long Island Consistory to call Rev. Freeman of Schenectady, *ERNY*, III, 1507.
[34] Letter from the Church of New York to the Classis of Amsterdam, June 10, 1706, *ERNY*, III, 1668.
[35] Edward Tanjore Corwin, "Calendar of Documents," entry dated May 23, 1706.
[36] *ERNY*, III, 2228.
[37] *ERNY*, II, 1279.
[38] Collegiate Reformed Protestant Dutch Church, *Bicentennary of the Charter of the Reformed Protestant Dutch Church in the City of New York, May Eleventh, 1896* (New York: printed by the Consistory, 1896), 18.

formed as the American congregations became independent also showed very little concern. The "Plan of Union" which brought an end to the Coetus-Conferentie schism among the American congregations in 1771, and which established the Dutch Church in America as an independent body in practice if not in name,[39] held that, "the above Articles [sic] shall not be binding in cases where they are inconsistent with any privileges granted by charter to any Church [sic]."[40] It should be noted that the Collegiate charter and those that followed left the Dutch congregations subject to the church order of Dort, as did the Plan of Union, which should have meant that there was no conflict. Furthermore, the *Explanatory Articles* 0f 1792, which adapted the Articles of Dort to an American religious situation, made no special provision for local congregational charters,[41] even though they are intended to "exhibit the true nature and form of government of our Dutch churches in America."[42] Indeed, the local charters and the *Explanatory Articles* were to work hand-in-glove to afford the Reformed Dutch churches appropriate civil protections.

> ... the PROCEEDINGS OF THE NATIONAL SYNOD, HELD AT DORDRECHT [the proper name of the town also called Dort], are the basis of the government of all Reformed Dutch churches throughout the world, and that all churches which have been given to the Dutch churches in the States of New York and New Jersey are founded thereon... The committee, therefore, judge it advisable that the Rev. Synod further direct and authorize there [sic] committee upon this subject to frame out of said proceedings a suitable plan which will continue to whole ecclesiastical discipline and government of the Dutch Reformed churches in America, as now

---

[39] As it provides for the "General Body" of the American church to approve ordinations by the "Particular Bodies" while not naming any body a classis or a synod.

[40] Article I of the Concluding Articles, "Plan of Union," *MGS*, 1771, 16. This recognizes that congregations in Kingston, Albany, Schenectady, Hackensack, the Raritan Valley of New Jersey, Hillsborough, and Bergen were also granted charters; only Dutch Reformed and Anglican congregations were granted such status in British North America (Corwin, *Digest*, 122). Of those, as we have noted above, only Trinity and Collegiate charters received formal recognition in later colonial and New York State law.

[41] The *Explanatory Articles* are cited in Corwin, *Digest*, vii-lxxxvii. William Linn and John Henry Livingston, both Collegiate ministers, are members of the committee that prepared these articles (*MGS*, 1788, 185), making Collegiate's representation fully a quarter of the committee.

[42] *MGS*, 1788, 185.

situated, and which shall be the only rule by which said churches are directed to abide, and by which they shall be known and distinguished as Dutch churches. This, in our estimation, will answer the expectations of the public, satisfy the desires of the civil government, and serve for the direction of all the members of our Church [sic]; since it will likewise appear from this plan, that the proceedings of the National Synod of Dordrecht are the basis of the government of the Dutch churches in America...[43]

This addresses what John Henry Livingston saw, according to his writings, to be two principal concerns for this newly independent denomination: civil protections of the sort that are provided by legal incorporation, and maintenance of his own high view of the authority of the unified church over competing interests of local classes and congregations, evident in the *Explanatory Articles*[44] and the "Plan of Union" a generation earlier; it is strongly stated in the use of "our Church"—as opposed to a reference to churches—in the excerpt cited above. It is hard to believe that Livingston would think that a local congregation, even his own, could flaunt the authority of classis and synod. Besides, Collegiate never needed to worry about exercising its will in the denomination of Livingston's day, where it was easily the largest and most influential of the congregations. The need for asserting charter rights over against ecclesiastical authority was probably the furthest thing from its collective mind.[45]

The special provision for church charters made in the "Plan of Union" was apparently abrogated in 1815, when the General Synod adopted a report by Philip Milledoler—Livingston's successor as a Collegiate minister, later to be his successor as Professor of Theology[46]—that "as these articles were framed to answer a temporary, though at that time highly valuable purpose, they ought to be preserved, as an important link in the history of our church, but contain, in the

---

[43] Interim report of the committee assigned to translate and adapt the Articles of Dort, *MGS*, 1791, 218.

[44] In the requirement, for example, that all congregations sing from *Psalms and Hymns of the Reformed Protestant Dutch Church*, Article LXV, Corwin, *Digest*, lxviii-lxx, and in Article XXXVIII, concerning "Middle ground" held by the denomination regarding church polity, xiviii-l.

[45] It has been shown in other places, not the least of which is Alexander Gunn's *Memoirs of the Rev. Dr. John Henry Livingston* (New York: Board of Publication of the Reformed Protestant Dutch Church, 1856), that Livingston's thinking had an inordinate impact on the course of the Reformed Church in America.

[46] Corwin, *Manual*, 628-29.

opinion of your committee, no regulations which make it necessary at this period for your ministers to subscribe the same."[47] The Constitutions of 1833 and 1874 each make the same lone reference to any congregational charter: "Consistories possess the right of calling Ministers [sic] for their own congregations, except where otherwise provided for by charter."[48] This, however, would seem to refer to charters which would limit the power of their consistories, and there are no known claims that the Collegiate charter does that in any way. In all other matters, there is simply no mention of local charters, nor any instance of conflict between the Collegiate charter and the denominational government, not because one deferred to the other, but because both were based on the polity of the Synod of Dort. There was silence on the subject for several decades. William H. S. Demarest, in his *Notes on the Constitution*—for many years the standard polity text for the Reformed Church in America—dismissed local charters as a historical curiosity of no current relevance,[49] and it began to appear that, as an interest within canon law, the Collegiate charter was simply going to fade away.

John F. Kennedy would be President of the United States and Norman Vincent Peale would be a Collegiate minister when the Collegiate charter again became an issue. The Synod of 1960, in adopting the *Book of Church Order* as a complete revision of the church order provisions of the *Constitution*, deleted from the methods for electing consistory members the one which read "Consistory as representing all the members of the Church [sic] shall choose the entire number" of elders and deacons. It simply did not occur to anyone on the revision committee that this method was still in use.

> Since the Collegiate Reformed Church of New York City had from its beginning elected the members of its Consistory according to the deleted subsection, namely by the members of the Consistory, and since this method of electing members of the Consistory was written into its Charter granted it in colonial days and later affirmed by the Legislature of the State of New York, the Collegiate Church continued to elect its elders and deacons as it

---

[47] *MGS*, 1815, 36.
[48] Article 58 in the Constitution of 1833, Article 51 in the Constitution of 1874, cited by Corwin, *Digest*, xliii.
[49] *Revised with Amendments, 1928-1946* (New Brunswick, NJ: New Brunswick Theological Seminary and the Reformed Church in America, 1946), 97.

had done through all of its history.

Since this method of electing elders and deacons was no longer authorized by the Constitution, the question arose in the Classis of New York whether members of the Consistory of the Collegiate Church could properly represent Collegiate at denominational ecclesiastical assemblies.[50]

Classis New York overtured the General Synod for an advisory opinion, and the Synod's Judicial Business Committee retained New York attorney Arad M. Riggs, who determined that, according to the Collegiate charter and the laws of the State of New York, "the appointment of Elders and Deacons by the Consistory of the Collegiate Reformed Church of the City of New York in 1961 was legal." The Synod of 1962 then concluded that, "if it is required by the laws of the State of New York, that the consistory of the Collegiate Church of New York earnestly consider petitioning the legislature of the State of New York to modify its method of election," the Synod should instead amend the *Book of Church Order* to accommodate Collegiate's situation.[51] This went beyond the recommendation of the Judicial Business Committee in 1962, which suggested that Synod and New York Classis simply allow Collegiate to keep doing what it was doing. It probably also went beyond any requirement of New York civil law: if the civil law of New York indeed recognized the whole of the Collegiate charter, then the consistory still retained the power to change those rules as long as the resultant rules are not contrary to civil law or the church order of Dort—the rules governing the denomination, hence the *Book of Church Order*.[52] The Judicial Business Committee advised against amending the *Book of Church Order* unless the Classis of New York initiated such an action.[53] The Synod elected to solicit the advice of Arad Riggs once again, and added a clause to the election procedures allowing for Collegiate's method of elections.[54]

It was this action that allowed the entire matter of the Collegiate Charter to live again over three centuries after is was written: the Collegiate Corporation and the Classis of New York cited the actions

---

[50] Report of the Permanent Judicial Committee, *MGS*, 1963, 118. It is interesting that the Classis had no question as whether those elders and deacons could be the legal Consistory of the church.
[51] *MGS*, 1963, 119.
[52] Charter of the Reformed Protestant Dutch Church in New York, *ERNY*, II, 1158.
[53] *MGS*, 1963, 120.
[54] *MGS*, 1963, 125.

of 1962 and 1963 and the report of attorney Riggs in their claim that, under the laws of the State of New York, the Collegiate charter does—indeed must—supersede the rules set out in the RCA Constitution.[55] While, as a matter of civil law, there might be a question, as a matter of canon law, only the General Synod may grant such an exemption from its *Book of Church Order*.[56] The Regional Synod did not, in the end, resolve the question of whether church and state were separate on this issue, but simply said that it did not have the authority to make a decision.

As a matter of history, the weight of evidence would seem to go against the Collegiate Consistory of 1997. Over the centuries, elders and deacons and ministers of the Collegiate church have used the charter to defend their congregation against civil authorities—and then, except in the matter of property taxes and sales, limited themselves to defense against British royal authority; the US government was never seen as a problem. Collegiate ministers, including Selyns, Livingston, Linn, Milledoler, and Coe, have affirmed the authority of the denomination over the proceedings of their Consistory, no matter what the charter might say. It is ironic that, in attempting to invoke history to buttress its wishes, the Collegiate Consistory had to deny some of its own history and negate the opinions of some of those people who it has claimed as honored historical figures and forebears in the faith.

In the end, the historical argument prevailed: the General Synod agreed that the Collegiate charter did not supersede the Constitution of the RCA, but at the same time ruled that the provision of the *BCO* 1.I.2, sec. 10 did not apply to this particular property, which was never intended for that consistory's own worship.[57] Ironically, this issue could also have been resolved at the classis level, and much more easily than the charter question, had the parties involved done their historical research.

This case study reminds us why it is important for all seminarians to stay awake in their Church History classes and take copious notes. It is also a reminder of the value of historical records and the work of archivists who maintain and help the church to access them. Even

---

[55] Letter from the Consistory of the Collegiate Reformed Protestant Dutch Church, April 9, 1997, and "Response of the Classis of New York to the Report of the Permanent Committee on Judicial Business," Minutes of the meeting of the Regional Synod of New York, May 10, 1997.
[56] Minutes of the Regional Synod of New York.
[57] *MGS*, 1998, 97-105.

after centuries, the questions of establishment of religion, separation of church and state, and the authority of ancient royal documents are not as clear-cut as we would like to think, and issues of seventeenth century and earlier polities can still be raised in the twenty-first century. It is the people who know their history who can make the best argument for moving into their future, and archives that will provide the best foundation for that work.

CHAPTER 8

Prophetic Teachers: Reflections on the Office of the General Synod Professor in the Reformed Church in America

Micah L. McCreary

Introduction

> But each of us was given grace according to the measure of Christ's gift (Eph. 4:7).

This Festschrift essay is written in honor of the history and legacy of the Reformed Church in America, particularly as it has been represented and remembered by the work of the great archivist Russell Gasero. I congratulate Mr. Gasero for his forty plus years of service to the church and the art of archives. Since July 2017, when I was called to serve New Brunswick Theological Seminary as President, I have developed a sincere appreciation for "Russ" and have used the Archives extensively to learn of my presidential and institutional lineage, especially the important role that New Brunswick Theological Seminary and John Henry Livingston have played, and continue to play, in the Reformed Church in America as a theological agent.

In searching for and praying about a topic to write on that would be relevant and essential to our shared history and current reality, I settled upon producing an essay about the Office of the General Synod Professorate of the Reformed Church in America, which originated at New Brunswick Theological Seminary. This composition reflects the views of this writer, with input and consultation of current and former General Synod professors.

My introduction to the General Synod Professorate began as I was preparing to interview for the presidency of New Brunswick Theological Seminary (NBTS). I sought to know more about the seminary's structures and vicissitudes. I was interviewing for the leadership of a historic reformed seminary while coming from the Methodist, Pentecostal, and Baptist Protestant faith traditions. I was a minister cultivated in process, liberation, and Catholic theologies. However, I had always been drawn to Reformed Theology, and to my delight, found astounding congruence between Reformed Theology and my existing theological perspective.

As I assumed my new position in 2017 and began the process of having my American Baptist Ordination received by the RCA, I humbly began to study the *Book of Church Order* (*BCO*) of the Reformed Church in America (RCA). I read articles on the Classis, the Consistory, Commissioned Pastor, the Elder, the Deacon, and the Minster of Word and Sacrament. Unsurprisingly, I was drawn to Article 8 section 1 of the *BCO*, which stated that the Office of the General Synod professor is a collective and individual ministry. It is a ministry that: (1) offers the *ministry of teaching* within the RCA as a whole, and (2) is to represent the *living tradition* of the Church in the preparation and certification of candidates for its ministry."[1] I found this description of an office within the RCA to be "fresh" and both intellectually and vocationally exciting. I perceived it as an epic teaching tradition.

As a former senior pastor, tenured professor of psychology, licensed clinical psychologist, and business owner, I was instantaneously drawn to this "Office of the General Synod Professor." I discerned that there was something extraordinary about this office. Further, as I continued the process of being "grafted into" the RCA as a member of the Classis of New Brunswick, I discovered the legacies of John Henry Livingston, the General Synod Professorate, and NBTS. This was even more intellectually stimulating and vocationally appealing. I felt honored to be acquainted with such a storied institution and its faithful and forward-thinking leaders, from the iconic Rev. Dr. John Henry Livingston to the illustrious Rev. Dr. Gregg Mast.

---

[1] *Book of Church Order* http://images.rca.org/docs/bco/2019BCO.pdf, 72

I was formally introduced to my first General Synod professor when I met the Rev. Dr. Gregg Mast, the retiring President of NBTS, during my 2017 introduction to the RCA at the General Synod. I met the current collective body of General Synod professors soon afterward, during their fall meeting at NBTS that year. I perceived them all, then and now, as gifted teachers of the church and the seminaries. Since assuming the NBTS presidency, I also have had the honor of "sitting" on the floor of the General Synod annual session for three years and observing the personal character and corporate professional interactions of the General Synod Professors within the august body of delegates, correspondents, and RCA staff.

Nevertheless, to gain deeper insight into the historic legacy of the Office of the General Synod Professorate, this writer reviewed (1) John Calvin's 1541 Draft Ecclesiastical Ordination,[2] (2) former NBTS Affiliate Professor and General Synod Professor emeritus Dr. Allan J. Janssen's *Constitutional Theology: Notes on the Book of Church Order of the Reformed Church in America*[3]; and (3) former NBTS President Dr. Norman Kansfield's essay, "Teacher of the Church: The Office of Professor of Theology in the Reformed Church in America"[4]; and (4) held an enlightening conversation with Dr. John W. Coakley, NBTS emeritus L. Russell Feakes Memorial Professor of Church History and General Synod Professor emeritus.

The RCA Office of General Synod Professor

> "I know that whatever God does endures forever; nothing can be added to it, nor anything taken from it; God has done this, so that all should stand in awe before him. That which is, already has been; that which is to be, already is; and God seeks out what has gone by (Eccl. 3:14-15)."

Calvin believed that the "extraordinary offices were raised up by the Lord at the beginning of his kingdom." He also stated that Apostles,

---

[2] Citing Schaff's analysis of Calvin's 4 Offices, articulated in the Ecclesiastical Ordinances of 1541 (https://www.ccel.org/ccel/schaff/hcc8.iv.xiii.vii.html).

[3] Dr. Allan J. Janssen (2019). *Constitutional Theology: Notes on the Book of Church Order of the Reformed Church in America* (2nd edition). The Historical Series of the Reformed Church in America No. 100. Grand Rapids, MI: Reformed Church Press pp. 235-243.

[4] Norman J. Kansfield, in James Hart Brumm, ed., *Tools for Understanding: Essays in Honor of Donald J. Bruggink*, number 60 in *The Historical Series of the Reformed Church in America* (Grand Rapids, Michigan: Eerdmans, 2008), 141-188.

Prophets, and Evangelists were raised up on special occasions when required and necessary[5]. It is Calvin's understanding and belief that he and other church reformers were to be regarded as "a secondary class of Apostles, Prophets, and Evangelists" because they were performing extraordinary works for God's church, which was the office of teacher.[6] Calvin embraced the belief that God was performing the work of the extraordinary offices through him and other reformers. He seemed to state that the crises the Church was facing in his time called for extraordinary persons to help the Church recover and reconstitute itself.

In addition to the extraordinary offices, Calvin did provide directions for the four ordinary offices of the Church. The first office is the office of the Pastors. Calvin seemed to prefer to call pastors "ministers of the gospel," and he outlined their responsibilities as preaching the Word of God, instructing, admonishing, exhorting and reproving members. Pastors are also to administer the sacraments, and, jointly with the elders, exercise church discipline."[7] Calvin's second office will be discussed and explored later in this section; next we move to the third office.

Calvin's third office was the office of the Ancients or Lay-Elders.[8] The Lay-Elders were assigned to watch over the good conduct of the people. According to Calvin, the Lay-Elders must be God-fearing and wise men, without reproach and above suspicion. According to Schaff, the Lay-Elder was an office of governance. The fourth office was the office of the Deacons. The Deacons are responsible for the care of the poor and the sick and of the hospitals. Two classes of Deacons were distinguished: those who administer alms, and those who devote themselves to the poor and sick.

The second office presented by Calvin, and most important to this article, is the Office of Teacher.[9] This office is to instruct the believers in sound doctrine, in order that the purity of the gospel be not corrupted

---

[5] *Citing Schaff's analysis of Calvin's 4 Offices, articulated in the Ecclesiastical Ordinances of 1541.*

[6] *Citing Schaff's analysis of Calvin's 4 Offices, articulated in the Ecclesiastical Ordinances of 1541.*

[7] *Citing Schaff's analysis of Calvin's 4 Offices, articulated in the Ecclesiastical Ordinances of 1541.*

[8] Ibid

[9] Allan J. Janssen, Constitutional Theology: Notes on the Book of Church Order of the Reformed Church in America, second edition, number 100 in The Historical Series of the Reformed Church in America (Grand Rapids, Michigan: Reformed Church Press, 2019), 235-243.

by ignorance or false opinions. Calvin derived the distinction between Teachers and Pastors from Ephesians 4:11, and states the difference to consist in this,

> that Teachers have no official concern with discipline, nor the administration of the sacraments, nor admonitions and exhortations, but only with the interpretation of the Scripture; whereas the pastoral office includes all these duties.

This writer notes that none of the modern Bible translations separate the pastors and teachers by comma; and many of the modern churches no longer separate the office of the Pastor and the office of the Teacher. Calvin also stated that Teachers sustain a similar resemblance to the ancient Prophets as the Pastors to the Apostles.

This writer finds power in Calvin's proposition and position. Whether we examine the Prophet Nathan, Elijah and the school of the Prophets, or the teaching of the Prophet and Christ Jesus of Nazareth, there is always a critical emphasis on teaching.

Schaff suggested that, because of its connection to the ancient Prophets, the office of the theological professor occupies the highest rank among Teachers.[10] Taking a cue from the Greek word διδάσκαλοι (doctors) in Ephesian 4:11 and surmising that there is an office of the Teachers, it would then be conceptualized as one occupied by those who would instruct the believers in sound doctrine in order that the purity of the gospel not be corrupted by ignorance or false opinions. Proudly, and sometimes problematically, the Reformed Church in America is the only Reformed denomination to continue this tradition.

Importantly, according to the Ephesians 4 pericope and the teachings of Calvin, the Offices of the Church are people. Our conceptualization of the church as the *ecclesia* (called out ones) parallels this interpretation and connects the church offices to the Old Testament Church, New Testament Church, current Testament Church and future Testament Church. It is, in a powerful way, where death and distraction are no longer sentences of extermination: they are opportunities to reassess ministry. As churches, ministers, and denominations examine their ministries and roles in the Body of Christ, instruction will become even more critical to church survival. We tend to elevate the office of Pastor and ignore the office of Teacher, but whether we conceptualize them as one office or two, the office of the Teacher is critical to the life

---

[10] Janssen, 235-243.

and breath of the church. Jesus is recorded by Luke in the first chapter of Acts as teaching, or instructing, the disciples at that crucial time.

The Church always needs inspired and inspirited teachers who proclaim the will of God. However, Calvin elevates this office when he invites us to consider the reality that there are ministers among us who "have no official concern with discipline like the consistory of the local congregation; who do not primarily focus on the administration of the sacraments like the consistory of the local congregation; nor focus primarily on admonitions and exhortations, but focus on, studies for years, to enhance and promote their abilities and insights to interpret the Scripture, theology, and the likes, for the betterment of the offices of the Pastor, Elder, and Deacon."

Janssen powerfully points out that Calvin's placing the office of the professor near the office of the minister and closely joining the office with the government of the church was both descriptive and symbolic.[11] Janssen correctly references and interprets Calvin's instruction that the office of the doctor is to instruct the faithful in true doctrine, and to "remind the church continually that Scripture is never exhausted in its interpretation."[12]

Kansfield, in his vital record of "very important business,"[13] chronicles and accurately interprets the legacy and history of Teacher in the Reformed Church in America (RCA). Dr. Kansfield joins Schaff and does the office of the Teacher a great service in his review and argument that the historical record clearly demonstrates that the office of the Teacher was present from the very foundation of the Christian church.

Specific to this article is his assertion and correct interpretation that RCA has done something "different" from other denominations in establishing the office of the Teacher. Kansfield reports that most denominations established theological seminaries and then empowered either the superintending boards of those schools, or the schools' administrations, to elect (or simply hire) theologians to teach within the schools. But the RCA simultaneously established the professorate and the seminary. That is, the RCA focused on calling persons to serve within an office of the church (Doctor or Teacher of the whole church), whose very embodiment and ministry of teaching ministers helped establish the seminary.

---

[11] Janssen, 235-243.
[12] Citing Schaff's analysis of Calvin's 4 Offices, articulated in the Ecclesiastical Ordinances of 1541.
[13] Kansfield, 143.

Dr. Kansfield reviewed the history of how the Classis of Amsterdam in 1771 sent to the "American church," a "Plan of Union" via a newly graduated Doctor of Sacred Theology, John Henry Livingston (1746-1825). According to Kansfield and the public record, the Classis of Amsterdam's plan separated the teaching of theology from the American college system and created the Professorate by allowing the selection of one or two Professors of Theology to teach Foundational, Constructive, and Exegetical theology, and related disciplines in accord with the Dutch Reformed confessions.[14]

Dr. Kansfield understood, as does this writer, that the use of the collective noun (Professorate) is the same as Calvin's "company of pastors" in Geneva. Further, as a faithful former president of New Brunswick Theological Seminary, Kansfield interpreted the collective noun—"the professorate"—with the 1784 election of two persons to teach theology. That is, on October 6, 1784, John Henry Livingston was elected to the office of Professor of Theology and Hermanus Meyer was elected to complete the faculty as "Instructor of the Students in the inspired languages.[15]" Thus, 1784, the date of beginning of the RCA Professorate is also the founding date of New Brunswick Theological Seminary, establishing it as the "earliest Seminary in America."[16]

Dr. Kansfield's essay illustrated that, from the election of the first professor to the office in 1784, and throughout the RCA's history until 2011, the election to the office of General Synod Professor was defined entirely in terms of serving on a seminary faculty. Indeed, for most of history, occupying the office of Professor (General Synod Professor) was synonymous with being a faculty member of Arcot Mission in India, New Brunswick Theological Seminary in New Jersey, or Western Theological Seminary in Michigan.

This writer would refer the readers interested in the history of the professorate from 1784 to 2005 to the Kansfield article and those interested in New Brunswick Theological seminary from 1874 to 2014 to the *New Brunswick Theological Seminary: An Illustrated History, 1784-2014* by Dr. John W. Coakley.[17] Critically important to this discussion on the general synod professorate is Kansfield's commentary on the "General Synod Professors Task Force," first established in 2005, and

---

[14] Kansfield, 163-164.
[15] Kansfield, 167.
[16] See Kansfield for additional information on Hermanus Meyer and the activities between the Classis of Amsterdam and the Consistory of New York.
[17] Number 83 in *The Historical Series of the Reformed Church in America* (Grand Rapids, Michigan: Eerdmans, 2014).

authorized by The President of the Synod of 2007. The task force was given this agenda:

1. To clarify the processes of accountability, appeal, and pastoral care for General Synod professors of theology currently outlined in the *Book of Church Order*, including any needed revisions to the *Book of Church Order*.
2. To coordinate the development of relevant policies and practices within the seminaries and/or commissions or agencies of the church that do not require changes to the *Book of Church Order*, but that relate to the role of General Synod professors within the seminaries and within the life of the church.
3. To review the nature of the office of General Synod professor.
4. To review criteria for eligibility to that office.
5. To clarify the responsibility of the office of General Synod professor of theology to the General Synod.
6. To examine the means by which the General Synod professors could be established as an ongoing body within the order of the church.[18]

The task force made its first report to the General Synod in 2009.

A Conversation with Dr. John W. Coakley

To learn more about the internal work of the General Synod Professors Task Force of 2005, this writer consulted with Dr. John Coakley. Dr. Coakley recalled that the committee was "very intentional" about all that they were charged to do and that they addressed, to the best of their abilities, all aspects of their assignment. Dr. Coakley informed this writer that he believed the substance and soul of their report was approved by the General Synod and by the requisite number of RCA classes. The recommendations were then included in the *BCO* in 2011.

Dr. Coakley acknowledged that their principal contributions were to the new description of the office. That is, The General Synod Professorate would:

(1) offer the *ministry of teaching* within the RCA as a whole, and
(2) represent the *living tradition* of the church in the preparation and certification of candidates for its ministry."[19]

---

[18] *Acts and Proceedings of the . . . General Synod of the Reformed Church in America*, 2007, 301; 2008, 111. Hereinafter cited as *MGS*.

[19] *BCO* 1.IV.8, sec.1.

The recommendations from the task force also included a revised procedure for discipline of a professor, found in *BCO* 2.I.3.5.

During our conversation, Coakley recalled that the two major matters of debate among task force members were (1) how professors were to be accountable to the church, and (2) whether and how the professorate's role in the church could widened, so as not to be solely defined in terms of service as a faculty member at Arcot Mission, New Brunswick Theological Seminary, or Western Theological Seminary.

The matters of General Synod professor accountability and discipline were given generous consideration, according to Coakley. How were they to aid the RCA, the General Synod Professorate, and the Church with these critical issues?

On the matter of accountability, Coakley reported that the committee's recommendation was that a General Synod Professor become a member of a classis, and therefore subject to its discipline. However, in matters of "doctrine," the committee reasoned that the General Synod Professor must remain accountable and subject to the General Synod. The reasoning and concern for this exemption lay behind the fact that "Matters of doctrine that affect the preparation of students for ministry throughout the church were not the domain of the classis, as a local body, but the domain of the General Synod."[20]

According to Dr. Coakley, the committee concluded that the only plausible course of action was to establish the aforementioned double accountability provision. Coakley did state, however, that he wished then and now that "some other solution might have presented itself to them."[21] He reasoned that the double accountability provision, with its ambiguous category of doctrine, did not alleviate the difficulty of the General Synod as a body to adjudicate disciplinary cases. Additionally, Coakley argued that the double accountability potentially increases the General Synod Professors' responsibilities as faculty members, members of Classis, and teachers to the Church. Considering the nature and importance of the office of the General Synod Professorate, it is not surprising that matters of accountability and discipline were challenging and weighty for all parties. However, like the committee, this writer is hopeful that these new *BCO* provisions will bare positive fruit moving forward.

---

[20] Personal written communication (10/19/2020) and Zoom Interview with Dr. John Coakley (12/10/2020).
[21] Coakley written communication.

In turning our discussion to the issue of widening the role of professor in the church, Dr. Coakley became very excited. He reflected that the seminary teaching role of General Synod Professors, over the last half of the twentieth century, began to include faculty members who were not RCA members. He further mentioned that, by the end of the century, the professors of NBTS and Western Theological Seminary had begun to meet and imagine a collective role for themselves in the church—as "Teachers of the church."[22]

Dr. Coakley explained that he and the Task Force began to imagine and dream about "what such a role might mean, how it might be formalized, and what implications it would have for *who* could take on the office."[23] According to Coakley, this became the primary focus of the task force. Thus, the final product of the Task Force centered on the expansion of the role of the General Synod Professor, and this recommendation is included in the revised version of the *BCO* article (*BCO* 1.IV.8) on the office of Professor. The *BCO* now states that the Professorate should be defined as having two functions: (1) the important traditional role of a RCA seminary faculty member preparing and certifying candidates for ordination and ministry, and (2) the new and exciting ministry of teaching within the RCA as a whole, by incorporating the role of "Teachers of the church" into the office of the General Synod Professor.

Additionally, the 2005 Task Force envisioned that this broadening of the role would result in the broadening of the membership beyond the seminary faculties, to include other ordained persons in the Church with recognized teaching ministries, who also have some "substantial and continuing role" in the formation of RCA students for ministry.[24] It was not surprising and not insignificant that, in the *BCO*, the matter of widening the role of the professors in the church was listed as the first defining characteristic of the General Synod Professor and its role in preparing students for ordination was listed as second.

This first General Synod Professor "role and function" of being "teachers of the church" was based on the novel idea of recasting the role of General Synod Professors to perform both an "individual" and "collective" ministry. Dr. Coakley saw many possibilities in this expanded role but warned of an underlying danger—of the Professors

---

[22] Coakley, written communication and Zoom interview.
[23] Coakley, written communication and Zoom interview.
[24] Coakley, written communication and Zoom interview.

being perceived as pontificating lecturers. John Coakley wisely stressed that the Professorate must envision themselves, and help others envision them, as enablers of the learning and growth of others. Coakley and the Task Force were envisioning the professorate as Teachers of the church in a collegial, non-superintendent sense.

Dr. Coakley and I also discussed the notion of the General Synod Professorate serving as a "preservative" critique and renewal for the RCA. This enabled us both to think on the Professorate. We surmised that the Office of the General Synod Professorate could be preservative of the church in the sense that professors functioning to develop and prepare ministers is preserving the church, and as collegial teachers of the church, they would continue to critique and enhance the church. This would constitute the "living tradition" of the office as envisioned by Calvin, Livingston, Kansfield, and the RCA.

Coakley mused that "perhaps no one person or group of persons in the church has quite that relation to tradition and overarching commitment to the critical cultivation of tradition as the Office of the General Synod Professorate." He then offered his dream and vision for the Office of the General Synod Professor, stating that he envisioned "a group of persons, ordained to the ministry of the Word, who realize a collective sense of call to be teachers of the Church; collegial and not giving themselves airs, but willing to try to be leaven for the loaf; that is, for the whole body of Christ that is the RCA."

Coakley's vision incorporates and expands on the wisdom of Allan Janssen, who emphasized the reality that the office of Teacher is not an office to be ordained to, but a specialized office to be installed into[25] and authorized as a profession to teach theology to the Church.[26]

The Professorate, the Seminary, and the Reformed Church

> The gifts he gave were that some would be apostles, some prophets, some evangelists, some pastors and teachers, to equip the saints for the work of ministry, for building up the body of Christ, until all of us come to the unity of the faith and of the knowledge of the Son of God, to maturity, to the measure of the full stature of Christ (Eph 4:7-13).

---

[25] Dort, 1619, XVIII.
[26] Janssen, 235, 236. Janssen does a marvelous job of exploring the context of this decision.

This writer affirms the work of the General Synod Professors Task Force of 2005 and comprehends the reasoning behind proclaiming the simultaneous individual ministry and corporate ministry of the General Synod Professorate of the RCA. Biblically speaking, Christ gave the gifts of individual offices to the corporate body to perform individual and corporate ministry and ministries. We must acknowledge and address personal sin and evil things people do, while we simultaneously acknowledge and address the connections between the sinful structures people create.[27]

What more effective structure is there than the office of the General Synod Professorate, for our church to address the powers, the sovereignties, and the principalities (Romans 8:38; Col. 2:15; Eph. 6:12) manifesting themselves in institutions and social systems? Our only vocation, as a Church, is to be the Christ, and to serve as ambassadors of Christ's grace and mercy.

Biblically, theologically, psychologically, and sociologically, we are to be the Church that is constantly on the edges—seeking the lost, the least, the able and the unable. It is easy to take sides and play the antagonist. It is more difficult to love all souls and to be the love that the world needs. We must not be a church that defines itself by excluding others. If you recall, the only groups that Jesus seriously critiqued were those who "include themselves and exclude others from the always-given grace of God."[28] Jesus majored in healing and converting marginalized people and sending them back into the village, back to their families, or back to the Temple to show themselves as healed to the priests and their acquaintances.

To that end, the professorate is positioned to convene teaching conferences on issues that are of importance to individual students and to the Church as a whole, and to offer a venue that allow members of the RCA to give frank expression and deep discussion to the weighty matters confronting our Church is a powerful way to engage a variety of views. This writer has been honored to empower and embolden the Reformed Church Center of NBTS to serve in this important and necessary capacity. Rev. Dr. John W. Coakley called this a "leaven in the lump" for the Church.[29]

---

[27] Adapted from Richard Rohr , ed. John Bookser Feister, *Radical Grace: Daily Meditations* (Cincinnati, Ohio: St. Anthony Messenger Press, 2019), 28.
[28] Rohr, 28.
[29] Coakley, written communication and Zoom interview.

According to John Calvin, the office of the prophetic teacher is in the DNA of the seminary, denomination, and church. A Biblical conceptualization for the prophet teacher is found in 2 Kings 2:2-15. Here, the reader is reminded of the people of Israel's trip to the Promised Land, via Gilgal to Bethel to Jericho. It further calls attention to the prophetic successions of Joshua's following Moses, as well as the double portion of the Elijah mantel falling to Elisha.[30] According to House, the passages in 1 King and 2 King stress "the continuity of God's message and God's messengers in Israel's history, and places Elijah on par with Moses.".[31] This important ministry is separated from the ministry of the pastor or, in our tradition, the Ministers of Word and Sacrament.

The Office of the prophetic teacher incorporates the responsibilities and tradition of the prophet into its living work. The Bible presents the prophetic tradition as being both fringe and establishment. James Cone argued that the prophet is a minister who is willing to take risks and speak out in righteous indignation against society's treatment of the oppressed and marginalized, even risking one's life, as we see in the martyrdom of Jesus Christ.[32] A prophetic teacher then, as suggested by Calvin,[33] is a minster possessing the prophetic gift of brilliant and convincing teaching. The beauty of the seminary is the positioning of prophetic teachers to humbly add their gifts of prophetic instruction to the minister of Word and Sacrament's administration of the sacraments and admonition and exhortation, and in concert with the elders' efforts to exercise discipline.

The issue here is that the definition of the Professorate has been narrowly conceptualized and defined. This writer suggests, as many already perceive, that the office of the General Synod Professorate must be biblically, theologically, sociologically and psychologically conceived, and that those holding the office must bear the burden of possessing the biblical knowledge, communal knowledge, ecclesiastical knowledge, and self-knowledge crucial to the denial of one's own shadow, projections, issues, and politics that would hinder the prophetic teaching work. Jesus, the consummate prophetic teacher, named brilliantly the issues of "denial," "defense mechanisms,"

---

[30] House, P. R., *1, 2 Kings*, (Nashville, Tennessee: Broadman & Holman Publishers, 1995), volume 8, 257-8.
[31] House, volume 8, 257-8.
[32] James H. Cone, *The Cross and the Lynching Tree* (New York: Orbis Books, 2011). Kindle Edition.
[33] *Citing Schaff's analysis of Calvin's 4 Offices, articulated in the Ecclesiastical Ordinances of 1541.*

"projections," and "the shadow self," that plagued His community, while advancing a ministry that provided inner healing of hurts. This writer is honored to partner with a body of prophetic teachers that reflects Jesus' instructions to communities then and now.

CHAPTER 9

When the Bonds Break: Reflections on the History of Divorce in the RCA

Lynn Japinga

Russ Gasero has been a great friend and wise guide for more than thirty years. I could not have written my dissertation or *Loyalty and Loss*[1] without his vast knowledge of the Archives and patient retrieval of box after box of materials. We have had many conversations about the state of the Reformed Church in America (RCA), past and present. By his careful attention to history and the preservation of stories and documents, Russ has maintained and nurtured the bonds between the various members and congregations of the RCA. I am grateful for the ways he has so faithfully served the RCA and wish him the best in his retirement.[2]

Divorce may seem like an inappropriate topic to honor Russ Gasero, who has been married to Maria for more than forty years. She

---

[1] *Loyalty and Loss: The Reformed Church in America, 1945-1994*, number 77 in *The Historical Series of the Reformed Church in America* (Grand Rapids, Michigan: Eerdmans, 2013).

[2] I am grateful to New Brunswick Theological Seminary and Mary and Norman Kansfield for the gift of the Hazel Gnade Fellowship. This grant enabled me to do research in the RCA Archives in February, 2020 just before everything shut down because of Covid.

has graciously accompanied him on many long road trips to General Synod, usually in a bumpy van loaded with archival boxes!

The documents Russ has so carefully preserved in the archives tell many stories of heroic witness to the gospel in congregations, mission fields, and denominational programs. The papers also tell the less heroic story of denominational disagreements and conflict. Some conflict leads to schism. Sometimes schism is averted. On rare occasions, conflict leads to creativity and revitalization.

The RCA is currently wrestling with disagreements which seem to be leading toward schism. The most controversial issue is the status of LGBTQ+ people in the church. Can they be members? Can they be ordained? Can they be married? Can their children be baptized? Some RCA members argue that the purity of the church demands that sinful homosexual behavior (relationships, marriage) cannot be tolerated. Other RCA members argue that the grace and justice of the church demand that anti-homosexual behavior (denying the opportunity for marriage and ordination) cannot be tolerated.

How does a denomination resolve such a sharp difference of opinion? Can the denomination be a big tent where different views are tolerated? Should the denomination make a statement that homosexual behavior is sinful and that anyone who disagrees is subject to discipline? Should the denomination make a statement that homosexual behavior is not sinful and that anyone who disagrees is subject to discipline? What is the role of a denominational statement in deciding moral questions and church polity? Some members insist that the RCA clearly articulate its beliefs about homosexuality, and make sure that all ministers act accordingly. Others insist that RCA members do not agree on this topic and that it is not the role of the denomination to make such statements.

In this essay I will explore a similarly controversial issue from the twentieth century. How should the church deal with divorce and remarriage? RCA members did not agree! In the 1930s, some RCA congregations, but not all, suspended divorced people from church membership and denied them the sacraments. They discouraged or forbade remarriage in order to retain the possibility of reconciliation. These rules about divorce were thought to be rooted in the Bible and the desire to maintain the purity of the church and take a firm stance against sin.

A century later, however, almost all RCA churches contain couples who have been divorced and remarried. Elders are not sent to investigate when a church couple gets a divorce. Divorced and remarried people are elected to Consistory. Indeed, even some pastors divorce and continue fruitful ministry in a gracious congregation.

How did this transition occur in the RCA? Is there anything to learn from the conversations about divorce that might be instructive in our current debates?

The two topics are similar in significant ways. The Bible criticizes both divorce and homosexuality based on what seems like clear biblical teaching, and yet biblical scholarship has noted that these texts are complicated, nuanced, and rooted in ancient cultural practices. Public opinion about divorce and remarriage has become more accepting in the last fifty to seventy-five years, although the church often criticized this acceptance. Finally, both issues have been viewed as a potential source of destruction for the family, the church, and the nation. The two topics can be compared because they both challenged the church to reconsider long held beliefs about the Bible and nature of grace.[3] Both topics dealt with questions of biblical interpretation, the role of culture, the purity of the church, and the nature of sin and grace. Disagreements over divorce, however, did not lead to heated debates at General Synod, or angry letters in the *Church Herald*, or threats to divide the denomination, all of which have occurred in response to disagreements over homosexuality.

In this essay I will explore some of the ways that RCA members responded to divorce during the twentieth century. Around 1900, the RCA tried to prevent divorce using secular laws. When the laws failed, RCA churches tried to prevent and punish divorce using discipline and education. In the 1960s and 1970s the RCA engaged in deeper study of the pastoral, biblical, and theological issues involved in divorce, and some congregations began demonstrating more grace and understanding to divorced people. On several occasions, the General Synod of the RCA was asked to provide definitive rules for handling divorces. Each time the Synod refused to provide such a directive

---

[3] The two topics are quite different, however, because divorce is an example of a breakdown in a relationship. Homosexual orientation is a question of sexual attraction and identity. It is not inherently hurtful or sinful or damaging, although certainly LGBTQ+ people wrestle with sin as all human beings do. The understanding of homosexuality is one of the most disputed aspects of the debate in the RCA, as some people argue that the orientation itself is a sin, others say acting on the orientation is a sin, and others say that orientation is simply part of the diversity of creation and is not sinful. The question is far more complex and nuanced that I can discuss in this paper.

and said the issues must be resolved at the pastoral level.[4] There were sharp differences of opinion regarding biblical interpretation and appropriate pastoral practice, but with time, study, and a move toward grace, the denomination came to a place of general agreement.

Preventing Divorce Using the Law

Understanding the practices of the RCA regarding divorce requires a basic understanding of divorce law in the United States. At the end of the nineteenth century, divorce laws were far more restrictive than in current practice. Divorce was relatively rare, difficult to obtain, and often limited to the grounds of adultery and desertion. Some states granted divorces for cruelty and drunkenness. Each state made its own rules. New York allowed divorce only on the grounds of adultery until the 1960s. South Carolina did not permit divorce at all until 1949. Western states often advertised their more flexible divorce laws. A New Yorker seeking a divorce could live in Indiana or South Dakota for three to six months and be granted a divorce with few questions asked. These migratory divorces caused serious legal problems, as a man might return from three months away with a new wife.

Most Protestant churches argued that adultery was the only biblical, and therefore the only legitimate, ground for divorce. The "innocent" party in a divorce granted for adultery should be allowed to remarry, but not the "guilty" party. If a divorce was obtained on unbiblical grounds such as desertion, cruelty, or drunkenness, neither party should be allowed to remarry. In practice, pastors did occasionally officiate at the weddings of the "guilty" party and the non-biblically divorced.

The actual number of divorces was relatively small, but the rate of increase caused anxiety. This chart shows the absolute number of marriages and divorces per year. Much of the increase can be attributed to the rapid growth in population, but notice that the number of

---

[4] Missing from this essay, unfortunately, are examples of actual divorce and discipline cases in congregations. These stories would tell the history of divorce in the RCA more realistically than the pronouncements of General Synod or denominational magazine editors. Those anecdotes are hidden deep in the pages of Elders' Minutes, or were not recorded in order to preserve privacy. The denomination might make statements, but the actual experiences of people who divorced were complicated and painful and not easily categorized into guilt and innocence. If readers of this essay know of past incidents of divorce in their congregations, I would be happy to hear about them. I am especially interested in the kinds of discipline churches used and whether it was effective in bringing about reconciliation.

marriages doubled between 1867 and 1900, but there were five times as many divorces in 1900.

Year	Number of Marriages	Number of Divorces
1867	357,000	10,000
1890	570,000	33,000
1900	709,000	56,000
1920	1,274,000	171,000
1940	1,596,000	264,000
1946	1,613,000	610,000
1967	1,927,000	523,000

The number of divorces dropped during the Depression, sharply increased after World War II, and then leveled off during the 1950s and 1960s to about 1.5 million marriages and 400,000 divorces per year.[5]

As the divorce rate slowly increased, denominations and congregations became increasingly anxious about the evils of divorce. When rhetoric and persuasion did not reduce the divorce rate, they turned to coercion. Divorce reformers called for a uniform national divorce law, which would force all states to abide by the same rules.[6] Because states held the power to enact their own laws, however, a national law was possible only if the United States Constitution was amended.

The RCA entered into this divorce reform conversation for the first time in 1898. Opponents of divorce had discovered that Congress could legislate for Washington D.C. and the American Territories and proposed a bill that would allow these residents to divorce only on the ground of adultery. The RCA agreed to support this, and Synod instructed the Stated Clerk of General Synod to sign a petition to the Senate and the House of Representatives encouraging the passage of this law. In 1899, Synod again expressed its opinion on divorce by passing a resolution opposing the remarriage of the guilty party in divorce cases, even if the state permitted them.[7]

---

[5] Statistics about divorce rates are incomplete and inconsistent. Records of divorce were not always maintained. Sometimes the number of divorces is stated per 1,000 people and other times per 1,000 marriages, which makes them difficult to compare. https://www.cdc.gov/nchs/data/series/sr_21/sr21_024.pdf.

[6] A national law would have included lengthy residency requirements in the state where one obtained a divorce, adultery as the only legitimate ground, and a mandatory waiting period before remarriage.

[7] *Acts and Proceedings of the General Synod of the Reformed Church in America* (hereinafter referred to as *MGS*), 1898, 255-56; 1899, 502-3. Prior to this, the General Synod had not dealt with divorce.

A few years later, the General Synod was more cautious. The RCA belonged to an ecumenical group called the Alliance of Reformed Churches. In 1903 the Alliance made a statement about divorce and invited the RCA to endorse it. In the typical rhetoric of the time, the Alliance described the high level of divorce and remarriage as "an evil of growing proportions and a serious menace to our Christian civilization." The Alliance cited the teaching of Jesus that marriage was permanent and could only be dissolved by death or unfaithfulness. The Alliance then asked RCA ministers not to officiate at the marriages of divorced persons except for the innocent party in a divorce granted for adultery.

Rather than endorsing the request immediately, Synod referred it to a special committee[8] which reported in 1904. The committee sympathized with the problem of divorce but did not think Synod had the authority to instruct clergy because divorce was not a matter of doctrine or polity. "Your committee is unable to find that either the standards or the Acts of the General Synod define the Scriptural grounds for divorce. Therefore, your committee is unable to recommend the passage of such a resolution."[9] The committee members believed that Synod should not legislate on pastoral matters that minister and elders should decide. The proper role of Synod regarding controversial social issues was to *encourage* members and clergy to act in certain ways, not to *require* compliance with hard and fast rules.

The General Synod refused to bind the consciences of its pastors, and yet tried to use laws to make divorce more difficult for American citizens. Synod sent delegates to the Interchurch Conference on Marriage and Divorce, which met several times between 1903 and 1905. The Conference continued to ask for a national uniform divorce law and tried to limit remarriage to the innocent party. It also encouraged churches to insist that their ministers marry only the innocent party in the divorce, after a one year wait. Most states ignored their advice, preferring to preserve their current laws and keep their distance from church interference.

These Christian groups tried to impose a high view of marriage on their fellow citizens, but lofty words about marriage did not change the fact that people behaved badly. Divorce could be made more difficult to obtain, but new laws did not reduce the demand for it. In their efforts

---

[8] The committee was composed of Cornelius Wells, James Vance, Alfred Myers, and two elders.
[9] *MGS*, 1904, 777-779.

to discourage divorce and remarriage, churches often appeared rigid, legalistic, and eager to punish unhappy people by forcing them to stay in a bad marriage.[10]

The editors of the weekly RCA magazine, the *Christian Intelligencer*, expressed a similar condemnation of "monstrous" and "scandalous" divorce laws. Between 1900 and 1920, the editors published one or two columns a year lamenting the high divorce rate. One cited statistics that showed 12.8 million marriages and 946,000 divorces between 1898 and 1906.[11] While eight percent seems low compared to the current forty percent divorce rate, the editors saw the numbers as a sign of national moral decay. They criticized famous people who divorced, because their bad example made divorce seem acceptable. They criticized other Protestant clergy for being willing to remarry anyone who asked, regardless of the reasons for divorce. They lamented the absence of a proper idea of marriage as sacred and binding. Finally, in a time of stark poverty and social inequity, the editors argued that nothing in social life was more urgent than strict national divorce laws and penalties for disobeying them. They called for church and state to form an alliance against evil doers.[12]

Like many Protestant churches, the RCA thought of itself as the conscience of the nation, with the duty to protect the fragile but essential institution of marriage. Was the church imposing its religious ideals of marriage and asking the state to enforce them? When churches insisted that marriage was sacred, and could only be ended on the basis of a biblical ground, was the church misusing its authority and influence?

In general, the RCA said relatively little about divorce in the first third of the twentieth century. Divorce happened to wealthy society people. or movie stars, or poor people, but not to most RCA members. Divorce was an evil to be condemned in others but not a reality that affected RCA people.

Preventing Divorce Using Discipline and Education

In the 1920s the divorce rate started to rise more rapidly. Between the 1920s and the 1950s, divorce increasingly occurred among RCA members. In response, some churches called for increased education,

---

[10] Editorial note, "Interchurch Conference on Marriage and Divorce," *Christian Intelligencer*, June 8, 1904.
[11] Editorial note, *Christian Intelligencer*, "The Divorce Evil," Dec. 2, 1908, 783.
[12] Editorial note, *Christian Intelligencer*, Sept. 20, 1911, 601.

in the hope that learning about marriage would help people succeed at it. Others insisted that church discipline would both discourage divorce and punish it if it did occur. Churches denied the Lord's Supper or suspended the membership of people who committed adultery or divorced on non-biblical grounds. This could mean that a spouse who sought a divorce on the grounds of abuse or abandonment or addiction did not have a biblical ground and was therefore considered sinful and subject to discipline.

Pastors began to realize, however, that divorces defied the simple categories of guilt and innocence, biblical and non-biblical. Even small towns full of Dutch Reformed people were not immune from divorce cases. In 1936, John TerLouw, a pastor in South Holland, Illinois, sought advice from an older pastor, J.F. Heemstra, of Hudsonville, Michigan. TerLouw wondered whether it was appropriate to remarry divorced people, even those who were presumed innocent. He told three complicated stories of divorce in his congregation.

A widowed woman married a man but quickly left, saying she could not live with him. They lived separately for several years but he provided no support. She taught school and, when married women were no longer allowed to teach during the Depression, she divorced him in order to keep her job.

A man's wife left him and their daughter and refused to reconcile. He countersued for divorce in order to retain custody. Should he be denied access to the Lord's Supper when it was not his choice to divorce? She was not a member of the church. Could the elders ask her what had happened?

A widowed man married a woman who hated his children. She left him but constantly asked him for money, until the judge pronounced her a "gold-digger." They divorced and he married again.

What constituted guilt and innocence in these cases? Who could remarry? What was appropriate church discipline? Should a spouse who had been deserted be punished with permanent singleness? TerLouw was trying to follow the rules, but some of his parishioners considered him intolerant compared to other local pastors who were more flexible. TerLouw wanted some clear and consistent rules to govern all RCA churches.

In his response, Heemstra acknowledged the difficulty of cultural pressure on churches and pastors. Most people who divorced expected to remarry, and they assumed that, if the court permitted remarriage, the church should, also. It was difficult for a pastor to be labeled intolerant, Heemstra said, but the church needed to maintain its purity by opposing all remarriages except for the innocent party in a divorce granted for adultery. All others sinned by remarrying, and their sin could not be erased by repentance. The church must exclude from membership those who continued in their wrong relationships. That would include all the examples TerLouw cited. God might choose to be gracious to them, but that was God's prerogative. The church could not be lenient. Heemstra defined the church as "composed of moral men under God's strict orders," so it must act in the fear of God, according to God's word. Congregations should not be too gracious and tolerant.[13]

These pastors seem to believe that church discipline would solve the divorce problem. People would not divorce if they knew they would be suspended from church membership. If they did divorce, then discipline would force them to reconcile, or to repent and atone for their sin by never marrying again. Unfortunately, the reality was that discipline did not prevent divorce, but punished a person who did not choose a divorce.

These pastors (and others like them) were bound up in both legalism and a literal reading of the Bible. They knew God was forgiving and gracious. They knew people were trying to make the best of a bad situation. They wanted to be more gracious, but they were held back by what they perceived as God's strict orders.

Over time, some members of the RCA came to see divorce in a less legalistic and more nuanced way. It was not an evil which must be condemned, but a sign of problems in the larger society. People divorced not necessarily because they were selfish or adulterous but because of challenging social circumstances beyond their control. For example, the divorce rate increased in the years following World War II as people extricated themselves from hasty war marriages.[14] In 1946, the RCA's Committee on Social Welfare advised churches to emphasize the sanctity of marriage[15] and teach courses on marriage and the home.

---

[13] John TerLouw file, Joint Archives of Holland, Michigan.

[14] Some people entered into marriages on the eve of a soldier's departure and later found they had little in common. Other marriages did not survive the stress of separation. Some soldiers may have been seriously damaged by their war experience. Those who divorced under these circumstances usually wished to marry again.

[15] The report noted that, although the Reformed Church did not believe marriage was a sacrament, as the Roman Catholics did, it did believe marriage was sacred, because it had been instituted of God and confirmed by Jesus Christ.

In the same year, the RCA's Board of Education noted that movies and novels often glamorized divorce. Churches needed to counter that powerful influence by insisting that "divorce is not freedom but calamity and that the Christian Church in her teaching, worship, and fellowship can save marriages from catastrophe."[16] Education, however, would be no more effective at preventing divorce than discipline. The church was no longer the primary shaper of opinion, and found it difficult to compete with the influence of popular culture.

In 1947, Albertus Pieters, a retired missionary and professor at Western Seminary, gave some advice about divorce at a meeting of the Holland Classis. He discouraged biblical literalism and strict discipline, as both could be misused in the absence of critical thinking and pastoral sensitivity. Pieters insisted that the Bible had to be interpreted. For example, the Bible says that a man can divorce his wife, but can a woman divorce her husband? If we agree that she can, he said, then we are interpreting the Bible and not reading it literally.

Interpreting the Bible also required reflecting on its cultural context. In the Sermon on the Mount, Jesus said that the marriage vow should not be broken, but he also advised cutting off a hand to avoid sin. Neither were meant to be taken literally. Jesus was presenting the ideal of lasting marriage, but he recognized the reality of human brokenness. Jesus did not give more laws, Pieters said, but principles which his followers can use to make ethical decisions.

Pieters then addressed a pastoral situation that had arisen in the Christian Reformed Church. A man divorced his wife for non-biblical reasons and remarried, but then acknowledged he had been wrong to remarry. The Christian Reformed Church (CRC) insisted that, if his first marriage has not been broken by the biblical ground of adultery, then the bond must still exist, and he was thus still married to the first wife while committing adultery with the second. Pieters wondered what true repentance meant in this situation. Should the man divorce the second wife and return to the first? Should he support both wives but live with neither of them? In the CRC, as long as the first wife was alive, he was technically married to her. No matter what he did, he was barred from the sacraments.

Pieters said this was a case of excessive discipline and legalism. He argued that, when the man married again, the bond of the first marriage was broken. The church must accept the legitimacy of a

---

[16] *MGS*, 1946, 182-3, 98.

second marriage that has been validated by the state. The man should be allowed to repent, be forgiven, and restored to church membership, without undoing his second marriage for the sake of legalistic obedience.[17] Marriage was not a magic rope that bound spouses who did not want to be together.

Pieters was a voice of calm during a tense time in the RCA. Midwestern RCA churches were often in competition with their CRC neighbors. Christian Reformed churches sometimes criticized RCA congregations for being too liberal and "soft on sin." Some RCA churches may have felt they needed to prove their orthodoxy by their rigorous church discipline, but Pieters gave them permission not to follow the CRC lead. Within the RCA during the post-war period, fundamentalism, purity, and biblical literalism were gaining traction in the RCA.[18] Pieters advised the Holland Classis that the Christian faith did not have to be rigidly literal and legalistic.

The desire for clear answers to questions about divorce reappeared in 1948, when the Classis of Pleasant Prairie asked General Synod to formulate a "definite and authoritative directive." The committee assigned to study the request reported in 1949 that the General Synod did not have the constitutional right to make binding rules about divorce and remarriage. Such directives would be a form of legalism that was inconsistent with both the New Testament and the Reformed tradition. On matters which were not clearly articulated in the Standards or *Book of Church Order*, Synod can give advice, but it cannot bind pastors to particular actions. Instead, decisions about the remarriage of divorced people needed to be made by the individual pastors who knew the couple and their history.

The committee recognized that divorce cases were complicated and that the grounds cited did not necessarily represent the facts in the case.[19] Pastors should take time to evaluate requests for marriage,

---

[17] Pieters argued that incurable insanity, life imprisonment, or a contagious disease could also break the marriage bond. People who divorced for these reasons should be free to remarry. The paper Pieters can be presented can be found in his file in the Joint Archives of Holland.

[18] See Japinga, 23-53.

[19] New York State became well known for its orchestrated divorce cases. Since adultery was the only ground for divorce, unhappy couples had to prove it had occurred. A man might get a hotel room, hire a woman to pretend to be his mistress, hire a photographer to provide evidence, and arrange for the wife to "discover" the scene. Judges and lawyers participated in the falsehoods. See Nelson Manfred Blake, *The Road to Reno: A History of Divorce in the United States* (New York: Macmillan, 1962).

but if divorced people (whether "innocent" or "guilty") confessed their sins, repented, and experienced forgiveness, ministers should feel free to marry them, "since neither the church nor its ministers are punitive agencies."[20] There was a growing recognition that people could not be prevented from remarrying and that it might actually be healthier for the church to encourage remarriage than to enforce punitive discipline.[21]

Despite this caution about the limits of legalism, literalism, and discipline, some RCA pastors sought clear rules about how to carry out punitive discipline. In 1954, the Particular Synods of Michigan and Chicago appointed a joint committee to provide churches with specific guidance about divorce and remarriage.[22] In 1957, the Committee published a substantive pamphlet containing its advice. Its work had been guided by three core values: marriage was a sacred institution so church policies had to be determined by the Bible; the church should not allow the state to establish the criteria for legitimate divorces and remarriage; divorce was a last resort and should be delayed as long as possible to provide opportunity for reconciliation.

The Committee recognized that people divorced for different reasons and gave specific advice for the innocent party, guilty party, and couples who obtained non-biblical divorces. The innocent party in adultery cases was counseled to remain single in case the spouse wanted to reconcile. She or he was not disciplined but might be admonished if he or she had contributed to the problems that caused the adulterer to stray. The guilty party must be suspended from church membership until he or she repented, and could not remarry until the innocent spouse died or remarried.

---

[20] *MGS*, 1949, 196-7.
[21] One possible contemporary way forward suggested for the RCA has been that the denomination should allow decisions about the marriage and ordination of LGBTQ+ people to occur at the congregational and classis level. No one would be forced to ordain or marry LGBTQ+ people, but no one could deny the right of other classes and congregations to do so. This has been dismissed by other RCA members as "too soft on sin" and "kicking the can down the road." They demand a definitive rule from General Synod, but if this committee was correct in 1949, it is not the appropriate work of the General Synod to offer such a rule.
[22] Members of the Committee from the Chicago synod were Gordon Girod, Spencer DeJong, Raymond Olthoff, Cornelius Reynen, John Van Harn, Bert Van Soest, and Charles Wissink, and from the Michigan synod, Abraham Rynbrandt, Gradus Aalberts, Theodore Schaap, John Damon, David Santman, and Garrett VanderBorgh. The Committee reported to the Particular Synods in 1957. The pamphlet can be found in the Pamphlet Files in the Joint Archives. It is 24 pages long, half on marriage and half on divorce and remarriage.

If a couple divorced for reasons other than adultery, the bond of their marriage had not been broken and they remained married in the sight of God. They were subject to discipline until they repented and reconciled. Neither should remarry, but if one did, that second marriage was considered adultery and broke the bond of the first marriage. At this point, the other spouse could repent of the sin of an unbiblical divorce and be restored as a full member of the church, even if she or he chose to remarry. The first spouse to remarry was still subject to discipline.

One of the crucial issues in this discussion was the definition of marriage as a sacred bond that could only be broken by death, adultery, or desertion for religious reasons.[23] The authors suggest there was something holy or supernatural about marriage. This led to serious relational knots. Was a divorced man married to his first wife? His second wife? Both? Most people who divorced saw this very differently. Their marriage bond had been broken by adultery, cruelty, absence, addiction, or by the decision that the marriage was over. The legal act of divorce simply acknowledged what had already occurred.

The pamphlet also emphasized the role of ministers and elders in investigating, evaluating, and disciplining members who divorced. If a marriage showed signs of trouble, elders were dispatched to talk to the couple. If they divorced, elders asked why, in an attempt to discern the innocent and guilty party. The goal of these inquiries was to help the couple forgive and reconcile, even if adultery had occurred. Couples who resisted this advice might find themselves suspended from church membership and denied the Lord's Supper. Surprisingly, some disciplined people remained connected to their congregation even in this state of limbo. Others left for a more hospitable church.

The members of this joint committee wanted to maintain the purity of the church by discouraging divorce, but the discipline more often punished those who failed at marriage. The efforts of the pastors and elders to intervene might have been experienced as intrusive and meddling rather than caring and gracious. Both the authors of the pamphlet and the pastors and elders knew that both spouses usually contributed to the failure of a marriage, and yet they treated the guilty and the innocent quite differently.[24]

[23] One example of the specificity of these instructions is the insistence that the only legitimate desertion was a non-Christian spouse leaving the Christian spouse for religious reasons. A shrewish woman could not drive her husband away and claim he deserted her.
[24] Anecdotal evidence suggests that the RCA churches in New York and New

The RCA tried to reduce the divorce rate with laws, with church discipline, and with education, but the divorce rate kept rising. RCA members disagreed about divorce, as did the rest of American society. Was divorce a legitimate way to end a troubled marriage? Or should people be forced to stay in a bad relationship to protect the institution of marriage?

Responding to Divorce with Realism and Grace

As the RCA grew in the 1950s, its denominational structures also expanded. The establishment of the Commissions on Theology and Christian Action provided a way to help RCA members reflect on the big questions in church life. The Christian Action Commission (CAC) published a paper on divorce in 1962.

The CAC paper acknowledged the persistent dilemma of divorce. Ideally, marriages last a lifetime, but, in reality, many do not. People behave badly or grow apart, and their marriages break down. Churches had tried to resolve this dilemma in the past by refusing to recognize divorces or bless remarriages, but insisting on the permanence of the marriage bond did not keep marriages together.

The CAC, like Albertus Pieters fifteen years earlier, noted the significant cultural differences between first century and the present. Jesus discouraged divorce in part because he was trying to protect vulnerable women from being discarded for petty reasons. Divorce was not the ideal, but Jesus gave one example of how it might be justified. Several decades later, the Apostle Paul did not simply adopt the literal teaching of Jesus (divorce only for adultery), but recognized that, if an unbelieving spouse left the marriage, the desertion broke a marriage just as adultery did. The CAC argued that these were not the only two possible grounds for divorce, but two examples of the many ways a marriage could fail.

Marriage had a personal aspect: the desire for partnership and fidelity. In some marriages, when the personal aspect waned for a time, the marriage survived because the couple relied on the institutional aspect of marriage, the promises made before God and witnesses. The church has often tried to force unhappy couples to stay together and preserve the institution of marriage, but, if the love and affection are absent, it will not be a real marriage. The CAC observed, "The church's

---

Jersey did not use these practices of discipline as rigorously as some midwestern congregations did. As one pastor who served in New York in the 1950s said, "We treated divorced people as sinners like everyone else."

dilemma is that when she always places institutional over personal considerations, she finds herself in a legalistic straitjacket....Automatic priority for institutional welfare (church, society, marriage, *et al.*) gives law priority over grace which contradicts the nature of the church."

The CAC argued that the church should encourage permanent relationships, but when they failed, the church should be gracious and offer healing and acceptance rather than judgment, shame, and discipline. The Commission did not use the categories of guilt and innocence, because both spouses usually contributed to the breakdown of the marriage.[25] Remarriage should be a possibility for all divorced people, regardless of the grounds. A couple forced to marry because of an unplanned pregnancy may not have had the maturity to succeed in that marriage but should not be denied the opportunity to try again. The criteria for remarriage should be whether the divorced people have come to terms with their own failures and immaturities, forgiven the partner, and provided adequate support for the spouse and children.[26]

In the 1970s divorce became even more common. No-fault divorce laws enabled a couple to decide to end their marriage based on irreconcilable differences without having to prove one person's guilt. No-fault also made it easier for one spouse to obtain a divorce when the other objected.

In 1973 the Particular Synod of Chicago (PSC) asked the Theological Commission to offer biblical solutions to the problem of increasing divorce and remarriage. Apparently the 1962 paper did not answer their questions, and they were concerned that "neighboring churches of the same denomination may have a different interpretation as to the solution of these problems thus making cooperation difficult." It appears that some churches in the Particular Synod of Chicago with stricter policies resented RCA congregations that welcomed divorced people rather than disciplined them. Again, the PSC asked for a set of rules that should apply to all. Again, the Theological Commission refused to supply these rules.

The Theological Commission presented its report to Synod in 1975. The Commission took a different approach to interpreting Jesus'

---

[25] The courts used guilt and innocence to demonstrate that one spouse was guilty of causing the divorce against the other who was innocent. The legal process of divorce often exacerbated anger and conflict, especially in custody battles. See the recent Netflix movie, *A Marriage Story*, for a contemporary example.
[26] *MGS*, 1962, 205-216, 223-4.

teachings about divorce.[27] Instead of debating cultural context and ideals versus reality, the Commission simply noted that Jesus' words were difficult. Jesus set the bar high for marriage, higher than many people could reach, but more importantly, he taught forgiveness. Divorce and remarriage were sins that could be forgiven.[28]

Rather than provide consistent rules to deal with divorced people, as the PSC asked, the Commission gently chastised churches for not being gracious enough.

> The church is called to be a fellowship where those who falter and fail can rebuild and where the divorced can find love and patient support. Some congregations (including elders and ministers) have not developed their ability to exercise the forgiveness of Christ toward repentant adulterers and divorcees. Yet the Bible indicates that failures or sins in this area are no more grievous than other sins nor any less forgivable.[29]

This marks a striking shift from the older belief that discipline and punishment were essential to preserve the church's purity. The Commission did not believe that the church should shame or punish divorced people, or accuse them of grievous sin, as the 1957 pamphlet had done. Divorce happens, and churches earn no bonus points with God for making divorced people feel worse than they already do.

Unlike previous discussions of divorce in the RCA, this paper did not debate which grounds for divorce were legitimate. Adultery broke the bond of marriage, as did abuse, addiction, absence, and a mutual decision to end it. Elders no longer needed to investigate the reasons for marital break down in order to determine who could remarry. The

---

[27] The paper illustrates the difficulty of using biblical texts to address contemporary issues. The paper argued that marriage was for fellowship, human fulfillment, and the transmission of faith in the family. It quoted some bible verses to support these purposes. But studying the actual families in the Old Testament suggests that marriage was primarily for the production of children. Some marriages had genuine fellowship, others less so. The men appear to be more fulfilled than the women. Marriages in the Bible were very different than our current views of what marriage should be.

[28] The paper briefly discussed Paul's teaching in I Corinthians 7, noting that Paul allowed for divorce for reasons particular to his cultural context. The early church did not in this case apply the words of Jesus literally, because their problems with marriage were somewhat different than decades earlier in the time of Jesus. The paper advised that the church at all times needs to apply the principles of Scripture and seek the guidance of the Spirit when trying to answer questions that the Bible does not answer.

[29] *MGS*, 1975, 170.

Commission wrote, "Christian realism includes acknowledging the new possibilities included in God's forgiveness. Where the one flesh relationship has been irreconcilably shattered, there one has divorce (*de facto*) and it must be recognized."[30] Divorced people should take adequate time to repent, reflect, change their unhealthy patterns, and rebuild their lives, but they did not have to face a life of singleness to atone for the sin of divorce.

The Theological Commission suggested that churches could strengthen marriages with more realistic teaching about the inevitable stress and conflict couples will experience. Churches should teach people how to work through conflict and understand that difficult interludes were normal in a marriage. Conflict did not indicate the marriage was doomed to fail, but that it needed grace and healing. Marriage was a beautiful but fragile gift.[31]

The fact that the commissions urged grace and forgiveness did not mean that all RCA churches followed their suggestions. Often, divorced people felt excluded in a congregation centered around families. Anecdotal evidence suggests that even if people were no longer disciplined for being divorced, they might be treated as second class citizens. One interesting indicator of a congregation's full acceptance was when the first divorced and remarried person was elected to consistory. Another was the treatment of a pastor who was divorced.

The *Church Herald* printed a few first-person articles about divorce between the 1950s and the 1970s, but they were usually anonymous or written by someone outside the RCA. The stories describe the awkward experience of attending church after a divorce. People did not know how to respond to a divorced person. One woman wrote about how she forgave her cheating husband and became a better wife and they reconciled and lived happily ever after. This was admirable, perhaps, but not the experience of most divorcing couples. If thirty to forty percent of marriages were ending in divorce, the RCA probably had its share of divorces in its congregations, but it was difficult to talk about divorce and admit that it happened to church members.

As the divorce rate increased, many churches realized they needed to minister more effectively to divorced people, who often felt shunned and excluded and shamed by their churches. Some pastors organized divorce recovery groups, where divorced people were invited to gather for eight weeks in a supportive environment to listen to speakers and

---

[30] *MGS,* 1975, 170.
[31] *MGS,* 1975, 162-72.

begin to process the difficult emotions. Some groups met in churches, but others chose a neutral environment such as the social room of a large apartment complex. Non-churched people were more likely to attend if the group did not meet in a church. If several churches cooperated in starting the groups, divorced people were more likely to find and develop community with other divorced people that they did not know. The groups worked well. People found community and support. Some found new spouses, although they were encouraged not to date group members too early in the process.

The groups also provided a way for divorced people to demonstrate their listening and leadership skills. They might not have been elected to Consistory because of their divorce, but those who showed leadership skills were recruited to lead and facilitate future recovery groups. Rather than shaming or punishing, the groups enabled and facilitated lay leadership. People who felt uncomfortable in their congregations were encouraged to transform their difficult experiences into care for others.[32]

Some of the groups were led by clergy who had themselves been divorced. For some pastors, divorce meant the end of ministry, but others found that their churches were gracious and supportive of them. Several pastors report receiving extraordinary care from church members who reached out to them with regular invitations to meals or activities. Pastors recalled those demonstrations of grace three decades later and were still moved by the care they received.

In Grand Rapids, Michigan, some of the people in the divorce groups wanted to worship together, in part because they did not feel comfortable in their own churches. The result was a new church, The Good News Community Church. Some churches, such as Christ Community in Spring Lake, Michigan, Central Reformed in Grand Rapids, Michigan, and Christ Memorial in Holland, Michigan, developed a reputation as places where divorced people could find a home. Sometimes other churches in the community resented these churches and accused of them being liberal, or soft on sin, or places that took anyone in. One pastor of Christ Memorial said that the discipline imposed on divorced people in other churches was his most effective church growth technique.

---

[32] See Sue Poorman Richards and Stanley Hagemeyer, *Ministry to the Divorced: Guidance, Structure, and Organization that Promote Healing in the Church* (Grand Rapids: Ministry Resources Library, 1986). Hagemeyer started a number of divorce recovery groups in Grand Rapids, MI, and also served as pastor of the Good News Community Church.

Conclusion

It is striking to look back and see the degree of anxiety people felt about marriage and divorce. The editors of the *Christian Intelligencer* lamented the frightening rise in the divorce evil and feared that society would fail if marriage failed. Overtures to General Synod showed the desire to make rules for church and society which would force people to stay married even if they were miserable. People were anxious about the fast pace of change, and they worried about social problems like juvenile delinquency, crime, and poverty, which were often linked to living in a single-parent home. Over time it has become clear that democracy will survive a high rate of divorce, and even social conservatives no longer complain about the divorce evil. LGBTQ+ people have now become the focus of communal anxiety, and gay marriage is painted as sign of social breakdown, just as divorce used to be.[33]

It is also striking to observe the very different theological and pastoral perspectives evident in the RCA. One side insisted that the purity of the church must be maintained by following God's strict rules about marriage and divorce. Those who broke the rules were disciplined and shamed. Technically, God may have forgiven them, but they could not marry again, so in a sense their sin was remembered by the church. The other approach was to recognize both the power of human brokenness and the power of God's grace and forgiveness. Divorce was difficult and painful but people could be forgiven and make a fresh start. The church was not punitive, in this view, and it valued grace more than law.

What accounts for these significant differences and shifts in the denomination's view of divorce? And how did the denomination stay together despite very different opinions about divorce and the role of the church?

Biblical interpretation has changed, and many RCA members now read the Bible differently than they did a century ago. In 1961, the Theological Commission published a paper which stated that the Bible was a complex document with a social and historical context. Scripture was "infallible and inerrant in all that it intends to teach and accomplish concerning faith and life." This paper released people from a literalist reading of Scripture, which included the teachings of Jesus about divorce. One could take the Bible seriously as a guide to life

---

[33] It is rather ironic that two presidents most adored by conservative evangelicals, Ronald Reagan and Donald Trump, had been divorced once and twice respectively.

without seeing the words of Jesus as providing absolute and binding rules about divorce and remarriage.[34]

Some people saw the pain caused by the strict rules and discipline. One pastor recalled that, when he was a teenager, people in the church were shamed and forced to make public confession of the sin of divorce or a premarital pregnancy. He vowed to do ministry more graciously. When people saw someone in their own family affected by divorce, they were likely to relax their beliefs on strict discipline. When they saw happy second marriages, they realized the possibilities of grace and a new start.

The growing acceptance of divorce in the culture and media also played a role in the church, even though church members often decried the bad influence of the culture. Television shows, novels, and movies tell the complicated stories and make it easier to understand and empathize with people who are divorcing. On the questions of slavery, civil rights, women's rights, homosexuality, and a number of other issues, the church has often learned from the culture to seek justice and equality and acceptance.

The RCA realized over time that it was generally better to be too gracious than too legalistic regarding divorce. Harsh discipline did not usually change minds and behavior and often sent people away from the church. Grace was more likely to keep them connected. Grace was more healing and life-giving than discipline, which was often shame based. Several pastors who divorced over thirty years ago remembered, and were still moved by, the compassion of church members who made regular social connections with them during the most difficult parts of their divorce. The memories of discipline were rarely positive.

RCA members increasingly realized the complexity of divorce. In 1900, divorce was considered a moral evil, but by 1975 most people realized that divorce did not fit tidy categories of guilt and innocence. The more church members saw the complexity, the more they were inclined to be gracious. Divorce was not an evil "out there" in society. Divorce was not confined to "sinful" or non-Christian people. Divorce

---

[34] See Japinga, 96-101. The paper was written in response to a situation in New Jersey where a seminary student said in his classis exams that he did not believe in six twenty-four-hour days of creation. Some ministers wanted to deny him ordination. Others insisted his beliefs were legitimate and that the Reformed tradition had never been literalist in its reading of Scripture. The paper said the Bible was inerrant and infallible in what it intended to teach, which in the creation story was the power and presence of God from the beginning of time. The Bible was not a science book which intended to teach the mechanics and details of creation.

could affect anyone, even church members. It was a result of the flaws and limitations that are part of being human.

At the denominational level, the RCA took its time in working through policies about divorce. Committees were formed to study difficult questions. When papers were produced by Commissions, congregations were encouraged to study them. The world is not static, much as we might wish that it was. Culture changes, public opinion changes, biblical interpretation changes. Change is not necessarily evidence of sin, and it is not sinful or unfaithful to revisit and rethink the big questions. To think deeply and repeatedly about important issues is not "kicking the can down the road," but an awareness that church opinion has changed on many issues over time. It is wise to be open to the leading of the Spirit and not assume that an issue that affects people in deep ways may be decided once and for all.

Finally, the General Synod has been reluctant to legislate about controversial pastoral issues, even when the Bible seemed to provide clear instructions. In 1904 and 1949, the General Synod said it did not have the authority to legislate about issues that should be handled at the pastoral level. When the commissions spoke about controversial questions, their papers offered biblical, theological, and pastoral advice but did not attempt to compel everyone to act in the same way. Commissions could think through the issues and offer advice, but they also trusted the pastoral instincts of pastors and elders who were closer to the situation. Divorce was complicated and one rule rarely fit all circumstances.

In times of uncertainty, churches and other institutions are tempted to make rules, to make decisions, to set boundaries. In times of deep anxiety, absolutes are appealing. But history has shown that strict rules and an authoritarian style are not the healthiest approach in the long run. Divorce, sexuality, identity, and community have been and will always be complicated issues. They involve sin and grace, repentance and forgiveness, pain and loss, redemption and healing. In all these things, we rest in the mercy and the comfort and the transformation made possible by the God whose bonds with us are never broken.

CHAPTER 10

"[T]he Everlasting Gospel should be preached to them in their own language": The First Translation from Dutch to English in the Dutch Reformed Congregations of North America

Dirk Mouw

Jacob Schoonmaker, while a minister in Queens County, Long Island, in the 1840s, wrote a story about his grandfather, John Henry Goetschius, who had been preaching in the same congregations a century earlier. Goetschius had had a conversation with an Anglican clergyman with whom he was on good terms. The Anglican said to Goetschius, "It always seems to me, when I hear you preach, that the law must have been given in the Dutch language."

"Very likely," replied Goetschius, "and I have always thought that the English must have been the language in which the serpent spoke to our mother in Paradise."[1]

Queens County was a different place in the 1840s than it had been in the 1740s. Goetschius had been Dutch by choice not by birthright. Born in Switzerland, he came to New York by way of Pennsylvania. He

---

[1] Jacob Schoonmaker, "John Henry Goetschius," in William B. Sprague, ed., *Annals of the American Reformed Dutch Pulpit* (New York: Robert Carter and Sons, 1869), 17; Edward Tanjore Corwin, *A Manual of the Reformed Church in America*, fourth edition (New York: Board of Publication of the Reformed Church in America, 1902), s.v. "Schoonmaker, Henricus," and "Schoonmaker, Jacob."

probably only learned Dutch because of his contacts in the colonial Dutch church and his desire to minister in a Dutch Reformed congregation. For Goetschius, learning Dutch was one of the costs of admission to the Queens County pulpits; the Dutch language was strong on Long Island. But when Schoonmaker told the story about his grandfather a century later, he did so as one who had witnessed the end of Dutch worship in those congregations. Schoonmaker knew people who had welcomed the ascent of English worship; he also knew people who lamented the fact that Dutch was no longer the language of the church. If Goetschius' remark about the language of the serpent in 1740 had been in good fun, there was a certain edge to the story when Schoonmaker told it a century later.

The story of the transition from Dutch to English worship has often been told in terms of the triumph of forward-thinking leaders who led their churches into the inevitably English future or as a story of people who tenaciously clung to and fought for their native tongue and then lamented its passing. In either telling, hostility and anger often figure significantly in the story. And is that not what we would expect to find? Language, religion, culture, and personal identity are often intimately connected.

And, indeed, the best-known episode in the transition from Dutch to English worship, that of the Dutch Reformed church of Manhattan, easily supports either of these plotlines. The consistory, having received a request for English worship and observing the decline of the Dutch language in many of the households of the church, pursued a plan to call an English-speaking minister. They were met with strong resistance, opponents challenging them within the congregation, in the public square, and in courts, both secular and ecclesiastical. Still, Archibald Laidlie began preaching in English in Manhattan in 1764; those who had striven to keep him away then strove for years to drive him out.[2]

It is not the purpose here, however, to tell the story of what happened in Manhattan in the 1760s again. The story of what happened in other Dutch Reformed congregations in the Mid-Atlantic is different and less well understood. Those churches made the transition from

---

[2] For the English-language controversy in Manhattan, see Charles E. Corwin, "The Introduction of the English Language into the Services of the Collegiate Dutch Church of New York City," *Journal of the Presbyterian Historical Society* 10 (1919-20): 175-88; Joyce D. Goodfriend, "Archibald Laidlie and the Transformation of the Dutch Reformed Church in Eighteenth-Century New York City," *Journal of Presbyterian History* 81 (2003): 149-62.

mostly Dutch-language to universally English-language congregations at a variety of paces and by a variety of means—first in congregations on the fringes of Dutch culture areas and last in areas of concentrated Dutch settlement. Overwhelmingly, they did so with little sign of the sort of bitterness and strife one might expect. There is one common thread that connects all of the congregations, however, even Manhattan: the language of the church—the sermons, the liturgy, the music, and the records—went through a series of transitions from Dutch alone, to Dutch-and-English, to English alone.

The idea that ministers ordained in the Dutch Reformed Church should preach in English was hardly a novel one in the 1760s. Nor was it often controversial. Already in the 1650s, years before New Amsterdam became New York, the director-general of New Netherland, Peter Stuyvesant, wrote to the directors of the Chartered West India Company in the Netherlands to request another minister for New Amsterdam—specifically requesting one who could preach in English as well as Dutch.[3] After the English Conquest of 1664, the numbers of ministers who could and did preach in both Dutch and English grew. Petrus Tesschenmaecker preached in both languages in 1679 in what is now New Castle, Delaware.[4] As the number of English speakers grew in the now-British colonies, so did demand for English preaching. The number of Dutch Reformed ministers able to preach in both languages increased as well, though in 1695 congregations were still seeking ministers from the Netherlands able to preach in both languages.[5] By the middle of the eighteenth century, the number of bilingual Dutch Reformed ministers in the colonies had increased significantly. And Dutch ministers preaching in English to Anglophonic (e.g., Presbyterian) congregations *did* become the cause of some complaints by some Dutch clergy and laity during the early years of the controversy over American ordinations and the relationship of the colonial congregations to the church in the Old World. Complaints faded and disappeared, however, after the Classis of Amsterdam came out in favor of English preaching in the Dutch congregation in

---

[3] West India Company Directors to Stuyvesant, April 4, 1652, in Edward Tanjore Corwin and Hugh Hastings, eds., *Ecclesiastical Records: State of New York*, seven volumes. (Albany: James B. Lyon, 1901-1916), I:307. Hereinafter *ERNY*.

[4] Tesschenmaecker to Classis of Amsterdam, October 30, 1682, Amsterdam Correspondence, Archives of the Reformed Church in America, New Brunswick, N.J.

[5] Commissioners of Kings County congregations to Classis of Amsterdam, May 7, 1695, Amsterdam Correspondence, Archives of the Reformed Church in America.

Manhattan, insisting that "the Everlasting Gospel should be preached unto them in their own language."[6]

The fact that other congregations introduced English preaching at about the same time as Manhattan seems to have gone unnoticed by historians. Only nine months after Laidlie preached his first sermon in New York, the consistories of the Raritan Valley in New Jersey decided that, in the congregation of North Branch, a portion of the services would be in English.[7] Scarcely a year later, the consistory of Freehold and Middletown decided that a portion of the worship services in its Middletown sanctuary would be as well.[8] Thus, two Reformed congregations were very close behind the Manhattan church.

The consistory minute marking the introduction of regular English worship in North Branch suggests that it was peacefully decided and easily implemented. In these respects, it was far closer to the norm for congregations that would follow than had been the experience in Manhattan.

> ... [I]t was proposed to the h[onorable] meeting that [since] a portion of the congregation of North Branch, who are not strong in the Dutch language, request that a portion of [worship] services be conducted in English, whereupon it was resolved that Rev. Hardenbergh, every other turn, will do one of the [Sunday] services in English.[9]

Thus, first, the change appears to have been made by the consistory without controversy in response to desires voiced by some of the congregation. Second, the minister of the congregations, Jacob Rutsen Hardenbergh, was bilingual; introducing English preaching did not involve calling another clergyperson, it was just a matter of asking the pastor to preach certain sermons in English. In Middletown,

---

[6] See, for example, Anthonius Curtenius to Classis of Amsterdam, November 5, 1754, in *ERNY*, V:3519. Wilhelmus Jackson to Classis of Amsterdam, n.d. [1762], Amsterdam Correspondence, Archives of the Reformed Church in America; Classis of Amsterdam to the "Thirteen Members who have declared themselves against the call of the Rev. (Archibald) Leadly [sic]," October 3, 1763, in *ERNY*, VI:3898.

[7] Raritan Valley consistories, minute, January 13, 1765, "Baptismal Register of the Ref. Protestant Dutch Church Raritan, New Jersey, Commencing in the year 1699 March 8 and extending to Dec 29, 1839," United Reformed Church, Somerville, New Jersey.

[8] Freehold and Middletown consistory, minute, February 3, 1766, Church of Freehold: Records, 1709-1851, Monmouth County Historical Association, Freehold, New Jersey.

[9] See note 7. My translation.

the introduction of English preaching thirteen months later appears to have been quite similar, though the consistory there did add provisos that those who wished to enjoy English services would have to "subscribe" (make pledges to contribute) to the minister's salary and agree "to submit to our church and church constitution." And since the minister there, Benjamin DuBois, was also bilingual, it was likewise an uncomplicated decision for the consistory to implement.[10]

The manner in which decisions were made to introduce regular English preaching—or to change the proportion of English-to-Dutch services—in individual congregations varied. In some instances, the consistory, presumably taking into consideration the desires as well as the best interests of the congregation, simply made the decision. For example, in 1791, the consistories of Hackensack and Schraalenburgh, "decided, that for the future, the services of Rev. Freligh [Froeligh] will occur in English in every other turn in the afternoon" service.[11] More often, it seems, the consistory acted (or did not act) upon formal or informal requests from churchgoers. In the foregoing cases in North Branch and Middletown, there is nothing in the surviving records to suggest a formal petition, so it is likely that those desiring English sermons made their requests orally to consistory members. In Albany, on the other hand, in 1799, the consistory received a formal petition for Dutch services signed by sixty-two people.[12]

The most common manner of determining which language should be the language of worship—or the ratio during the period of mixed-language worship—was probably the subscription. In the eighteenth century in particular, this was a common method employed by consistories to make important decisions. Proposals would be

[10] See note 8. My translation. Curiously, Corwin is vague about the timing of the introduction of English worship in Middletown and whether there was controversy. This may be because he was relying in part on the writings of Theodore Welles or the two relied on a common secondary source. Welles states that English preaching began in Freehold in 1764 and was only later introduced in Middletown, meeting resistance in the latter location. This does not comport with the surviving congregational records. See Corwin, *Manual*, s.v. "Du Bois, Benj." and Theodore W. Welles, "The Church—Her History, 1699-1905," in Abram I. Martine, ed., *Bicentennial Celebration, 1699-1899, Reformed Church of the Navasink and its Two Branches* (New York: P. F. Collier and Son, 1905), 54.

[11] Hackensack and Schraalenburgh consistories, minute, June 19, 1791, v.3, Bergenfield, etc., Records of the Dutch Reformed Church of Schraalenburgh and Hackensack, New Jersey, Rutgers University Special Collections and Archives, New Brunswick, New Jersey. My translation.

[12] Albany consistory, minute, March 1, 1799, vol 1a, Records of the First Reformed Church of Albany (microfilm), Archives of the Reformed Church in America.

circulated among the congregation, either on separate sheets or on one sheet with two columns, and individuals would pledge a sum (to be paid annually) either in support of English preaching or Dutch preaching. Some individuals would pledge in both language columns, others would pledge only for one language. Assuming the minister was bilingual, or in case of congregations with more than one minister who were collectively able to preach in both languages, the consistory would assign the Dutch-to-English worship ratio in accordance with the sums pledged for each by worshippers. For example, in 1773, the consistories of the Raritan Valley congregations in New Jersey called Rev. Christian Frederick Foering to serve their congregations in order to increase the number of English services. When Foering declined the call, the consistory, "After deliberation, decided" to circulate "a new subscription list" for Hardenbergh, their current minister, and "let everyone sign for English services or Dutch services, as their judgment and inclination directs them" to pledge to pay toward the minister's salary, and "services will be regulated according to the subscriptions for the one and the other."[13]

While the subscription list was undoubtedly the closest the overwhelming majority of congregations came to democratic decision making with respect to the language of worship, at least one congregation did hold a congregational vote on the subject. When the Niskayuna consistory issued a call to Thomas Romeyn in 1805, they specified that he would perform half the services in English and half in Dutch—for ten years. The consistory added that, once the decade of evenly divided worship had passed, the congregation would then vote on the proportion of services in each language. Early in 1816 the congregation did, indeed, vote and chose to discontinue Dutch worship entirely.[14]

On some occasions, however, the hands of consistories were tied; circumstances did not permit them to strike the linguistic balance they wanted. In Albany, the Dutch-born Eilardus Westerlo began preaching

---

[13] Raritan Valley consistories, minute, December 27, 1773, "Baptismal Register of the Ref. Protestant Dutch Church Raritan, N.J. Commencing in the year 1699 March 8 and extending to Dec 29, 1839," United Reformed Church, Somerville, New Jersey. My translation.

[14] Niskayuna consistory, call to Thomas Romeyn, August 29, 1805, and minute, January 1816, in Royden Woodward Vosburgh, ed., *Records of the Protestant Reformed Dutch Church of Niskayuna, in the Town of Niskayuna, Schenectady County, N. Y.*, (New York: New York Genealogical and Biographical Society, 1919). See also Elizabeth D. Shaver, *A Serving People* (Schenectady, New York: Niskayuna Reformed Church, 1966), 29.

in English in addition to his native Dutch in 1782. The assistant pastor at the time of Westerlo's death in 1790, however, and the ministers subsequently called to serve the church were unwilling, or unable, to preach in Dutch. There were certainly members of the congregation desirous of Dutch preaching. Circumstances had prevented the consistory from acceding, however: the church's financial condition as well as the reputation of the congregation as riven with conflict sometimes made it impossible for them to call a bilingual minister and at other times led clergy to decline calls. In 1794, a delegation from the General Synod stepped in to try to help but to no avail. When, six years after Westerlo's death, a young minister finally accepted a call to the church, he was not one who could preach in Dutch. Regular Dutch preaching did not resume for more than a dozen years after Westerlo's death, when a minister, William Linn, fleeing a raging epidemic in New York City, took refuge in Albany and conducted worship in Dutch for a while. Though he returned to New York for a couple of years, he soon retired in Albany and again offered Dutch pulpit supply. Throughout the years from the death of Westerlo to the arrival of Linn, the consistory received requests and petitions for Dutch worship. Although there were certainly moments of strong tensions over the matter, most of the requests seem to have been more plaintive than angry. In a 1799 letter to the consistory, petitioners averred,

> [W]e wish not to create Dissentions in the Church of Christ . . . but while we respect the Feelings of others, we entreat you to . . . save us the Mortification of either abandoning public Worship, or attending it, in <u>to us</u> an unknown or imperfectly known Tongue, by making effectual provision, not for an occasional & interrupted service in the <u>Dutch Language</u> but for its regular & Stated Continuance.

While the consistory did set aside funds for Dutch pulpit supply, its decision "to procure a Dutch Minister from time to time," probably was not the "regular & Stated" preaching the petitioners had sought.[15]

---

[15] Robert A. Naborn, "Eilardus Westerlo (1738-1790): From Colonial *Dominee* to American *Pastor*" (Ph.D. diss., Vrije Universiteit, 2011), 210; Robert S. Alexander, *Albany's First Church and Its Role in the Growth of the City* (Albany: The First Church in Albany, 1988), 160-67; Albany consistory, minutes, volumes 1, 1a, 2, Records of the First Reformed Church of Albany (microfilm), Archives of the Reformed Church in America. Consistory quote is from April 12, 1799, volume 1a. Quote from the letter to the consistory is from Photocopy of Petition for regular service in Dutch, February, 1799, Rutgers University Special Collections and Archives.

In 1811, the Kingston consistory was presented with a similar petition; like the consistory of Albany, Kingston felt its hands were tied. The transition to English worship in Kingston had been unusually abrupt. Up to 1808, all worship had been in Dutch; their pastor, George Doll, could preach in three languages—but not English. In that year the consistory called John Gosman, partly because Doll had grown somewhat infirm. There was also, however, desire in the congregation for English preaching. Gosman, could only preach in English. While Doll continued to preach occasionally in Dutch after Gosman arrived, he retired and moved away soon after. The consistory responded to the 1811 petition by agreeing to six Dutch services per year, provided that funds could be raised. Those petitioning for Dutch services took the matter to the Classis of Ulster, stating that they had had an agreement with the Kingston consistory to call a second minister to preach in Dutch. The consistory took the position that calling a second minister to preach in Dutch was not in the "spiritual interests" of the congregation but also that "the Church revenue is not competent to the decent support of two settled ministers." Thus, the consistory felt that its hands were tied. While the petitioners felt that the consistory had failed to live up to agreements made, and found support in the Classis of Ulster, the consistory held that it was unable to comply with the decision of the Classis of Ulster. The consistory decided to be annexed to the Classis of Poughkeepsie.[16]

By the eve of the American Revolution, the options for ministers like Doll, who could not preach in English, began to grow more limited. Martinus and Henricus Schoonmaker, born in 1737 and 1739 in Rochester (Ulster County), New York, were, likewise, both weak in English. They both probably attempted preaching in English but the reception was such that they quickly abandoned the effort. Martinus's first call included Gravesend, and he eventually came to serve several congregations in Kings County (where Dutch remained strong) to 1824. Even there, however, in 1787, these congregations called Peter Lowe to preach in English.

[16] Corwin, *Manual*, s.v. "Doll, George J.L." Kingston consistory, minutes, 1811-1812, "Consistory Minutes 1795-1841, Deaths 1701-1841," volume 5B, Records, First Reformed Protestant Dutch Church of Kingston, Old Dutch Church, Kingston, N.Y. Quote is from December 9, 1811. Perhaps those desiring Dutch worship left the congregation or perhaps there was some disingenuousness on the part of the consistory. On July 3, 1812, the consistory decided that there were few desirous of Dutch preaching and resolved to stop attempting to procure it for the congregation. See also note 12.

Where congregations were unable to support two ministers, they were faced with the choices of either trying to force a unilingual minister out or delaying regular English services longer than they would otherwise have chosen. In Fishkill and Poughkeepsie, where Henricus served for the first nine years of his career, he had come under increasing pressure to preach in English. Unable or unwilling to do so, he accepted a call to Acquackononck in 1774, and then to both Acquackononck and Totowa from 1799-1816. Evidently there had been a desire in the congregations of Acquackononk and Totowa for English preaching that went unsatisfied until Henricus retired in 1816. Both congregations then called bilingual ministers, and both called upon their new pastors to preach in both languages.[17]

In theory, consistories that called bilingual ministers were free to set the proportion of Dutch-to-English preaching that they thought best for their congregations. Such was not always the case, however. William Eltinge served three congregations that were (then) in Bergen County. In one of them, Saddle River, he had been voluntarily preaching extra sermons in English beyond what his call stipulated. In 1811, however, the consistory ordered him to reduce the number of services he conducted, specifically requiring him to preach no more English sermons than his call specified. Eltinge refused and resigned his call to that congregation in a somewhat bitter letter, on two grounds. First, it was contrary to the spiritual welfare of the congregation, particularly the youth. Second, "under these discouraging circumstances, your minister is gradually losing his habit of preaching English, and his stimulus to accuracy in said language...." Unless he were allowed to preach regularly in English, he would become less useful in a land where English was overtaking Dutch. His resignation was approved by the Paramus consistory, the classis, and the particular synod. While the consistory of Saddle River had tried to establish the ratio of Dutch-

---

[17] Corwin, *Manual*, s.v. "Schoonmaker, Martinus," and "Schoonmaker, Henricus;" Henry Whittemore, *History of the First Reformed Protestant Dutch Church of Breuckelen, Now Known as the First Reformed Church of Brooklyn, 1654-1896* (Brooklyn: First Reformed Church, 1896), 23-24; Eric Nooter, "Between Heaven and Earth: Church and Society in Pre-Revolutionary Flatbush, Long Island" (Ph.D. diss., Free University of Amsterdam, 1994), 92; A. P. Van Gieson, *Anniversary Discourse and History of the First Reformed Church of Poughkeepsie* (Poughkeepsie [N.Y.]: First Reformed Church, 1893), 57; John Gaston and Ame Vennema, "The Reformed Church of Acquackanonk," in *A History of the Classis of Paramus of the Reformed Church in America*, ed. Joseph H. Whitehead, et al. (New York: Board of Publication, R.C.A., 1902), 184.

to-English worship it thought best, there was evidently a limit to what it could force its minister to do involuntarily.[18]

While for many congregations the surviving record does not contain information about when English preaching was introduced or when Dutch preaching ended, it is nevertheless possible to make some observations about the transitionary period. In most congregations founded before the Revolution,[19] the first regular (or stated) English sermons were preached in the 1780s or 1790s and the last stated Dutch sermons were preached in the decade after 1800. As noted above, two congregations in New Jersey had already introduced English preaching in the 1760s and a congregation in Bucks County, Pennsylvania, began trying to introduce English in 1775. These were all near the margins of the Dutch culture area of New Jersey.[20] At the other end of the spectrum were congregations in and around Bergen County. Stated English preaching was not introduced in the congregations of Acquackanonk and Totowa until 1816 and Dutch preaching continued in the Old North congregation until 1833.[21]

The pattern in New York (excluding Manhattan) was not as straightforward. In Fishkill, stated English preaching commenced in 1772, and in Lansingburgh a lay reader was reading equal numbers of sermons in each language beginning in 1774.[22] And while the majority

[18] Eltinge to the Paramus consistory, September 30, 1811, Classis of Paramus, minutes, October, 1811, Edward Tanjore Corwin, *Manual and Record of the Church of Paramus*, revised and enlarged edition (New York: Hosford and Co., 1859), 64-69. See also 70-72 in the same volume.

[19] My general observations about language and worship focus chiefly on congregations founded before the American Revolution.

[20] Subscription list for a call to Solomon Freligh (Froeligh), February 31, 1775, Registers, 1737-1833, vol. 1., North and Southampton Reformed Church, Churchville, Pennsylvania, Records, Presbyterian Historical Society, Philadelphia, Pennsylvania. The call was declined.

[21] As noted above, Henricus Schoonmaker did not preach in English and he was the sole minister of these congregations until 1816. For Old North, John Beardslee, *et al.*, *The Old North Reformed Church of Dumont, New Jersey* (Dumont, New Jersey: The Old North Reformed Church, 1976), 20.New Jersey</style> (Dumont, N.J.: The Old North Reformed Church, 1976

[22] Minutes of the General Meeting of Ministers and Elders of the Reformed Dutch Church, October 1772, in "Minutes of the General Synod of the Reformed Protestant Dutch Church in North America, 1771-1812," in *The Acts and Proceedings of the General Synod of the Reformed Protestant Dutch Church in North America*, Vol. I, *1771-1812: Preceded by the Minutes of the Coetus (1738-1754) and the Proceedings of the Conferentie (1755-1767), and followed by the Minutes of the Original Particular Synod (1794-1799)* (New York: Board of Publication of the Reformed Protestant Dutch Church, 1859), 31; Arthur James Weise, *History of Lansingburgh, N.Y., from the year 1670 to 1877* (Troy, New York: W. H. Young, 1877), 8.

of New York congregations seem to have followed the same pattern as the majority of New Jersey congregations—initiating English preaching in the 1780s or 1790s and discontinuing Dutch preaching in the early 1800s—the outliers at the other end of the spectrum were not concentrated in one area but two: Long Island and Ulster County. In Kings County, for instance, two ministers began taking turns preaching in a number of congregations in 1787, one preaching in English, the other in Dutch until 1824. In Ulster County, the Kingston congregation had a late and also extremely short transition from Dutch to English preaching—English sermons began in 1808 and Dutch sermons ended the same year. A more typical and slower transition commenced in Katsbaan in 1808, though regular Dutch sermons were not discontinued until 1825.[23]

While preaching was central to Dutch Reformed worship throughout this period, the sermon was by no means the whole of worship, and other elements presented a range of difficulties when English worship was introduced. The easiest, of course, was the reading of scripture, as an acceptable English translation of the Bible was available. The Heidelberg Catechism, the Belgic Confession, and the Liturgy or Forms and Prayers of the Reformed Church of the Netherlands presented more of a challenge, but the New York City church had produced a translation of those when the decision had been made to introduce English worship. Adapting and improving parts of previous translations and producing new translations of others, the church produced versions that historian Daniel Meeter has described as "a complete success."[24]

The transition to English singing in worship was not equally smooth. Meeter describes the stakes in 1763, when the New York City congregation set about to produce an English Psalter. Abandoning the Genevan tunes of the Dutch Psalter "would have been an enormous price to pay for introducing English into worship." The goal in 1763 was a rhymed translation of the Psalms that could be sung simultaneously in English and Dutch to the Genevan tunes. The result

---

[23] Gerald F. De Jong, *The Dutch in America, 1609-1974* (Boston: Twayne Publishers, 1975), 104; Corwin, *Manual*, s.v. "Doll, George J. L."; Benjamin Myer Brink, *The Early History of Saugerties* (Kingston, New York: R. W. Anderson and Son, 1902), 285.

[24] Daniel James Meeter, *"Bless the Lord, O My Soul": The New-York Liturgy of the Dutch Reformed Church, 1767*, number 6 in Kenneth E. Rowe and Robin A. Leaver, eds., *Drew Studies in Liturgy* (Lanham, Maryland: Scarecrow Press, 1998), 48-75, 81-82.

was a disappointment in large part because the tunes familiar to the Dutch were altered when the adaptation was composed. As a result, congregations outside Manhattan broadly rejected it. Two decades later, the young American denomination saw fit to assemble a new English Psalter for use in its congregations. It abandoned the Genevan tradition of the Dutch and adopted the Common Meter tradition of the English. Successive denominational versions were further adapted to Anglo-American culture.[25]

Meanwhile, congregations were evidently struggling with the transition to English singing. A couple of years before the first denominational English Psalter appeared, the consistory of Freehold and Middletown was evidently attempting to resolve differences of opinion among their own worshippers regarding Dutch and English Psalm-singing. In what was an extraordinarily (if not uniquely) long document produced by the consistory to be read to the congregation, the consistory laid out its position on the music in worship, through nine queries and answers, complete with proof texts. Recommending "order and decensy" in singing, and acknowledging that tunes and "mode[s] of singing" were "matters indifferent," the consistory nevertheless held that it was "a lawful duty to improve musick" and "Resolved unanimously, that it is sutteable for a Christian on a chearfull occasion to sing a chearfull tune," though "the flat key" was "suteable to be used on mournfull occasions." The congregation that had been among the very first to introduce English preaching, clearly sided with English traditions over the Dutch Genevan tradition.[26]

Making the transition to English singing was evidently a common problem for consistories and congregations for decades after English preaching was introduced. While the Freehold and Middletown consistory had embraced new English meters, in 1797, the consistory of Millstone and Neshanic—on the same day that they decided that sermons should be equally divided between the languages—also appointed a committee to find "a certain set of tunes suitable to the different Metres in the low Dutch Psalm book & proper to be sung in Church." Though the minute is somewhat cryptic, the consistory

---

[25] Meeter, 47-49, 77-81; James L. H. Brumm, *Singing the Lord's Song: A History of the English Language Hymnals of the Reformed Church in America*, number 2 in the *Occasional Papers* (New Brunswick, New Jersey: Historical Society of the Reformed Church in America, 1990), 11-21.

[26] Freehold and Middletown consistory, minute, February 26, 1787, Church of Freehold: Records, 1709-1851, Monmouth County Historical Association.

appears to have been seeking to introduce English singing in the Dutch style.[27]

Adjusting to the English style of singing remained an issue into the nineteenth century. The Albany consistory had appointed a committee to decide "what Psalm Tunes are proper to be Continued in use;" in early 1800 the committee reported a list of long, common, and short meter tunes that appears to include only one Genevan tune. Still, in 1803, the consistory received a petition advocating for "improvements" in congregational singing. While the consistory found itself unable to meet the costs associated with the petitioners' request, by 1806 it had agreed to a petition along similar lines, allowing "a number of young gentlemen" to sit in the front row of the gallery, to assist the congregation in singing. There had always been leaders for congregational singing in the Dutch Reformed Church and, though more competent in the English language than the Dutch, some evidently believed the congregation needed leadership when they sang in both languages.[28]

The language of a congregation is not, of course, only the language of sermons, scripture, and songs but also the language of its records. In this, congregations generally made the transition from all Dutch to all English records over the course of years or decades, most often beginning in the decade after the end of the Revolution. The general pattern is that English did not appear in congregational records for a number of years after regular English worship commenced in a congregation and Dutch typically disappeared from the records before regular Dutch worship ceased. Not surprisingly, some English appeared in congregational records as early as 1774 in places like Bucks County, Pennsylvania, and Dutch persisted long in the records of Tappan, only disappearing completely from the records in 1830.[29]

---

[27] Neshanic consistory, minute, December 20, 1797, Memberships, Consistory Minutes 1786-1875, Copies of the accounts of the Church Builders, 1759-1772, Archives of the Reformed Church in America.

[28] Albany consistory, minute, February 18, 1800, volume 2, "Minutes of Consistory, Jan. 1, 1800-March 21, 1808, Records of the First Reformed Church of Albany (microfilm), Archives of the Reformed Church in America; Alexander, *First Church*, 247-48.

[29] Smithfield, Pennsylvania, Reformed Records, 1741-1814, Historical Society of Pennsylvania, Philadelphia, Pa.; Records of the Reformed Dutch Church, Tappan, N.Y., Tappan Reformed Church, Tappan, N.Y. I have ignored occasional words or entries that fall well outside the period of linguistic transition as well as documents regarding legal or financial matters clearly written so that people who did not know Dutch could read them.

Written as they were by many individuals—ministers, both in the churches to which they were called or those that they visited and supplied, elders, deacons, lay worship leaders—they represent a myriad of individual choices and unconsidered actions. Some consistories and authors, at various points in time, clearly knew what the language of the church was, or should be. In Kingston, the consistory decided in 1809 that its records "be hereafter kept in the English language."[30] Seldom was the change abrupt, however. A 1779 Raritan Valley record suggests that while the writer considered Dutch to be the language of the church, English was the language of much of the rest of his life: the consistory minute was written in Dutch on the back of an English broadside, along with English notes about finances and a colt, and a recipe for cough syrup.[31] And the records, in very many cases, indicate a bilingual people, living their lives in two or more linguistic spheres. The baptismal registries often remained in Dutch longer than of any record type; entering a baptism in Dutch the writers very often used the English word for the month of March, and similarly, used various spellings of the Dutch word for the same month sometimes while writing in English. In a particularly striking example of language mixing, outgoing Katsbaan consistory members in the early 1810s made annual financial notes mostly in Dutch but with a little English mixed in: "Ende vinde aen geld [and find in cash] the summe van Seven Dollars and Twenty Four Cents ende zekere summe aan noten end bande [and certain sums in notes and bonds]. . . ."[32]

In addition to records, sermons, liturgy, and worship, there is at least one other sphere in which one can speak of the language of a congregation: the congregational community. This is much harder to gauge in retrospect, but Dutch remained in some respects the language of at least some congregational communities long after Dutch worship and Dutch record-keeping were memories. George Sharpe, who was born in Kingston about two decades after regular Dutch worship had disappeared, wrote later in life that he could remember a time when, at "the close of the service," the "pronunciation of the benediction

---

[30] Kingston consistory, minute, May 30, 1809, "Consistory Minutes 1795-1841, Deaths 1701-1841," Records, First Reformed Protestant Dutch Church of Kingston.

[31] Consistory minute, December 23, 1779, Johannis Demott (1716-1780) Papers: Neshanic Reformed Church Accounts, Subscription Lists, etc., 1759-79, in Demott (John) Papers, Rutgers University Special Collections and Archives.

[32] Consistory records, 1811-1813, Saugerties Reformed Church Records, Hoes Collection, Senate House State Historic Site, Kingston, New York.

[in English] was followed by an immediate resumption of the Dutch language by the congregation passing down the aisles and issuing from the doors." Just a little upriver in Katsbaan, a sermon was preached by Abram Lansing in 1886 in the nineteenth-century "colloquial dialect" of the Hudson Valley Dutch—more than sixty years after the last regular Dutch service in that town—it was "thoroughly enjoyed" by the hundreds of people "who were able to understand it...." The language had in most senses left the church, but it had not entirely left the church community.[33]

It is perhaps ironic—a Dutch Calvinist might say providential—that even though Dutch had ceased to be the language of worship in New York and New Jersey, both Dutch and English were the languages of the future for the American denomination. The minister who preached the 1886 sermon in Katsbaan was born in 1829, probably near Schenectady. In his forties, Lansing served as a missionary, part of the church plant that became Third Reformed Church in Pella, Iowa.[34] He was among a number of Reformed ministers, descended from New Netherland ancestors, who were able to preach and serve a new wave of Dutch immigrants who arrived beginning in the 1840s.[35] Though English would eventually prevail as the language of the churches, the unilinguality that had seemed inevitable in 1835 was no longer so certain two decades later.

The case of Manhattan notwithstanding, the transitions of the languages of the congregations were generally peaceful and gradual transitions—spanning more than seven decades. Language, culture, religion, and identity are often intimately connected and, together, often resistant to change, so one might expect to find evidence of acrimony in the archives, and yet there is little to be found. The transition from the Dutch to the English sermon was made much easier by the wide availability of clergy who could preach in either language, allowing consistories and congregations to make the transition at the pace they wanted and thought best for their constituents. At the congregational level, the final stage, that of discontinuing Dutch preaching entirely, seems to have been the most difficult. Ironically, introducing the language of the "serpent" went quite smoothly; discontinuing sermons

---

[33] "Oration," in *Year Book of the Holland Society of New-York*, 1886-87, 46; Brink, *History of Saugerties*, 285.

[34] Corwin, *Manual*, s.v. "Lansing, Ab. G.," and "Pella 3D, 1869"

[35] Frederick G. Dekker and Theodore W. Welles, "The First Holland Reformed Church of Paterson," in *A History of the Classis of Paramus*, 432; Martin Flipse, "The First Holland Reformed Church of Passaic," in *A History... Classis of Paramus*, 504.

in the language of the "law" more often occasioned hard feelings. The transition to the English liturgy was eased by people who were well educated in theology and who also intimately understood nuances in both languages, providing congregations with fully acceptable alternatives for services in either language. And while the language of the song was a more difficult hurdle to overcome, a series of both linguistic and cultural adaptations at both the denominational and congregational levels eventually found overwhelming acceptance. Meanwhile, the language of some congregational communities helped preserve a language that would prove to be an important part of the future of the denomination even as others helped prepare worshippers for a future in the United States.

The Reformed Church in America has an international past, even when one looks solely at the early congregations of New York and New Jersey. Planted in a Dutch colony, it flourished and began to develop a distinct identity and organization in British colonies. But by the time Rev. Peter Van Pelt, Rev. John Romeyn, and Rev. John Johnson delivered funeral orations for George Washington from pulpits in Flatbush, Rhinebeck Flatts, and Albany, in early 1800, it had become very much a church of the United States of America, nonetheless significantly shaped by its Dutch and British past.[36] The stories of those transitions and many others are to be found in the archives of the congregations and denomination. I have deep gratitude to Russell Gasero for his decades of service, collecting and preserving a vast body of documents in which many stories and the answers to many questions lie. His extensive knowledge and documentation of other historical resources in congregational and other repositories is likewise an invaluable resource. His contributions to the denomination, assistance to scholars, and aid to the curious from many walks deserve acknowledgement and celebration. I, for one, could not have done much of the work I have done since I first visited the Reformed Church Archives two decades ago, had it not been for his broad and deep expertise, and generous spirit.

---

[36] Peter I. Van Pelt, *An Oration, in Consequence of the Death of General George Washington, Late President of the United States* (Brooklyn, New York: Thomas Kirk, 1800); John B. Romeyn, *A Funeral Oration, in Remembrance of George Washington* (Poughkeepsie, New York: John Woods, 1800); John B. Johnson, *Eulogy on General George Washington* (Albany, New York: L. Andrews, 1800).

CHAPTER 11

Saving the Stories of RCA Women: A Tribute to Russell Gasero

Mary L. Kansfield

Introduction

This essay will focus on some of the ways in which Russell Gasero, as Reformed Church in America (RCA) Archivist, has played a pivotal role in helping to recognize the dedication, the giftedness, and the ministries of RCA women and to memorialize RCA women in the identity and history of our beloved Reformed Church in America.

The gifts and skills of RCA women have, for the most part, gone unrecognized; their dedication to their "jobs" has been taken for granted; and their struggles within the cultures of their communities have gone mostly unnoticed. RCA women have long been under-valued. Reformed Church women have long known what it's like for their gifts and for their commitments to the church to go unrecognized. Russell Gasero, our highly distinguished denominational Archivist, helped to change that.

In Joshua 4: 4-7, we read:

"So, Joshua called together the twelve men he had appointed from the Israelites, one from each tribe, and said to them, "Go over before the ark of the LORD your God into the middle of the Jordan. Each of you is to take up a stone on his shoulder, according to the number of the tribes of the Israelites, to serve as a sign among you. In the future, when your children ask you, 'What do these stones mean?' tell them that the flow of the Jordan was cut off before the ark of the covenant of the LORD. When the Ark crossed the Jordan, the waters of the Jordan were cut off. These stones are to be a memorial to the people of Israel forever."

This well-known Biblical text reflects the high point of the Exodus—the entrance of God's people, at last, into the Promised Land. What it reveals to us is the need to remember, preserve, and memorialize the pivotal events of our lives as signs of God's presence among us. Women's lives need to be remembered as fully as any other, because they also show God's presence. It is important for those who follow us to know the various ways that women have come to know God, to feel sustained by God and God's people, and to faithfully serve God.

The stories of individual women, of women's groups, and of wives and husbands working together within Christ's church, have largely gone untold. The story I am about to tell is intended to show how painfully slow the RCA has been in recognizing women's stories and valuing the broader history of RCA women. This story is equally committed to demonstrating how important our Archivist has been in seeking to correct that situation. To be sure, some of this history has gone unwritten due to the laws of the land or the culture of the times. But women's stories and their collective narratives need to find a larger, better, and more secure place in our denomination's history.

This essay is rather personal, because the life of the person being honored and the life of the author over the past fifty years have been intertwined in rather unusual ways. It began in New York City in 1965. Russ Gasero grew up in the borough of Queens, where he and his family were members at the Steinway Reformed Church. As newlyweds, my husband, Norman J. Kansfield, and I moved to Astoria, Queens, where we began our ministry at the Second Reformed Church of Astoria. Change was in the air. Decisions by the Second Vatican Council brought changes to the Roman Catholic Church, and Christian denominations sought to come together in new and exciting ecumenical ways, challenging the status quo and encouraging the culture and the church to think differently about inclusion, and about women in particular. As inner-city RCA churches sought to deal with declining membership, four Long Island City congregations in

Queens formed a consortium.[1] The young people from each of the four churches formed a single youth group. Young Russell was part of this youth group.

My next opportunity to interact with Russell occurred when he was a student majoring in chemistry at Hope College. To fulfill his required religion courses, Russ had taken two courses taught by my husband. At some point in his college career, Russ wasn't sure he wanted to become a scientist and to continue with his college studies. His parents weren't so keen on the idea of Russ dropping out of college, so Russ's mother, Virginia, contacted my husband, Norm, to ask if she and Russ and Russ's sister, Carol, could come for a visit. As we sat drinking lemonade in our back yard in Holland, Michigan, Virginia Gasero voiced her hope that Norm would use his influence to help convince Russell not to drop out of college. In the end, Russ stayed the course and finished his degree in philosophy at Hope College.

During his college career, Russ sensed a call to ministry and, following his graduation from Hope, signed up for a New Testament course at Princeton Theological Seminary. However, instead of pastoral ministry, Russ' career moved in a different and unexpected direction. During his high school days at the New York School of Printing, Russell became enchanted with typography and the offset printing process. He loved ink! Instead of pursuing ministry, Russ found a job at the United Nations as an archival assistant. He loved his job, and Russ quickly became immersed in what would become his ministry and lifetime career as an archivist.

The Commission on History and the Growth of the Archives

In 1841, the denomination's archives existed in a single case located in the consistory rooms of the Collegiate Church. But, beginning in 1876, the archives were moved to New Brunswick Theological Seminary's Gardner Sage Library, which at the time was a brand new and a state-of-the-art library building. Today the denomination's archives continue to be housed in the Gardner A. Sage Library.

Prior to 1966, the archives were overseen by the General Synod Permanent Committee on History and Research, and the denomina-

---

[1] These four Long Island City churches included First Reformed Astoria, Second Reformed Astoria, the Reformed Church of Long Island City, and Steinway Reformed. See "The Astoria Line" by Norman J. Kansfield, *Youth Highlights*, a quarterly publication of the RCA Division of Youth Evangelism, ed. Lynn T. Joosten, vol 2, no 3, (Lansing, IL:, 1967), 6-9.

tion's archives continued to function as a small and scattered operation.[2] But, in 1966, the Commission on History assumed responsibility for oversight of the archives.[3] In their 1972 report to General Synod, the Commission noted:

> The home of the commission is the Dutch Church room in Sage Library, on the campus of New Brunswick Theological Seminary. The commission is indebted to the seminary for providing it with facilities to deposit valuable archive materials, office space for cataloging and correspondence, duplicating equipment, and free rent and utilities. Without this kindness, the commission would be unable to operate at all because its budget remains small in comparison with its responsibilities. The daily operation of the Commission on History is supervised by Dr. John W. Beardslee III, who serves as the official archivist of the denomination.[4] Mrs. Cecil Roberts (Emma) and Miss Elsie Stryker carry on the work of the commission, answering requests for information, handling sales of the *Directory*, and cataloging and maintaining the general archives collection. Each of these persons is devoted to the work, and contributes invaluable service to the denomination at very minimal wage.[5]

The 1972 report also noted that the General Synod approved the Commission's recommendation:

---

[2] *Acts and Proceedings of the General Synod* (hereinafter *MGS*), 1961, 394.

[3] Specifically, the newly formed Commission on History was charged to 1) collect and preserve the official records and documents of the RCA, its churches, judicatories, boards and institutions, 2) maintain a permanent archive where such data will be available for historical research, 3) promote an interest in the history and traditions of the RCA, and 4) furnish information about and further research on the history of the RCA. Membership on the Commission was to include six members each serving three-year terms, plus the Stated Clerk, *ex officio*, and an archivist to serve a five-year term to assist the Commission in its work. *MGS*, 1966, 315.

[4] Use of the tern "archivist" seems to go back to 1966, when "the new" RCA Historical Directory was published. Peter N. Vandenberg was editor of this new directory, and served as the librarian at Sage Library (1957-1967). Publishing the *Historical Directory* was a herculean job, since well over forty years had passed since the fifth edition of Corwin's *Manual of the Reformed Church in America* had been published. Work on the new manual extended over four years, and once finished, the Stated Clerk, Marion deVelder, by the authority of his office, designated Peter N. Vandenberg the denomination's official archivist. Although the term "archivist" may have been referenced before, conferring this title on Mr. Vanden Berge did reveal a gracious gesture by the denomination to acknowledge his work.

[5] *MGS*, 1972, 267.

That all commissions, committees, agencies and boards of General Synod file regularly with the Office of the Stated Clerk a copy of all minutes and documents as soon as they are prepared and ready for distribution....The Stated Clerk [General Secretary] shall be responsible for depositing these records in the denominational archives.[6]

This involved a huge step forward for the archives. Needless to say, the amount of material in the archives grew exponentially.

Recognizing the need for a plan, the Commission on History in 1977 drew up a comprehensive plan for the future of the archives. This plan articulated the necessary components of a modern and adequate denominational archives.[7] It called for a full-time archivist, who was trained in archives management and "should be sensitive to and knowledgeable in the history and character of the RCA."[8] The General Synod passed the plan, Russell Gasero applied for the job, and the rest is history. Russ began his tenure as RCA archivist in May 1978.

It is important to note just how comprehensive this plan was.[9] In addition to hiring a full-time archivist, the plan called for hiring an assistant archivist (or assistants equal to one full-time person). In passing this plan, the General Synod clearly committed itself to the future of the archives and in a very substantial way. Looking backward in time, it seems as if the plan anticipated an archival future that used technology unknown at the time. Although the plan identified microfilm preservation, a program that had begun in the 1960s, future cyber space and preservation tools could hardly have been imagined at the time. Russell's interest in computers and technology skills were well suited to move the archives into an exciting yet unknown future.[10]

[6] *MGS*, 1972, 268.
[7] This archival plan was written by Norman J. Kansfield, whose doctoral work at the University of Chicago was in library science, and who at that time served as the Librarian at Western Theological Seminary and was a member of the Commission on History, which then included John W. Beardslee, III, Arie R Brouwer, Donald J. Bruggink, Elton J. Bruins, Gerald De Jong, Barbara Fassler, Leroy A. Suess, Chairman, and Sharon T. Scholten. It should be noted that Barbara Fassler served as chair of the Commission on History 1980-1982, and the first woman to serve in that capacity.
[8] *MGS*, 1977, 241.
[9] MGS, 1977, 239-242.
[10] A year after Russ's arrival as Archivist, the General Synod approved a plan put forth by the Commission on History to establish an RCA Historical Society, whose primary purpose was to promote RCA history and share in the ongoing expenses of the archives. The plan also sought to establish a Council of Reformed Church Archivists. It was hoped that both the Historical Society and the Council of

At its 1967 meeting, the General Synod took a giant step forward by approving a way to capture and preserve the stories of our denomination. Approving the History Commission's oversight of *The Historical Series of the Reformed Church in America* meant our stories would have a home. With Donald J. Bruggink as General Editor, the first volume in the series was published in 1968.[11] By the time Russell Gasero became Archivist in 1978, five additional volumes had been published as part of the series, and the third volume, it should be noted, was written by a woman. As an *ex officio* member of the Commission, Russ immediately became involved in making manuscripts camera-ready for publication, where his love of journalism and ink served him well. In 2001, the General Synod recognized Russ' production work for the *Historical Series* noting he "provided corrected photo-ready copy to the printers, totaling over 6,000 pages, for the last eighteen volumes of the series through the donation of his time, expertise, and resources without remuneration or compensation."[12]

RCA Women's Groups Transition to Meet the Changing Times

The early stories of RCA women are known mostly through minutes that attest to how women functioned as mission society groups.[13]

Reformed Church Archivists would help fund the archives. A quarterly newsletter called *Historical Highlights* as well as a series of *Occasional Papers* were written and distributed by Russ. (See Report of the Commission on History in MGS, 1981, 125). Although membership in the Historical Society reached a highpoint of approximately 300 members, both plans lacked sustained support. See MGS, 1980, 133-134.

[11] The first title in the series was *Ecumenism in the Reformed Church in America*, written by Herman Harmelink, III (Grand Rapids, Michigan: Eerdmans, 1968). This was followed by *The Americanization of a Congregation* by Elton J. Bruins (Grand Rapids, Michigan: Eerdmans, 1970), and *Pioneers in the Arab World* by Dorothy F. Van Ess (Grand Rapids, Michigan: Eerdmans, 1974). These volumes were followed by *Piety and Patriotism*, edited by James W. Van Hoeven, (Grand Rapids, Michigan: Eerdmans, 1976), *The Dutch Reformed Church in the American Colonies*, by Gerald R. De Jong, (Grand Rapids, Michigan: Eerdmans, 1978), and *The Historical Directory of the Reformed Church in America, 1628-1978*, edited by Peter N. Vanden Berge (Grand Rapids, Michigan: Eerdmans, 1978).

[12] MGS, 2001, 161.

[13] Minutes were not the only means giving voice to the missionary work of women. In 1878, the denomination's Board of Foreign Missions began publishing the *Mission Monthly*. One quarter of the space in that publication was given to women's mission work. From 1883 to 1917, the Woman's Board of Foreign Missions published *The Mission Gleaner*. This was the Woman's Board's own periodical "entirely for women, by women, and, mostly about women." See Renée S. House, "Women Raising Women: The Urgent Work of the Mission Gleaner, 1883-1917" in Renée S. House and John Coakley, eds., *Patterns and Portraits: Women in the History*

The Minutes of the Woman's Board of Foreign Missions (WBFM) and the Women's Board of Domestic Missions (WBDM), founded in 1875 and 1882 respectfully, spell out in significant detail how these networks of mission societies worked together as an organizational whole. Local mission societies were yoked to one another in classical unions, and regional unions related one to another as a national organization. Organizationally, the system reflected the denomination's structure, and detailed minutes were kept of missionary society meetings at all levels. It is within all these minutes and reports that the stories of women were first captured.

For over seventy years this organizational structure functioned well. By the end of World War II, however, the organizational framework for women's ministries began to change. Challenged by the enormous success of women's mission work, and the ability of women to raise money in support of missions, the two national women's mission boards were unceremoniously subsumed into the structure of the larger church.[14] Although women were included in the leadership of the denomination's newly created Foreign Mission Board and Domestic Mission Board,[15] in so doing women lost the self-awareness and cohesion brought about by coming together as local and regional groups to form a national network of church women. Having begun as grassroots organizations of "women supporting other women and children," the movement lost its separate place in the denominational structure and was diminished by the loss of the direct involvement of women at the local, regional, and national levels.

---

of the Reformed Church in America, number 31 in *The Historical Series of the Reformed Church in America* (Grand Rapids, Michigan: Eerdmans, 1999), 103-118.

[14] The Woman's Board of Foreign Missions merged with the denomination's Board of Foreign Missions on May 1, 1946, and the Women's Board of Domestic Missions joined the Board of Domestic Missions on January 1, 1951. The reasoning behind the mergers lay in the success of the women's boards. As noted in *Letters to Hazel: Ministry within the Woman's Board of Foreign Missions of the Reformed Church in America*, number 46 in *The Historical Series of the Reformed Church in America* (Grand Rapids: Eerdmans, 2004), 131, "When considering the tremendous grassroots involvement of church women and their amazing success in raising and administering "their own" money for missions, there was no doubt that "woman's work for woman" had placed the WBFM in a position of power. In recognition of this success, the General Synod encouraged a merger of the WBFM with the denominational BFM largely in the name of corporate efficiency."

[15] "In agreeing to the merger, the women agreed also to a representation of fifteen women on a new Board of Foreign Missions composed of forty-two members, or a 37 percent share of the leadership on the new board, thereby losing majority control over their organizational structure and their considerable finances." Kansfield, 132.

Until the women's mission boards were merged with the denominational boards to form single Boards of Foreign Missions and Domestic Missions, the stories of church women had a home. After the mergers, the stories of women lost their place in the former treasury of minutes and publications that was kept safe within the women's networks and later within the denomination's archives.

Following the mergers, the women in local auxiliaries, mission societies, and Ladies' Aid Societies soldiered on, but, without a place of their own in the denominational structure, they felt disconnected and separated from one another. Women needed other women. This need, coupled with the hoped-for income provided by women's groups, became glaringly apparent to the General Synod, and, during the late 1950s,[16] steps were taken to create a new National Department of Women's Work. Renamed Reformed Church Women (RCW) in 1972, and subsequently renamed Reformed Church Women's Ministries (RCWM) in 1993, this new structure involved Guilds organized in congregations throughout the denomination around the need for prayer, spiritual growth, education, and service. During its ministry from 1959 to 2001, immensely gifted and dynamic leaders served the organization. Anita Wellwood served as president from 1959-1972, Beth Marcus 1973-1986, Diana Paulsen Walker 1986-1994, Christina

---

[16] This became especially apparent in 1956 when the retiring president of General Synod, the Rev. Dr. Daniel Y. Brink gave his "Report of the State of Religion to the General Synod" saying:

> Dare a mere man venture a few comments regarding the work of the women? We have some organizations of their interests on the higher levels of our denominational life, but could there not be improvement in the women's programs of many of our local congregations? In some places, of course, they are splendidly organized and enlist the support of a large number of the women in the church in a comprehensive program. But in far too many churches the women's work is a hit-and-miss affair, beautifully disorganized, consisting of the remnants of organizations of a by-gone day that are dying out and the beginning of others that have not yet found themselves. In some churches there are too many groups, with little coordination of effort. Some, with no program, seem to have no reason for being, except that someone once started them, and they don't know how to go gracefully out of existence. Because it seems so difficult to correct these situations on the local level, could there not be more help given from higher up? Other denominations have patterns of organization for the women's program in the individual church. In that way they have developed an integrated work, in which all women of the congregation have a responsibility, that includes study and support of both local and denominational projects. And, could there not be a national assembly of the women of our church, something like the laymen's convention?

VanEyl 1994-1996, and Arlene Walters Waldorf 1996-2000.[17] This leadership brought back a spark, a renewed sense of dedication and a more settled feeling among lay women, who once again recognized they had a place in the denominational structure.

From Mission to Commission on/for Women

Throughout the 1960s and 1970s, the roles that women played in church life began to reflect a new day for women. Nowhere could this better be observed than the 1969 General Synod. Women interrupted the business of synod by marching into the meeting with signed petitions requesting the ordination of women to the offices of deacon and elder. That memorable General Synod was only the beginning. In 1972, the offices of deacon and elder were opened to women, and, in 1973, Joyce Stedge was the first RCA woman ordained to the office of minister of Word and Sacrament. But it wasn't until 1979 that the General Synod approved the ordination of women to that office.[18]

In 1974, the Christian Action Commission brought before the General Synod a paper titled "Feminism and the Church," and recommended that "the church reaffirm the equality of all men and women (persons) in Christ." This was adopted.[19] Church women seeking ordination needed to find a place within the church structure. To this end, the General Synod established the Commission on Women (COW) in 1980. In 1993, the Commission requested a name change from the Commission on Women to the Commission for Women and offered this reason for the change. "The Commission on Women and many within the RCA find the name of the commission unfortunate. The preposition "on" has an oppressive connotation. The word "for," however, expresses the commission's intent." The General Synod agreed and approved the name change.[20]

The absence of information about the lives of RCA women and the need to capture women's stories were initially acknowledged in 1975, the 100th anniversary of the WBFM. However, it took until 1988, when the World Council of Churches declared 1988-1998 the "Ecumenical Decade: Churches in Solidarity with Women," for General Synod "to

---

[17] See *MSG*, 2001, 222-223.
[18] In 1979, Joyce Borgman de Velder was ordained by the Classis of Albany to the Office of Word and Sacrament, the first woman to be "legally" ordained.
[19] *MGS*, 1980, 53.
[20] *MGS*, 1993, pp. 282-283.

instruct the Commission on Women to disseminate the stories of women in ministry throughout the church that the history of women in the denomination may be known, understood, and appreciated fully."[21] With Reformed Church Women, the Commission on Women, and the denomination's Publications Office behind the effort, Beth Marcus, then Executive Director of RCW and Director of Promotion and Communication, approached Una Ratmeyer to gather the stories of women. Seeking to have the book published in time for the 1996 Triennial,[22] Una pressed ahead with the herculean task of gathering the stories of RCA women amid the pressure of a looming deadline. Using a survey to reach a cross-section of church women, Una began putting together small biographical pieces of ninety-five women. To accomplish this, Russ Gasero and Professor John W. Beardslee, III, the seminary's archivist, offered immense help to Una, and Eloise VanHeest, who was serving as church administrator at Hope Church, Holland, proofed Una's pieces, offering advice and encouragement. In 1995, *Hands, Hearts, and Voices: Women Who Followed God's Call* was published by the Reformed Church Press. The publication served as the first of its kind.[23]

The Standing Seminar Committee

My working relationship with Russell as Archivist began in June1993, when our family moved into the President's House at New Brunswick Theological Seminary (NBTS), then located not more than forty feet from Sage Library. Welcome to the neighborhood! I was invited to serve on the Standing Seminar Committee. This permanent committee came into existence in 1985, at a time when Western Theo-

---

[21] *MGS*, 1988, 183.

[22] In 1957 RCA women gathered in Buck Hill Falls, PA for the First National Women's Assembly. Beginning in 1962, RCA women came together in national gatherings called Triennials. Every third year, from 1962 to 2007, these gatherings were organized by RCM and RCWM and took place in different parts of the country.

[23] Prior to 1995, three volumes in the RCA Historical Series had been penned by women: *Pioneers in the Arab World* by Dorothy Van Ess in 1974, *Sharifa* by Cornelia Dalenburg (Grand Rapids, Michigan: Eerdmans, 1983), and *Grace in the Gulf* by Jeanette Boersma (Grand Rapids, Michigan: Eerdmans, 1991). Additionally, *Doctor Mary in Arabia: Memoirs by Mary Bruins Allison, M.D.* was published by the University of Texas Press in 1994. Also extant was Mary A. Chamberlain's *Fifty years in Foreign Fields, China, Japan, India, Arabia: A History of Five Decades of the Woman's Board of Foreign Missions Reformed Church in America* (New York: Abbott Press, 1925). Please note that all of these biographies, plus Mary Chamberlains' anniversary history, are written by missionaries.

logical Seminary (WTS) and NBTS were both struggling to define their identities within the denomination.[24]

Out of this struggle, there emerged at NBTS a new format for hosting guest lecturers that was designed to be both informative and efficient.[25] At the suggestion of Professor John Coakley, and with the approval of President Robert White, a Standing Seminar Committee put in place what became a continuing annual lecture series. Although originally a lunchtime event, the majority of classes had become evening classes, and the format called for serving a simple meal at 5:00, and, following a lecture and discussion, students would have sufficient time to attend a 7:00 pm class. Of course, my role on the committee was to provide for the "simple meals" that accompanied each lecture.[26] From the start, Russell played a large part in planning each of the lecture series, and throughout his tenure as archivist he was present to videotape all of the presentations.

In 1993, after months of planning, the Standing Seminar Committee hosted a two-year lecture series titled "An Awakening Majority: Women in the History of the RCA." These were exciting and well-attended lectures, and each year Russ presented a lecture on the presence of RCA women in our denomination's past.[27] These

[24] Following the end of the Bi-Level-Multi-Site Curriculum in 1977, in 1993 both seminaries resumed having separate Presidents. Including the newly formed Theological Education Agency (TEA), all three educational entities were overseen by the Board of Theological Education. In 1985 the Board of Theological Education reported to General Synod, "It has been a year of retrenchment as the fiscal crisis at New Brunswick Seminary worsened and demanded immediate and drastic action resulting in faculty and staff reductions as well as reductions in non-personnel operating expenses." MGS, 1985, 198.

[25] Professor John Coakley originally came up with the idea for this continuing lecture series, and Professor John Beardslee, III, quickly agreed to join him in "making it happen." By the time we arrived in 1993, stories were legend of the two Johns opening cans of tomato soup for the "simple suppers" accompanying lecture presentations.

[26] As Manager of Hospitality, I was asked by the Moderator of the Board of Trustees "to create a welcoming atmosphere, promote the school, and 'to do things nicely.'" See report of meeting with Harold Brower, 9/28/1993, in possession of the author.

[27] Presenters the first year included: Diana Paulsen, "Pictures at an Exhibition: Snapshots of Women in the RCA;" Martha Shattuck "Dutch Women's Rights: The New Netherland Experience;" John Beardslee, "Male Domination and Two Ethnic Traditions: What Are the Questions;" Jennifer Reece, "Learning the Missionary Position: The Education of Sarah Couch;" Joyce Borgman deVelder and Joyce Stedge-Fowler, "The RCA and the Ordination of Women: Personal Memories;" Una Ratmeyer, "Prophetic Voices ... Discerning the Will of God: Work in Progress;" Carol Hageman, "The Rise and Fall and Rising Again of Women in the Reformed Church;" and Russell Gasero "The Silent Faithful: The Establishment

presentations were extremely well received. Not only were all the lectures video recorded by Russ, but under the leadership of Professor John Coakley and Renée House, the Seminary's librarian, many of the lectures were gathered into a new volume on RCA women titled *Patterns and Portraits* and published in 1999 as part of the RCA Historical Series. Following the publication of Una Ratmeyer's *Hands, Hearts and Voices* in 1995,[28] *Patterns and Portraits* became a second volume of studies on RCA women.

Within a year of our moving into the President's House at 25 Seminary Place, I was introduced vicariously to Frances Beardslee, because our family "lived in Frances Beardslee's house."[29] Alumni were keen to remember Frances Beardslee, the wife of John W. Beardslee, Jr., Professor of New Testament and President of the Seminary, 1935–1947. Alumni loved to recall stories of how they as students interacted with the Beardslee family. With the full support of both John Walter Beardslee, III, and William Armitage Beardslee, the two oldest sons of Frances and John Beardslee, I delved into the story of their mother with the intention of writing her biography. Russ certainly encouraged me, and both John and Will went to extraordinary lengths to have me come to know their mother. Having invested nine years of my time in this research, my book writing effort came to a screeching halt in 2003. I suddenly realized that, with no written context for Frances Beardslee's life, no story of her life could be told. It was that simple – no context, no biography. At this point, there were only two books on RCA women's history available, *Hands, Hearts and Voices* and *Patterns and Portraits*, and neither of these books provided sufficient context for my work.

---

of the Women's Boards." In 1995 the presenters included: Firth Fabend, "Pious and Powerful: Evangelical Mothers in Reformed Dutch Households, 1826-1876;" Ruth Stafford Peale, "A Personal Perspective on Women in the Reformed Church in America;" Renée House, "Women Raising Women: The Urgent Work of the Mission Gleaner, 1883-1917;" Russell Gasero, "The Silent Faithful: The Establishment of the Women's Board of Foreign and Domestic Mission;" Johan van de Bank, "The Lord's Loving Dealings with Dinah van Berg': An 18th century Woman's Reflections on the Spiritual Life;" Sara Smith, "One Woman's Experience with the RCA;" and Joyce Goodfriend, "Incorporating Women into the History of the Colonial Dutch Reformed Church: Problems and Proposals."

[28] Una H. Ratmeyer, *Hands, Hearts and Voices: Women Who Followed God's Call* (New York: Reformed Church Press, 1995).

[29] For over forty years, Frances Beardslee was a member of a local literary club called the Travelers' Club. Thirty members were expected to research and present papers, and each meeting concluded with a formal tea. I also became a member of this club. Because meetings were held in members' homes, I hosted my first meeting in the President's House only to have an elderly club member ask me "how does it feel to be living in Frances Beardslee's house?"

Russ Gasero fully understood my dilemma. Without batting an eye, he told me I needed to write a history of the RCA Woman's Board of Foreign Missions. He pointed out that all nine volumes of the *Minutes of the Woman's Board of Foreign Missions*[30] were just sitting on a shelf in Sage Library, and the story of Frances Beardslee and almost all other RCA women from 1875 to 1946 would find a place within this broad history.

Creating the Gnade Fellowship

Reading through all the *Minutes of the Woman's Board of Foreign Missions* was eye opening for me. After *Letters to Hazel: A History of the Woman's Board of Foreign Missions* was published in 2004, I was haunted by the lack of women's stories and the failure of the church to value the commitments of RCA women. In my utter frustration, I prepared a proposal for the Center for Reformed Studies as a way for more RCA women to tell their stories. This proposal called for two things. Following an application process, a man or woman would be invited to campus for two weeks to utilize the denomination's and the seminary's archives to research some aspect of the lives of RCA women,[31] for which they would receive a stipend. After completing the research, the fellow would make a presentation to the seminary community of his/her findings, much like other Standing Seminar fellowship recipients. The second aspect of the proposal had to do with a commitment to make the results of the fellow's research available to the whole church. As I recall, everyone on the committee thought my proposal had merit, and in November 2003, the Committee approved what was called the "RCA Women's Project." Of course, one of the first questions asked was, "And how do you plan to finance this proposal?"[32] I promptly replied that RCA women would support this, and I would also contribute all

---

[30] These *Annual Minutes of the Women's Board of Foreign Missions* extend over 65 years from 1874 through 1939 and are bound in nine volumes.

[31] The proposal quite specifically invited both women and men to apply for the Fellowship and noted that "although the Fellowship must involve RCA women's history, it could assume any number of forms. For example, research could be undertaken for a play, a dance, a dramatic reading, an oral or written presentation. It could be undertaken for liturgical use, for anniversary celebrations of women's groups or congregations, for Triennial presentations, or for civic uses." Taken from a bookmark brochure titled "Advocates for RCA Women's History."

[32] The original total cost was estimated at $50,000. A fund of $25,000 producing five percent would make available $1250 on an annual basis. In terms of time, it was hoped that the first fellow would be appointed in early 2005. On December 31, 2004, the fund stood at about $10,000.

profit from the sale of *Letters to Hazel* to what was initially called the "Women's History Project," and later became known as the Hazel B. Gnade Fund. Along with the Center's approval, both sons of Hazel Gnade provided substantial gifts in support of the project, and with the help of Russ Gasero, the leadership of RCWM, the Commission for Women and the Standing Seminar Committee, the project was off and running.[33] Little did we know at the time that it would take fourteen years before the first Hazel B. Gnade lecture was presented at NBTS.

At the time, the Center for Reformed Church Studies Committee approved the commitment to "make the results of each fellow's research available to the whole church," I could not envision exactly how this could be made to happen. Russ Gasero knew otherwise. If Russ had a passion for ink, he was no less in love with technology. The rapid development and growing use of technology called to Russ. Beginning around 1981, Russ began personally to invest in technology by purchasing a Commodore Vic-20 computer and then a Kay-Pro portable computer and C-Itoh Starwriter, or daisywheel, printer. Using these, he could publish RCA *Historical Highlights*. Then, in 1988, Russ purchased a Macintosh computer and Apple Laserwriter which allowed for desktop publishing. Russ kept updating and investing in various new computers, printers, software and VCR cameras that allowed him to digitize large collections of archival records and pictures. With this technology, Russ began to make available camera-ready pages for the RCA Historical Series. His skills also allowed him digitally to share archival collections and exhibits on the web, and to live stream videos, including the Hazel B. Gnade lectures, and to make them instantly available to the public.[34] Russ was ahead of his time, and the whole RCA benefitted from Russ' eagerness to embrace technology and personally to invest in a vision for using technology to help capture and share the stories of our denomination's past.

---

[33] A prospectus of the Gnade Fund project was prepared on NBTS stationery. This and a cover letter over the signatures of Dr. Jerry Gnade and Ken Gnade were sent to family and friends and to all Guilds and classes in the tri-synod area. Bookmarks promoting the cause were inserted in all copies of *Letters to Hazel* and handed out at General Synod. Presentations on behalf of the fund were made at the 2004 and 2007 Triennials.

[34] In 2016, Russ invested in using VIMEO, a live streaming video platform. He also began using OMEKA, a publishing platform for sharing digital collections and creating media-rich online exhibits.

A New Era—the Center for Reformed Church Studies

For fourteen years, from 1985 to 1999, the Standing Seminar Committee functioned well. However, as the composition of the NBTS student body changed, the Board of Trustees in 1999 approved the creation of the Center for Reformed Church Studies. The Center was designed to underscore an RCA presence within the seminary's increasingly ecumenical community, to encourage the study and reflection of the Reformed tradition world-wide, as well as the past, present, and future of the Reformed Church in America, and to serve as an umbrella organization for all Standing Seminar lectures, fellowships, guest lecturers, workshops, and scholarly conferences. Professor John Coakley became the first Director of the Center, and Russ Gasero continued to play an important role as Archivist.

Beginning in 2007, Rev. Dr. Barbara Fillette became the Center's second director. Over the course of seven years, Barbara Fillette brought to the position a new energy and dedication to broaden the discussion of issues in a forum setting. Of her time as Director of the Center, Barbara notes:

> I came to New Brunswick Seminary as more a shepherd than an erudite scholar...Russ was always encouraging to me. He was supportive and ever so patient. There were many things that I didn't know or understand about dealing with researchers in academic circles. Russ was wise and communicative, practical and creative in his strategies for getting things done. He had contacts everywhere. He was invariably generous in assisting me, and I remain grateful to him for the gracious way he carried out his calling.

In 2014, Rev. James Brumm was installed as the third Director of the Center for Reformed Church Studies and continues in that position today. With experience as Moderator of the Commission on History and a continuing role as General Editor of the RCA Historical Series, James Brumm has significantly broadened the role of the Center and expanded Internet access and Zoom presence to the programs of the Center and to the life of NBTS and the broader Reformed community.

The calls for major changes within the RCA cannot be traced to a single specific date, but instead reflect a growing movement to broaden the church's embrace.[35] When the RCWM organization came

---

[35] Among the major changes, the General Synod in 2003 approved and began to implement a new statement of Mission and Vision that articulated a ten-year

to an end in 2000, the women who comprised RCWM joined forces with ordained women supported by the Commission for Women and requested the denomination to create a single Office for Women that was funded through denominational assessments. This did not immediately happen.[36] But, in 2009, amid grudging but growing recognition that the church failed adequately to assure women equal gender and racial representation, especially among denominational staff, a new Office for Women was created with funding through assessments. Following a search, Claudette Reid was hired in 2010 as the new Coordinator for Women's Ministries. Claudette is an ordained elder, but, as an immigrant from Jamaica who had not grown up in the Reformed Church, Claudette began her new job without the usual networks created by life-long experiences in the RCA. She recalls:

> I quickly came to know Russell Gasero, and it seemed to me that Russ knew everyone and everything. Not only could he answer my questions about people, process and denominational history, but Russ took the time to share more than I asked. He became a kind of default setting for me. Russ prepared a display on the history and contributions of RCA women used at General Synod meetings and made sure he was available to speak up and explain the stories and the history of RCA women. Russ became my

---

plan called "Our Call." (*MGS*, 2003, 60-70). This was given a solid theological grounding when, in 2010, the Belhar Confession was adopted as a doctrinal standard (*MGS*, 2010, 45).

[36] On April 12, 2000, the General Synod Council (GSC) approved plans for an Office for Women at the unit level within the denominational structure of the RCA. (*MGS*, 2000, 261) Funding for the new office would rest on the shoulders of the women, who had to raise $800,000 above and beyond expenses to underwrite the cost of the new office. The following parameters were placed on the fund drive: "First, all monies raised in the "InStep Together" fund drive would be used for women's ministry. Second, $800,000 over and above expenses would need to be raised before hiring a full-time director of women's ministry. Third, if, by December 31, 2003, the stated end of the fund drive had not reached its goal of $800,000, whatever money was raised over and above expenses would be used to hire part-time staff to enhance the work of women in the Reformed Church in America. As of the end of 2003, the "InStep Together" had raised $300,000 over and above expenses, for the work of women's ministries in the RCA. Based on the previous actions of GSC, a job description was developed for a part-time coordinator of women's ministry. Following a review of all applications, initial phone interviews with five persons, and in-person follow-up interviews with three finalists, Mary Clark was hired in March of 2004 as coordinator of women's ministries." *MGS*, 2004, 128. Mary Clark served in this position for five years. In June 2009, Mary and her valued contributions to the work of women's ministries were recognized and honored by the General Synod (*MGS*, 2009, 323).

collaborator and my friend. When my time as Coordinator for Women's Ministries ended sooner than I expected, it was Russ Gasero and his family who reached out and gave me moral and spiritual support. I am honored to have worked with Russ.[37]

In 2013, the General Synod approved a fifteen-year plan for the future of the denomination. The plan is titled "Transformed and Transforming: Following Christ in Mission Together." "Women's Transformation and Leadership" is part of this plan, and the Office for Women is located within the space of New Brunswick Seminary's new building. Serving as Coordinator for Women's Transformation and Leadership is Rev. Elizabeth Testa, who came to the task in 2014 committed to finding new ways of involving and equipping women in the life and witness of the church. With offices within walking distance of one another, Liz Testa, James Brumm and Russ Gasero seized the opportunity not only to promote the work of women, but also to encourage sharing women's stories.

RCA Women's Stories Day

It is within this context that Liz, James, and Russ further collaborated to bring about the first Women's Stories Day. This event took place in May, 2017, and, as the first Gnade Fellow, Dr. Jennifer Reese presented her research project titled "Women's Work for Creation: Reformed Church Women's Missions and the Beginnings of the Environmental Movement." Additional presentations were made by Monica Schaap Pierce reflecting on what the Accra Confession means for women, justice and creation care, and Clara Woodson, who spoke on breaking barriers in the church. The day also held a worship service with Lynn Min preaching and an interactive session by Liz Testa encouraging women to tell their stories. Also present were Russell and Matthew Gasero, who sought to record the stories of women attending the conference for inclusion in the archives' growing women's oral history collection.

On May 12, 2018, the second Women's Stories Day took place, and the occasion celebrated several important anniversaries for RCA women. It had been 100 years since the first General Synod overture calling for all offices of the church to be open to women, and a century since Dr. Ida Scudder opened Velore Women's Medical College in India. Forty-five years had passed since the first woman was ordained to the

---

[37] Correspondence with the author, December 17, 2020.

office of Word and Sacrament, and five years later women began to be examined by classes for ordination. Thirty years had gone by since the first African-American woman was ordained as minister of Word and Sacrament, and it was twenty years since the General Synod elected the first woman Professor of Theology. These were all meaningful anniversaries, especially for RCA women.

That year, the Gnade Fellowship included five presentations, all by women who hold the distinction of serving first in their ministry. The "First Women" who participated included Bernita Babb, retired pastor of Mott Haven Reformed Church in the Bronx, who became the first African-American woman to become minister of Word and Sacrament; Carol Bechtel, who became the first woman professor of theology; Elizabeth Johnson, who served as the first woman full-time faculty member at NBTS; Joyce Borgman deVelder, who in 1979 became the first woman legally ordained to the approved office of Word and Sacrament; and Young Na, the first woman of Korean heritage to be ordained minister of Word and Sacrament.

The third Women's Stories Day focused on women who had taken a stand. Elizabeth Colmant Estes, pastor of the Readington, New Jersey, Reformed Church, served as the Gnade Fellow for 2018-2019 and presented her research on "Women Who Took a Stand for the Word." Additional speakers included Patricia Sealy, who spoke on "Mass Incarceration and Children of Incarcerated Parents;" Karen Jackson, whose presentation was titled "Here I Am, Lord: The Call to Local Advocacy;" and Liz Testa, who spoke on "Sharing Our Stories of Taking a Stand." Guests were treated to a viewing of the 2019 video "She Is Called," and Anna M. Jackson, served as worship leader.

With the pandemic rapidly spreading, the fourth Women's Stories Day, which was scheduled for March 21, 2020, was conducted via Zoom. While using the Zoom platform instead of meeting together in person, presenters rose to the challenge and adapted with grace to this new technology. As the Hazel B. Gnade Fellow, Lynn Japinga lectured on "The Courage to be Honest About Divorce." Additional presenters included Irma Williams speaking on "The Courage to be Honest About Domestic Violence;" Pamela Pater-Ennis, who spoke on "The Courage to be Honest About Mental Health;" and Lynn Min, whose presentation was titled, "The Courage to be Honest About Where We Fit." Using the Zoom "Chat," a robust question and answer period followed the presentations. Devotions for the gathering were led by Damaris Whittaker.

Although the schedule for Women's Stories Day for 2020-2021 is incomplete at this writing, the Hazel B. Gnade Scholar will be Anna M. Jackson.

Once again, at these and other events, Russell was present to record the stories of RCA women. In its 1988 report to General Synod, the Commission on Women noted "An item on the agenda of the commission in recent years has been the compilation of the oral history of women in the life of the church. Contemplated as a cooperative project with the archivist of the denomination, this project seeks to develop a permanent record for the future. Budgetary constraints have prevented the implementation of the project, but it has again been raised as a priority of the commission." Again, and again the subject comes up. Beginning with the 2004 Women's Triennial in California, Russ began interviewing and collecting the stories of RCA women. A brochure titled "What's yOUR Story: Women in the RCA Oral History Project" promoted the project. However, funds for advancing the project were limited, and denominational interest lagged.[38]

A Testimonial to the Future

Giving voice to the stories of RCA women did not come without struggle. In 2007, the last Triennial took place, and in the same year "the Commission for Women advocated for full-time remuneration for the coordinator of Women's Ministries, RCA."[39] There seemed at that time no clear path forward for women's ministries or for capturing their stories. Intervening with a proposal for the archives, Russ Gasero designed a plan for acquiring the written and oral records of RCA women throughout the denomination, digitizing them, and making them assessable to all using CDs and the web site. In the Introduction to his archival plan, Russ states:

> There is a serious lack of resources about the history of women in ministry. While women have been actively engaged in ministry and mission from the start of the church, the stories of that ministry and mission have been neglected. Both the Commission on Women and the Commission on History have raised concerns about this omission over the last few years.

---

[38] The brochure titled "What's yOUR Story? Women in the RCA Oral History Project" is held by the author. See also personal correspondence of November 18, 2020, from Russell Gasero to the author.

[39] *MGS*, 2007, 347.

Women's involvement has been neglected in general church histories. Many are not even aware of historical developments from Sara Doremus' efforts in the early nineteenth century that were pioneering efforts in ecumenical relations and mission support, to Joyce Stedge, the first woman ordained in the RCA in 1973, or Bernita Babb, the first African-American woman ordained in the RCA in 1988, or Beth Marcus, the first woman elected president of the General Synod in 1992.

Raising concerns, however, does not accomplish the task. The RCA needs a focused and deliberate program to capture and preserve these stories and documents so that the future is informed as the past is remembered. Such a program is within the scope of the Office of Historical Services and provides an opportunity to strengthen partnerships with other agencies.[40]

From his love of ink to his fondness for technology, Russ used his position as Archivist to advocate for recognizing and including the stories of all women in the history of the RCA. Although the plan noted above was never actualized, it serves as a testament to what might yet be. Russ's unfailing support for establishing a Hazel B. Gnade Fellowship and his willingness to advocate for including the stories of women in the broader history of the RCA is to be celebrated and remembered—just like that pile of stones mentioned in Joshua 4:4-7.

---

[40] Titled "Women in Ministry in the RCA," a copy of Russ Gasero's plan for the archives is in the possession of the author.

CHAPTER 12

Found in the Archives: Notes from Friends

Not everybody who has used the RCA Archives is a scholar or author. Not everybody who uses the Archives was able to write an essay for this book. The notes that follows are just a few notes from some of Russell Gasero's many friends and admirers.

Thank you, Russ, for being Russ. You've saved me a lot of grief and taught me a lot of stuff.

David Alexander
Retired RCA Missionary

Mr. Gasero has been the living treasure of Gardner Sage Library and its most eloquent and resourceful ambassador. He is worthy of honor and appreciation.

Benjamin Alicea-Lugo
Pastor, St. Paul's Reformed Church, Perth Amboy, New Jersey

Thank you, Russ, for your thorough research and thoughtful work in archiving information that many commissions, agencies, churches and individuals have been able to access to grow in understanding issues pertinent to the RCA! Well done!

Phil and Stephanie Doeschot

Russell Gasero has been a wonderful addition to our "Dutch Cousins of Kentucky" international group, donating his time, talents, and paying his own expenses to travel to Kentucky and conduct Sunday worship services open to the public in the restored Old Mud Meetinghouse built by our Low Dutch ancestors in 1800. The Dutchmen never secured a permanent Dutch-speaking pastor and eventually became Presbyterian. The building, originally constructed of mud and wattle, was used by many congregations over the years, so it became the "mother" church for many believers. At least thirty-five Low Dutch Revolutionary soldiers are buried here.

The Dutch Cousins of Kentucky
Tamara Fulkerson, President

Many years ago, my wife Nella and I were the beneficiaries of the hospitality of Russ and Maria overnight in their home, while I was doing research in the archives at the magnificent Gardner Sage. We have appreciated his unfailing helpfulness and friendliness when we were on the Commission on History—and also elsewhere—over the ensuing decades, including, only incidentally, the twirling of his luxuriant moustache.

Earl Wm.("Bill") Kennedy
Professor of History emeritus, Northwestern College, Orange City, Iowa
Senior Research Fellow, A.C. Van Raalte Institute, Hope College,
Holland, Michigan

Cornelia B.("Nella") Kennedy
Senior Research Fellow, A. C. Van Raalte Institute, Hope College

Meeting and getting to know Russell Gasero and his wife Maria through the Dutch Cousins of Kentucky organization has been a joy over the past few years. The Old Mud Meetinghouse near Harrodsburg, Kentucky, built by our ancestors in 1800, was in complete disrepair in 2005 with a shaky foundation and a leaky roof, no doors or windows when the Dutch Cousins first visited and took it on as a project. At our rededication service in 2017, Russell Gasero organized an 1800s-style service with Cousins serving as Voorlezer, deacons, and ushers, that was quite impressive and fun.

We all love Russell!

Carolyn Leonard
Organizer and Past President, The Dutch Cousins of Kentucky

He always pointed us to relevant material and was never too busy to take time for a chat.

Roland Ratmeyer
Retired RCA minister

Una Ratmeyer
Author and historian

Russ is a servant of the first order. It is my honor to call him a friend.

Douglas Van Aartsen
Retired RCA minister

I have found Russ to always be kind, understanding and very patient with answering my questions. I always enjoyed our conversations at General Synod. I recall an occasion where his position might be eliminated due to budget cuts. Thankfully it remained.

Albert Vander Meer
Retired RCA Minister and Regional Synod Executive

Publications in the Historical Series of the Reformed Church in America

The following Historical Series publications may be ordered easily through the Faith Alive web site at www.faithaliveresources.org

The home page has a search the site box. Either enter the specific title or author, or enter "Historical Series" to search for all volumes available. Titles will appear with the option of adding to cart. Books may also be ordered through your local bookstore.

You may also see the full list of titles on the RCA website at:

www.rca.org/series

1. *Ecumenism in the Reformed Church in America*, by Herman Harmelink III (1968)
2. *The Americanization of a Congregation*, by Elton J. Bruins (1970)
3. *Pioneers in the Arab World*, by Dorothy F. Van Ess (1974)
4. *Piety and Patriotism*, edited by James W. Van Hoeven (1976)
5. *The Dutch Reformed Church in the American Colonies*, by Gerald F. De Jong (1978)
6. *Historical Directory of the Reformed Church in America, 1628-1978*, by Peter N. VandenBerge (1978)
7. *Digest and Index of the Minutes of General Synod, 1958-1977*, by Mildred W. Schuppert (1979)
8. *Digest and Index of the Minutes of General Synod, 1906-1957*, by Mildred W. Schuppert (1982)
9. *From Strength to Strength*, by Gerald F. De Jong (1982)
10. *"B. D."*, by D. Ivan Dykstra (1982)
11. *Sharifa*, by Cornelia Dalenburg (1983)
12. *Vision From the Hill*, edited by John W. Beardslee III (1984)
13. *Two Centuries Plus*, by Howard G. Hageman (1984)
14. *Structures for Mission*, by Marvin D. Hoff (1985)

15. *The Church Speaks*, edited by James I. Cook (1985)
16. *Word and World*, edited by James W. Van Hoeven (1986)
17. *Sources of Secession: The Netherlands Hervormde Kerk on the Eve of the Dutch Immigration to the Midwest*, by Gerrit J. tenZythoff (1987)
18. *Vision for a Christian College*, by Gordon J. Van Wylen (1988)
19. *Servant Gladly*, edited by Jack D. Klunder and Russell L. Gasero (1989)
20. *Grace in the Gulf*, by Jeanette Boersma (1991)
21. *Ecumenical Testimony*, by Arie R. Brouwer (1991)
22. *The Reformed Church in China, 1842-1951*, by Gerald F. De Jong (1992)
23. *Historical Directory of the Reformed Church in America, 1628-1992*, by Russell L. Gasero (1992)
24. *Meeting Each Other in Doctrine, Liturgy, and Government*, by Daniel J. Meeter (1993)
25. *Gathered at Albany*, by Allan J. Janssen (1995)
26. *The Americanization of a Congregation*, 2nd ed., by Elton J. Bruins (1995)
27. *In Remembrance and Hope: The Ministry and Vision of Howard G. Hageman*, by Gregg A. Mast (1998)
28. *Deacons' Accounts, 1652-1674, First Dutch Reformed Church of Beverwyck/Albany*, trans. & edited by Janny Venema (1998)
29. *The Call of Africa*, by Morrill F. Swart (1998)
30. *The Arabian Mission's Story: In Search of Abraham's Other Son*, by Lewis R. Scudder III (1998)
31. *Patterns and Portraits: Women in the History of the Reformed Church in America*, edited by Renée S. House and John W. Coakley (1999)
32. *Family Quarrels in the Dutch Reformed Churches in the Nineteenth Century*, by Elton J. Bruins & Robert P. Swierenga (1999)
33. *Constitutional Theology: Notes on the* Book of Church Order *of the Reformed Church In America*, by Allan J. Janssen (2000)
34. *Raising the Dead: Sermons of Howard G. Hageman*, edited by Gregg A. Mast (2000)
35. *Equipping the Saints: The Synod of New York, 1800-2000*, edited by James Hart Brumm (2000)
36. *Forerunner of the Great Awakening*, edited by Joel R. Beeke (2000)
37. *Historical Directory of the Reformed Church in America, 1628-2000*, by Russell L. Gasero (2001)
38. *From Mission to Church: The Reformed Church in America in India*, by Eugene Heideman (2001)
39. *Our School: Calvin College and the Christian Reformed Church*, by Harry Boonstra (2001)

40. *The Church Speaks, 2*, edited by James I. Cook (2002)
41. *Concord Makes Strength*, edited by John W. Coakley (2002)
42. *Dutch Chicago: A History of the Hollanders in the Windy City*, by Robert P. Swierenga (2002)
43. *Doctors for the Kingdom*, Paul Armerding (2003)
44. *By Grace Alone*, Donald J. Bruggink (2004)
45. *Travels of an American Girl*, June Potter Durkee (2004)
46. *Letters to Hazel*, Mary Kansfield (2004)
47. *Iowa Letters*, Robert P. Swierenga (2004)
48. *Can Hope Endure, A Historical Case Study in Christian Higher Education*, James C. Kennedy and Caroline J. Simon (2005)
49. *Elim*, Robert P. Swierenga (2005)
50. *Taking the Jesus Road*, LeRoy Koopman (2005)
51. *The Netherlands Reformed Church, 1571-2005*, Karel Blei (2005)
52. *Son of Secession: Douwe J. Vander Werp*, Janet Sjaarda Sheeres (2006)
53. *Kingdom, Office, and Church: A Study of A. A. van Ruler's Doctrine of Ecclesiastical Office*, Allan J. Janssen (2006)
54. *Divided by a Common Heritage: The Christian Reformed Church and the Reformed Church in America at the Beginning of the New Millenium*, Corwin Smidt, Donald Luidens, James Penning, and Roger Nemeth (2006)
55. *Henry J. Kuiper: Shaping the Christian Reformed Church, 1907-1962*, James A. De Jong (2007)
56. *A Goodly Heritage, Essays in Honor of the Reverend Dr. Elton J. Bruins at Eighty*, Jacob E. Nyenhuis (2007)
57. *Liturgy among the Thorns: Essays on Worship in the Reformed Church in America*, James Hart Brumm (2007)
58. *Old Wing Mission*, Robert P. Swierenga (2008)
59. *Herman J. Ridder: Contextual Preacher and President*, edited by George Brown, Jr. (2009)

60. *Tools for Understanding*, edited by James Hart Brumm (2009) 404 pp. ISBN: 978-0-8028-6483-3

"Beginning with Donald Bruggink's own notion that 'history is a tool for understanding,' the dozen essays in this volume are tools for understanding four areas of his life and his fifty-five years of ministry. While all the contributors to this volume have benefited from Bruggink's friendship, teaching, and ministry, the first and last essays are by the contributors he has known longest, who had a formative role in his life"
— Eugene Heideman and I. John Hesselink.

61. *Chinese Theological Education*, edited by Marvin D. Hoff (2009) 470 pp. ISBN: 978-0-8028-6480-2

This book offers insight into the emergence of the Christian church after Mao's Cultural Revolution. While reports of Communist oppression have dominated American perceptions of church and state in China, this is an increasingly dangerous view as China changes. Dr. Marvin D. Hoff, as executive director for the Foundation for Theological Education in Southeast Asia, traveled at least annually to China for the period covered by this book. The original reports of his encounters with Chinese Christians, especially those involved in theological education, are a historic record of the church's growth—and growing freedom. Interspersed with Hoff's accounts are reports of essays by Chinese and other Asian Christians. Introductory essays are provided by Charles W. Forman of Yale Divinity School, Daniel B. Hays of Calvin College, and Donald J. Bruggink of Western Theological Seminary.

62. *Liber A*, edited by Frank Sypher (2009) 442 pp. ISBN: 978-0-8028-6509-0

Liber A of the Collegiate Church archives contains detailed seventeenth-century records of the Reformed Dutch Church of the City of New York, including correspondence, texts of legal documents, and lists of names of consistory members. Especially significant are records pertaining to the granting in 1696 of the royal charter of incorporation of the Church, and records relating to donations for, and construction of the church building on Garden Street. The full Dutch texts have never before been published.

63. *Aunt Tena, Called to Serve: Journals and Letters of Tena A. Huizenga, Missionary Nurse to Nigeria*, edited by Jacob A. Nyenhuis, Robert P. Swierenga, and Lauren M. Berka (2009) 980 pp. ISBN: 978-0-8028-6515-1

When Tena Huizenga felt the call to serve as a missionary nurse to Africa, she followed that call and served seventeen years at Lupwe, Nigeria, during a pivotal era in world missions. As she ministered to the natives, she recorded her thoughts and feelings in a diary and in countless letters to family and friends--over 350 in her first year alone. Through her eyes, we see the Lupwe mission, Tena's colleagues, and the many native helpers. Aunt Tena (Nigerians called all female missionaries "Aunt") tells this profoundly human story. Interesting in its own right, the book will also prove invaluable to historians, sociologists, and genealogists as they mine this rich resource.

The extensive letters from Tena's brother Pete offer marvelous insights into the Dutch Reformed subculture of Chicago's West Side. Because his scavenger company later evolved into Waste Management Inc., those letters are especially valuable. Pete's winsome descriptions and witty dialogue with his sister add a Chicago flavor to this book.

64. *The Practice of Piety: The Theology of the Midwestern Reformed Church in America, 1866-1966,* by Eugene P. Heideman (2009) 286 pp. ISBN: 978-0-8028-6551-9

"With the instincts of a historian and the affection of a child of the RCA, Gene Heideman has accessed both Dutch and English sources in order to introduce us to the unique theology and piety of the Midwestern section of our denomination from 1866 to 1966. Through the words of pastors, professors, and parishioners, he has fleshed out the Dutch pilgrims of the 19th century who found their roots in the Netherlands but their fruit in America. Accessing the Dutch language newspaper *De Hope,* and the writings and lectures of a century of Western Seminary professors, the history of the RCA in the Midwest has come alive. This book is a gracious and winsome invitation to its readers and other scholars to dig deeper and understand more fully the theological and ethnic heritage of those who have helped ground our past and thus form our future."

— Gregg A. Mast, president, New Brunswick Theological Seminary

65. *Freedom on the Horizon: Dutch Immigration to America, 1840 to 1940,* by Hans Krabbendam (2009) 432 pp. ISBN: 978-0-8028-6545-8

"It's been eighty years since the last comprehensive study of the Dutch immigrant experience by a Netherlands scholar—Jacob Van Hinte's magisterial *Netherlanders in America* (1928, English translation 1985). It was worth the wait! Krabbendam has a firmer grasp of American history and culture than his predecessor, who spent only seven weeks on a whirlwind tour of a half-dozen Dutch 'colonies' in 1921. Krabbendam earned an M.A. degree in the USA, is widely traveled, versed in American religious culture, and has written the definitive biography of Edward W. Box (2001). *Freedom on the Horizon* focuses on the ultimate meaning of immigration—the process by which one's inherited culture is reshaped into a new Dutch-American identity. 'Only the steeple was retained,' Krabbendam notes in his tale of a congregation that tore down its

historic church edifice in favor of a modern new one. This is a metaphor of the Dutch immigrant experience writ large, as told here in a masterful way."
   — Robert D. Swierenga, Kent State University

66. *A Collegial Bishop? Classis and Presbytery at Issue*, edited by Allan Janssen and Leon Vanden Broek (2010) 176 pp. ISBN: 978-0-8028-6585-4

   In *A Collegial Bishop?* classis and presbytery are considered from a cross-cultural, indeed cross-national, perspective of the inheritors of Geneva and Edinburgh in their contemporary contexts in the Netherlands, South Africa, and the United States.
   "Dutch theologian A. A. van Ruler compares church order to the rafters of a church building. Church order sustains the space within which the church is met by God, where it engages in its plan with God (liturgy), and where it is used by God in its mission in and to God's world. Presbyterian church order intends to be faithful to its root in God's Word, as it is shaped around the office of elder and governed through a series of councils of the church."
   Alan Janssen
   — Pastor, Community Church of Glen Rock, NJ

67. *The Church Under the Cross*, by Wendell Karssen (2010) 454 pp. ISBN: 978-0-8028-6614-1

   The Church Under the Cross: Mission in Asia in Times of Turmoil is the illustrated two-volume account of Wendell Paul Karsen's more than three decades of cross-cultural missionary work in East Asia.
   In one sense a missionary memoir of Karsen's life and ministry in Taiwan, Hong Kong, China, and Indonesia, the work also chronicles the inspiring story of the Christian communities Karsen served—churches which struggled to grow and witness under adverse circumstances throughout years of political turbulence and social upheaval.

68. *Supporting Asian Christianity's Transition from Mission to Church: A History of the Foundation for Theological Education in Southeast Asia*, edited by Samuel C. Pearson (2010) 464 pp. ISBN: 978-0-8028-6622-6

   "This volume, telling the story of how one North American ecumenical foundation learned to move from a 'missions' stance to one of 'partnership,' is at once informative, intriguing, and instructive for anyone curious about or interested in the development of contextual theological education and scholarship in China and Southeast Asia. It traces the efforts of Protestant churches and educational institutions emerging from World War II, revolution, and colonization to train an indigenous leadership and to nurture theological scholars for the political, cultural, and religious realities in which these ecclesial bodies find themselves."

— Greer Anne Wenh-In Ng, Professor Emerita, Victoria University in the University of Toronto

69. *The American Diary of Jacob Van Hinte*, edited by Peter Ester, Nella Kennedy, Earl Wm. Kennedy (2010) 210 pp. ISBN: 978-0-8028-6661-5

"This is a charming translation, scrupulously annotated, of the long-lost travel diary of Jacob Van Hinte (1889-1948), author of the monumental Netherlanders in America. Van Hinte's energetic five-week sprint in the summer of 1921 from "Dutch" Hoboken up the river by dayliner to Albany and on to the Dutch-settled towns and cities in the Midwest convinced him that the "migration to America had been a blessing" to the Dutch. But in his brief sojourn among the descendants of the immigrant generation, he also became aware of the "tales of misery" and the "noble struggles" of the settlers that will put readers of all ethnic backgrounds to wondering about their own poignant histories."

— Firth Fabend, author of Zion on the Hudson: Dutch new York and the New Jersey in the Age of Revivals

70. *A New Way of Belonging: Covenant Theology, China and the Christian Reformed Church, 1921-1951*, by Kurt Selles (2011) 288 pp. ISBN: 978-0-8028-6662-2

"As someone who spent much of my childhood on the mission field described in this book, I anticipated having my early memories refreshed by reading it. I did indeed find the book to be an accurate and thorough account of the work of the CRC China Mission as I remember it, but—more surprising—I also learned a good deal of new information. Kurt Selles has performed an important service for the history of missions by uncovering so much new information and doing such impressive research under difficult circumstances. Although the events took place more than a half-century ago, Selles has been able to retrieve a vast amount of detail. His analysis of the cross-cultural dynamics of this work is insightful. Anyone interested in the successes and failures of Christian mission should find this study interesting and informative."

— J. William Smit, professor of sociology, Calvin College, child of CRC China missionary Albert Smit

71. *Envisioning Hope College: Letters Written by Albertus C. Van Raalte to Philip Phelps, Jr., 1857-1875*, edited by Elton J. Bruins and Karen G. Schakel (2011) 556 pp. ISBN: 978-0-8028-6688-2

These letters between the colony's leader and the first president of Hope College in Holland, Michigan, are sequentially placed in historical context and richly footnoted. They offer an intimate view of Van Raalte as he seeks funding for his college from the Dutch Reformed Church in the east, as well as insights into his pioneer community in the midst of conflagration and war.

72. *Ministry Among the Maya*, by Dorothy Dickens Meyerink (Dec. 2011) 434 pp. ISBN: 978-0-8028-6744-5

Dorothy Meyerink entered her ministry among the Maya of Chiapas, Mexico, in 1956, and spent her entire service there. *Ministry Among the Maya* is an exciting account of persecution and success, relating the story of how, through the faithful witness of the laity and the early ordination of Mayan ministers, a strong, large, indigenous church was established and continues to flourish. Meyerink interweaves her personal experiences and the history of the church with reflections on the effective application of church growth principles.

73. *The Church Under the Cross, Vol. 2*, by Wendell Karsen (Dec. 2011) 802 pp. ISBN: 978-0-8028-6760-5

See volume 67.

74. *Sing to the Lord a New Song: Choirs in the Worship and Culture of the Dutch Reformed Church in America, 1785-1860*, by David M.Tripold (2012) 304 pp. ISBN: 978-0-8028-6874-9

As their privileged status evaporated in America's melting pot, the Dutch Reformed Church was forced to compete with a host of rising Protestant denominations in the New World. Survival became linked to assimilating within a new American way of life, with its own distinct language, culture, and religious practices. Gradually, organs, hymns and institutional church choirs were added to the traditional singing of the Psalter—innovations that altered the very fabric of Dutch Reformed religious life in America.

Sing to the Lord a New Song examines how choirs in particular revolutionized the Dutch Reformed Church in the nineteenth century, transforming the church's very nature in terms of worship, ecclesiastical life, institutional structures, and even social, fiscal, and moral practices. Moreover, the book examines how choirs helped break social barriers, particularly those regarding the status and role of women in the church.

Includes audio CD.

75. *Pioneers to Partners, The Reformed Church in America and Christian Mission to the Japanese*, by Gordon Laman (2012) ISBN: 978-0-8028-6965-4

Beginning with Japan's early exposure to Christianity by the very successful Roman Catholic mission to Japan in the sixteenth and seventeenth centuries, and the resultant persecution and prohibition of Christianity, Laman lays the groundwork for understanding the experience of nineteenth-century Protestant missionaries, among whom those of the Reformed Church in America were in the forefront. The early efforts of the Browns, Verbecks, Ballaghs, and Stouts, their failures and successes, are recounted within the cultural and political context of the anti-Western, anti-Christian Japan of the time.

Verbeck's service to the government helped bring about gradual change. The first Protestant church was organized with a vision for ecumenical mission, and during several promising years, churches and mission schools were organized. Reformed Church missionaries encouraged and trained Japanese leaders from the beginning, the first Japanese ministers were ordained in 1877, and the Japanese church soon exhibited a spirit of independence, ushering in an era of growing missionary/Japanese partnership.

The rise of the Japanese empire, a reinvigorated nationalism, and its progression to militarist ultranationalism brought on a renewed anti-Western, anti-Christian reaction and new challenges to both mission and church. With the outbreak of World War II, the Japanese government consolidated all Protestant churches into the Kyodan to facilitate control.

Laman continues the account of Reformed Church partners in mission in Japan in the midst of post-war devastation and subsequent social and political tensions. The ecumenical involvement and continued clarification of mutual mission finds the Reformed Church a full participant with a mature Japanese church.

76. *Transatlantic Pieties*, ed by Hans Krabbendam, Leon van den Broeke, and Dirk Mouw (2012) 359 pp. ISBN: 978-0-8028-6972-2

Transatlantic Pieties: Dutch Clergy in Colonial America explores the ways in which the lives and careers of fourteen Dutch Reformed ministers illuminate important aspects of European and American colonial society of their times. Based on primary sources, this collection reexamines some of the movers and shakers over the course of 250 years. The essays shed light on the high and low tides, the promises and disappointments, and the factors within and beyond the control of a new society in the making. The portraits humanize and contextualize the lives of these men who served not only as religious leaders and cultural mediators in colonial communities, but also as important connective tissue in the Dutch Atlantic world.

77. *Loyalty and Loss, the Reformed Church in America, 1945-1994*, by Lynn Japinga (2013) ISBN: 978-0-8028-7068-1

Offering a meticulously researched yet also deeply personal history of the Reformed Church in America throughout much of the twentieth century, Lynn Japinga's *Loyalty and Loss* will be of intense interest to the members of the RCA, reminding them of where they have come from, of the bonds that have held them together, and of the many conflicts and challenges that they have together faced and ultimately surmounted.

For those outside the RCA the questions of identity raised by this book will often sound very familiar, especially, perhaps, in its account of the church's struggle throughout recent decades to reconcile the persistently ecumenical spirit of many of its members with the desire of others within the denomination to preserve a real or imagined conservative exclusivity. Others may find the conflicts within the RCA reflective of their own experiences, especially as they relate to such issues as denominational mergers, abortion, the Viet Nam war, and women's ordination.

78. *Oepke Noordmans: Theologian of the Holy Spirit*, Karel Blei (tran. By Allan Janssen) (2013) ISBN: 978-0-8028-7085-8

Oepke Noordmans was one of the major Dutch theologians of the twentieth century, whose recovery of a vital doctrine of the Holy Spirit placed him at the center of thought on the nature of the church and its ministry.

In this volume Karel Blei, himself a theological voice of note, has provided a lucid introduction to and summary of Noordmans's thought and contextual impact. The book also includes substantial excerpts of Noordmans's writing in translation, offering a compact representation of his work to an English-speaking audience.

79. *The Not-So-Promised Land, The Dutch in Amelia County, Virginia, 1868-1880*, by Janet Sjaarda Sheeres (2013) 248 pp. ISBN: 978-0-8028-7156-5

The sad story of a little-known, short-lived Dutch immigrant settlement.

After establishing a successful Dutch colony in Holland, Michigan, in 1847, Albertus Van Raalte turned his attention to the warmer climes of Amelia County, Virginia, where he attempted to establish a second colony. This volume by Janet Sheeres presents a carefully researched account of that colonization attempt with a thorough analysis of why it failed. Providing insights into the risks of new settlements that books on successful colonies overlook, this is the first major study of the Amelia settlement.

A well-told tale of high hopes but eventual failure, *The Not-So-Promised Land* concludes with a 73-page genealogy of everyone involved in the settlement, including their origins, marriages, births, deaths, denominations, occupations, and post-Amelia destinations.

80. *Holland Michigan, From Dutch Colony to Dynamic City* (3 volumes), by Robert P. Swierenga (2013) ISBN: 978-0-8028-7137-4

Holland Michigan: From Dutch Colony to Dynamic City is a fresh and comprehensive history of the city of Holland from its beginnings to the increasingly diverse community it is today.

The three volumes that comprise this monumental work discuss such topics as the coming of the Dutch, the Americans who chose to live among them, schools, grassroots politics, the effects of the world wars and the Great Depression, city institutions, downtown renewal, and social and cultural life in Holland. Robert Swierenga also draws attention to founder Albertus Van Raalte's particular role in forming the city—everything from planning streets to establishing churches and schools, nurturing industry, and encouraging entrepreneurs.

Lavishly illustrated with nine hundred photographs and based on meticulous research, this book offers the most detailed history of Holland, Michigan, in print.

The volume received the Historical Society of Michigan 2014 State History Award in the Books, University and Commercial Press category

81. *The Enduring Legacy of Albertus C. Van Raalte as Leader and Liaison*, edited by Jacob E. Nyenhuis and George Harinck (2013) 560 pp. ISBN: 978-0-8028-7215-9

The celebration of the bicentennial of the birth of Albertus C. Van Raalte in October 2011 provided a distinct opportunity to evaluate the enduring legacy of one of the best-known Dutch immigrants of the nineteenth century. This book of essays demonstrates his unique role not only in the narrative of the migration to America but also in the foundation of theological education for Seceders (Afgescheidenen) prior to his emigration. These essays were all presented at an international conference held in Holland, Michigan, and Ommen, Overijssel, the Netherlands, with the conference theme of "Albertus C. Van Raalte: Leader and Liaison." Three broad categories serve as the organizing principle for this book: biographical essays, thematic essays, and reception studies.

Van Raalte began to emerge as a leader within the Seceder Church (Christelijk Afgescheidene Gereformeerde Kerk) in the Netherlands, but his leadership abilities were both tested and strengthened through leading a group of Dutch citizens to the United States in 1846. In his role as leader, moreover, he served as liaison to the Reformed Protestant Dutch Church in America in the eastern United States (renamed the Reformed Church in America in 1867) to the Seceder Church in the Netherlands, and to the civil authorities in the United States, as well as between business and their employees.

These fifteen essays illuminate the many facets of this energetic, multi-talented founder of the Holland kolonie. This collection further enhances and strengthens our knowledge of both Van Raalte and his Separatist compatriots.

82. *Minutes of the Christian Reformed Church, Classical Assembly, 1857-1870, General Assembly, 1867-79, and Synodical Assembly, 1880*, edited and annotated by Janet Sjaarda Sheeres (2014) 668 pp. ISBN: 978-0-8028-7253-1

"Janet Sheeres, noted scholar of the Dutch in North America, here turns her skill to the early years of the Christian Reformed Church in North America. She has painstakingly researched all the individuals who attended denominational leadership gatherings and the issues discussed and debated at these meetings. Her extensive annotations to a new translation of the minutes provides unprecedented and cogent insight into the early years of the denomination and the larger Dutch trans-Appalachian immigration of the nineteenth century. The annotations reflect Sheeres's characteristically detailed research in both Dutch and English. Scholars of immigration, religion, Dutch-American immigrants, and the Christian Reformed Church will benefit from data in this book, and the appendix of biographical data will be invaluable to those interested in family research."

— Richard Harms, archivist of the Christian Reformed Church

83 *New Brunswick Theological Seminary: an Illustrated History, 1784-2014.* John W. Coakley (2014) ISBN: 978-0-8028-7296-8

This volume marks the 230th anniversary of New Brunswick Theological Seminary and the reconfiguring of its campus by retelling the school's history in text and pictures. John Coakley, teacher of church history at the seminary for thirty years, examines how the mission of the school has evolved over the course of the seminary's history, focusing on its changing relationship to the community of faith it has served in preparing men and women for ministry.

In four chapters representing four significant eras in the seminary's history, Coakley traces the relationship between the seminary in New Brunswick and the Reformed Church in America, showing that both the seminary and the RCA have changed dramatically over the years but have never lost each other along the way.

84. *Hendrik P. Scholte: His Legacy in the Netherlands and in America.* Eugene P. Heideman (2015) 314 pp. ISBN: 978-0-8028-7352-1

This book offers a careful contextual theological analysis of a nineteenth-century schismatic with twenty-first-century ecumenical intent.

Hendrik P. Scholte (1803-1868) was the intellectual leader and catalyst of a separation from the Nederlandse Hervormde Kerk. Leaving the state church meant being separated from its deacon's funds, conflict with the laws of the state, and social ostracism. Due to poverty, Scholte emigrated with a group that settled Pella, Iowa. Schismatic tendencies continued in this and other nineteenth-century Dutch settlements with the most notable division being between those who joined the Reformed Church in America and those who became the Christian Reformed Church in North America.

As Heideman says: "Although this book concentrates on what happened in the past, it is written with the hope that knowledge of the past will contribute to the faithfulness and unity of the church in the future."

85. *Liber A:1628-1700 of the Collegiate Churches of New York, Part 2*, translated, annotated, and edited by Frank J. Sypher, Jr. (2015) 911 pp. ISBN: 978-0-8028-7341-5

See volume 62.

86. *KEMP: The Story of John R. and Mabel Kempers, Founders of the Reformed Church in America Mission in Chiapas, Mexico*, by Pablo A. Deiros. (2016) 558 pp. ISBN 978-0-8028-7354-5

"This faithful story reveals God's power to transform thousands of people's lives through a couple committed to spreading God's message of love and devotion. The Kempers' commitment to their slogan "Chiapas para Cristo" was evidenced in all that they did. They were our surrogate parents, mission colleagues, and mentors."
— Sam and Helen Hofman, career RCA missionaries in Chiapas, Mexico.

"Employing a creative narrative style, Pablo Deiros has fashioned a fully documented biography into a compelling story of the lives and witness of John and Mabel Kempers. *Kemp* is a must read for those who are interested in the intersection of the Christian Church and the social revolution in Mexico during the twentieth century, the struggles of Maya cultures in Chiapas, and the transformative impact of the gospel of Jesus Christ among the people of Chiapas. *Kemp* is an inspiring and engaging history."
— Dennis N. Voskuil, Director, Van Raalte Institute

87. *Yes! Well...Exploring the Past, Present, and Future of the Church: Essays in Honor of John W. Coakley*, edited by James Hart Brumm. (2016) 324pp. ISBN: 978-0-8028-7479-5

In this volume, authors from around the world present essays in honor of John W. Coakley, L. Russell Feakes Memorial Professor Emeritus of Church History at New Brunswick Theological Seminary in New Jersey. Following the pattern of Coakley's teaching, the contributors push readers to think about aspects of the church in new ways.

Contributors include: Thomas A. Boogart, James Hart Brumm, Kathleen Hart Brumm, Jaeseung Cha, James F. Coakley, Sarah Coakley. Matthew Gasero, Russell Gasero, Allan Janssen, Lynn Japinga, Mary L. Kansfield, Norman J. Kansfield, James Jinhong Kim, Gregg A. Mast, Dirk Mouw, Ondrea Murphy, Mark V. C. Taylor, and David W. Waanders

88. *Elephant Baseball: A Missionary Kids Tale*, by Paul Heusinkveld. (2017) 282 pp. ISBN: 978-0-8028-7550-1

This fascinating book recounts the up-and-down experiences of a missionary kid growing up overseas away from home in the 1960s. A sensitive autobiographical exploration of the universal trials of adolescence, Paul Heusinkveld's *Elephant Baseball* luxuriates in narrative fluidity—truly a riveting read.

89. *Growing Pains: How Racial Struggles Changed a Church and a School*, by Christopher H. Meehan. (2017) 240 pp. ISBN: 978-0-80287-570-9

In the 1960s, black parents from Lawndale Christian Reformed Church in Chicago tried to enroll their children in an all-white Christian school in the suburb of Cicero. A power struggle ensued, taking the matter to synod and inspiring the creation of the Office of Race Relations.

90. *A Ministry of Reconciliation: Essays in Honor of Gregg Mast*, edited by Allan J. Janssen. (2017) 272 pp. ISBN: 978-0-80287-598-3

Respect and affection for Gregg Mast permeates this volume of essays written by his colleagues across the fruitful years of his ministry. He certainly has much to show for his years of labor; the list of his accomplishments is long. But it is his heart that impresses me the most. I consider it a privilege to number myself as one of his colleagues, and I can attest, along with many others, to his generosity of spirit, kindness of speech, and faithful persistence of character. This book is a fitting tribute to his impact, and I warmly commend it to a wide readership.

— Leanne Van Dyk, President and Professor of Theology, Columbia Theological Seminary, Decatur, Georgia

91. *For Better, For Worse: Stories of the Wives of Early Pastors of the Christian Reformed Church*, by Janet Sjaarda Sheeres. (2017) 224 pp. ISBN: 978-0-80287-625-6

In *For Better, for Worse*, Janet Sjaarda Sheeres highlights the lives of the wives of the first ten pastors of the Christian Reformed Church.

Beginning in 1857, when the CRC was founded, Sheeres proceeds in the order in which the first ten pastors joined the church.

Drawing on genealogical and census data, church records from congregations their husbands served, and historical information about the position of women at the time, Sheeres brings the untold stories of these women's lives to light.

92. *In Peril on the Sea: The Forgotten Story of the William & Mary Shipwreck*, by Kenneth A. Schaaf. (2017) 382 pp. ISBN: 978-0-98914-696-8

"Historian Ken Schaaf has mined the rich holdings of the Library of Congress, the National Archives, and research facilities on both sides of the Atlantic to uncover the amazing story of the eighty-six Frisians who boarded the William & Mary en route to America. After weeks of sailing, they found themselves abandoned at sea by captain and crew aboard their sinking vessel. Readers interested in transatlantic passages under sail will not be able to put this book down. The story grabs the emotions and will not let go."

—Robert P. Swierenga, Senior Research Fellow, Van Raalte Institute

93. *Jack: A Compassionate Compendium: A Tribute to Dr. Jacob E. Nyenhuis, Scholar, Servant, Leader*, edited by Donald A. Luidens and JoHannah M. Smith. (2018) 366 pp. ISBN: 978-0-98914-697-5

A tribute to Dr Jacob E. Nyenhuis, scholar, servant, and leader. Nyenhuis served as a professor of Classics at Hope College (Holland, Michigan) and later served as its Provost, before becoming the director of the Van Raalte Institute.

94. *A Commentary on the Minutes of the Classis of Holland, 1848-1876: A Detailed Record of Persons and Issues, Civil and Religious, in the Dutch Colony of Holland, Michigan*, edited by Earl William Kennedy (three volumes). (2018) 2,080 pp. ISBN: 978-0-98914-695-1

"This much-anticipated, annotated edition in English of the Dutch-language minutes of the Classis of Holland (Michigan)—the seminal regional assembly of Dutch Reformed immigrants in the Midwest—is extraordinary for its scope and detail. Every substantive theological and ecclesiastical issue, whether Netherlandic or American in origin, is rooted in the foundational Synod of Dort (1618-19) and the Later (Nadere) Reformation. In addition, Kennedy provides biographical sketches of virtually every ministerial and elder delegate, likely hundreds of churchmen. Only a scholar grounded in Reformed theological and ecclesiastical history, fluent in languages, and skilled in genealogical search engines could have written such an extensive work. This multivolume sourcebook will be indispensable to anyone interested in Reformed church history."

—Robert P Swierenga, Research Professor, A. C. Van Raalte Institute, Hope College

95. *Hope College at 150: Anchored in Faith, Educating for Leadership and Service in a Global Society*, Jacob Nyenhuis et alii (two volumes). (2018) 1,414 pp. ISBN: 978-1-950572-00-7

A comprehensive survey and history of 150 years of Hope College, edited by Jack Nyenhuis with contributions by James C. Kennedy, Dennis N. Voskuil, Robert P. Swierenga, Alfredo M. Gonzales, John E. Jobson, Michael J. Douma, Thomas L. Renner, and Scott Travis. The two volume set includes many full-color images of the buildings on the campus and the history of Hope's architecture as well as lists of alumni, faculty, enrollment data, summaries of student life and housing, ending with a plan for the future.

96. *Remembrance, Communion, and Hope: Essays in Honor of Allan J. Janssen*, edited by Matthew J. van Maastricht. (2019) 261 pp. ISBN: 978-1-9505-7201-4

This festschrift in honor of Allan Janssen's service as a General Synod Professor looks at his work as a theologian, ecclesiologist, and polity expert, who was, first and foremost, a pastor and teacher. Featuring essays by Carol M. Bechtel, Abraham van de Beek, Karel Blei, Leon van den Broeke, John W. Coakley, Daniel M. Griswold, Eugene P. Heideman, Paul Janssen, Leo J. Koffeman, Christo Lombard, Matthew J. van Maastricht, Gregg Mast, Daniel J. Meeter, and Micah L. McCreary.

97. *Before the Face of God: Essays in Honor of Tom Boogaart*, edited by Dustyn Elizabeth Keepers. (2018) 336 pp. ISBN: 978-1950572021

A collection of essays in honor of the long-time professor of Old Testament at Western Theological Seminary on the occasion of his retirement, including works by Jeff Barker, Carol M. Bechtel, Tim Brown, James Brownson, Pam Bush, John W, Coakley, Benjamin Conner, Christopher Dorn, Jaco J. Hamman, Christopher B. Kaiser, Dustyn Elizabeth Keepers, Zac Poppen, Alberto La Rosa Rojas, Kyle

Small, David L. Stubbs, Lyle VanderBroek, Travis West, and Stephen J. Wykstra.

96. *Remembrance, Communion, and Hope: Essays in Honor of Allan J. Janssen,* edited by Matthew J. van Maastricht. (2019) 261 pp., ISBN: 978-1-9505-7201-4

This festschrift in honor of Allan Janssen's service as a General Synod Professor looks at his work as a theologian, ecclesiologist, and polity expert, who was, first and foremost, a pastor and teacher. Featuring essays by Carol M. Bechtel, Abraham van de Beek, Karel Blei, Leon van den Broeke, John W. Coakley, Daniel M. Griswold, Eugene P. Heideman, Paul Janssen, Leo J. Koffeman, Christo Lombard, Matthew J. van Maastricht, Gregg Mast, Daniel J. Meeter, and Micah L. McCreary.

98. *A Constant State of Emergency: Paul de Kruif, Microbe Hunter and Health Activist,* by Jan Peter Verhave. (2018) 656 pp. ISBN: 978-1-950572-06-9

A biography of the Dutch Reformed health care champion whose influence on the fields of immunology, medicine, and microbiology in the mid-twentieth century was world-changing. De Kruif fought for the reform of the American health care system, the presentation and treatment of diseases, and affordable health care for all.

99. *Register of Marriages from 1783 to 1905 in the Collegiate Churches of New York,* edited by Francis J. Sypher, Jr. (2019) 447 pp. ISBN: 978-1-9505-7203-8

Meticulously transcribed and annotated records of the oldest Protestant congregations with a continuous ministry in North America, providing invaluable data to church members, genealogists, biographers, social historians, demographers, and anyone curious about people in New York through the eighteenth to twentieth centuries.

100. *Constitutional Theology: Notes on the book of Church Order of the Reformed Church in America, second edition,* by Allan J. Janssen. (2019) 328 pp. ISBN: 978-1950572045

This is the updated, second edition by one of the RCAs foremost researchers. The volume offers commentary that explains the proper roles of elders, deacons, classes, and synods and details the procedures necessary for successful church life. Based on the Book of Church Order, this helpful volume will assist church leaders in their callings and prevent the myriad difficulties that arise when appropriate procedures are not followed. A necessity for every pastor, elder, and deacon.

101. *The Church Remembers: Papers of the RCA Commission on History, 1977 to 2019,* edited by James Hart Brumm. (2020) 174 pp. ISBN: 978-1-9505-7211-3

A collection of seventeen papers presented by the Commission on History covering the historical development of the Constitution of the Reformed Church in America, the General Synod, RCA Ecclesiology, and the relationship of the Church to the world. These papers look at events from the sixteenth century Reformation to the present, always with an eye toward how these past events inform the present and future work of the church.

102. *Called to Serve: Essays on RCA Global Mission,* edited by Charles Van Engen, Jean Van Engen, and Sally Tapley. (2020) 162 pp. ISBN: 978-1-9505-7213-7

A collection of brief a=essays primarily my missionaries who worked in the field, sharing stories of this work that is integral to the fabric of the Reformed Church in America and giving readers a glimpse of faithful people doing their best to follow God. Contributors include Alan Beagley, Jeanette Beagley-Koolhaas, James Hart Brumm, William DeBoer, Lind Walvoord deVelder, Eugene Heidemann, J. Samuel Hoffman, John Hubers, Derrick Jones, LeRoy Koopman, Gordon D. Laman, Jacob Moss, Richard Otterness, Sally Tapley, Carles E. Van Engen, and Jean Van Engen.

103. *Tongue of a Teacher: Essays in Honor of the Rev. Dr. Timothy Brown,* edited by Trygve Johnson. (2021) 162 pp. ISBN: 978-1-950572-17-5

The Tongue of a Teacher celebrates Tim Brown's forty-five-year ministry in the Reformed Church in America as pastor, teacher, and seminary president. On the occasion of his retirement, as he is declared General Synod Professor of Theology Emeritus, his friends and colleagues present this collection of essays on homiletics, church history, biblical studies, and theology, representing a snapshot of the best seminary scholarship of the time. Edited by Trygve Johnson, director of chapel at Hope College, in Holland, Michigan, the other essays in this festschrift are authored by Karen Bohm Barker, David

Bast, J. Todd Billings, Jon Brown, Gail Ebersole, Fred Johnson, III, Kristen Deede Johnson, Han-luen Kantzer Komline, Jeffrey Munroe, and Leanne Van Dyk.

104. An RCA Reader: Outlining the History of the Reformed Church in America in Seventy-Five Documents, edited by James Hart Brumm. (2022) 568 pp. ISBN: 978-1-950572-23-6

An RCA Reader is a welcome addition for teaching the history of the Reformed Church in America (RCA) in college and seminary classes. A sourcebook of seventy-four documents from the earliest years of the RCA in the 1600s to the present. This volume is not just for the classroom but will be a welcome addition to the libraries of all history lovers. The document covers the colonial period, including the Leisler Rebellion, New Netherlands' settlement, and the coetus-conferentie controversy: the early American period including the True Dutch Reformed Church, institution building, and slavery and slaveholding; the mission efforts of the RCA around the world; the 19th-century immigration and the establishment of the Christian Reformed Church and Hope College; the rise of denominationalism in the RCA; the growth of social justice issues including the Black Manifesto, ecumenism, women's ordination, and denominational identity.

Each section includes a practical contextual analysis to place the documents in their historical context and suggestions for further reading. This is not a volume that needs to be read from cover to cover; it will provide helpful insights into the significant issues the RCA was involved in over nearly four centuries of its life and ministry.

SCRIPTURE INDEX

Colossians. 2:15, 110
Ecclesiastes 3:14-15, 101
Ephesians. 4:7, 99
Ephesians 4:7-13, 109
Ephesians. 4:11, 103
Ephesians. 6:12, 110
Exodus 2:24, 2
Exodus 24, 4, 5
Genesis 1, 4
Genesis 8:1, 1
Genesis 9:15, 2
Genesis 19:29, 1
Genesis 30:25, 1

Joshua 4: 4-7, 151
Joshua 4:4-7, 170
Judges, 7–8
1 Kings, book of, , 7–8
2 Kings, book of, 7–8
2 Kings☐ 2:2-15, 111
2 Kings 20:20, 7
Matthew 13:31–32, 9–20
Nehemiah 8, 5
Revelation 2:17, 31
Romans 8:38, 110
2 Timothy 2:15, 31

SUBJECT INDEX

A

Aartsen, Douglas Van, note about Russell Gasero, 173
Alexander, David, note about Russell Gasero, 171
archives, and the Holy Spirit, 6-7; community nature of, 8; definition of, ix-x; growth of the, 153-57; purpose of, 69; start of formal program, x; theology for, 1-8

B

Babb, Bernita, 168, 170
Bayard, Nicholas, 88
Beardslee, Frances, 162, 163
Beardslee, Jr., John Walter, 74
Beardslee III, John W., 154
Bechtel, Carol, 168
Beemsterboer, Erie, 21
Beemsterboer, Stef, 21
Bellomont, Earl of. *See* Coote, Richard.
Benjamin Alicea-Lugo, note about Russell Gasero, 171
Bethany church. *See* New York, NY. Bethany Reformed Church.
Bevier, Ann DeWitt, 47; bio sketch of, 54-55; urging investigation into Murphy, 50-52
Bevier, Philip, 54
Bi-Level-Multi-Site Curriculum, 161

Board of Domestic Missions, 157
Board of Foreign Missions, 157
Board of Theological Education, 161
Book of Church Order, a complete revision of the constitution, 95
Boyles, Walter, 21
Breda, Treaty of, 87
Brink, Daniel Y., 158
Brinks, Herbert, 44, 45
Brower, Harold, 161
Bruggink, Donald J., 156; chapter by, 33–45; note about, xiii
Brumm, James Hart, 165, 167; chapter by, 85–98; note about, xiii; preface by, ix–xi

C

Calvin, John, 18, 101, 111; and the offices of the church, 101–103
Capitein, Jacobus Elias Joannes, and view on slavery, 62
care, pastoral, and link with discipline, 82–83
Center for Reformed Church Studies, 165–67
Certificate of Fitness for Ministry, 29. *See also* professorial certificates.
Clark, Mary, 166
Coakley, John W., 101, 105, 161, 162, 165; chapter by, 25–32; conversation on the professorate, 106–09; note about, xiv
Coe, Edward B., 92, 97
Coetus-Conferentie schism, 93

Collegiate church. *See* New York, NY. Collegiate church.
Community Development Corporation, 13
Cone, James, 111
Cooperative Colonial Origins Project. See DAHC.
Coote, Richard, 90
Cornbury, Lord, 92
Corwin, Charles, 49
Cox, Jane, mother of James Murphy, 51
Crosby, Jane Murray Livingston, 26
Curtenius, Anthonius, 138

D

DAHC, beginning of, 43–45; founding of, 34; history of, 33–45
de Koster, Lester, 43, 44
Demarest, David D., 73
Demarest, William H. S., 75, 95
Design Ideas, 14
deVelder, Joyce Borgman, 159, 168
DeVries, Laura, 14
Dina's Dwellings, 21; origin of, 13–15; *See also* Town Clock Community Development Corporation.
discipline, and link with pastoral care, 82–83
divorce, and remarriage, 120–25; CAC paper on, 126–27; in the Christian Reformed Church, 122–23; in the RCA, 113–33; law, reform in the RCA, 117–19; pastoral attitude toward, 129–30; preventing using

discipline and education, 119–26; preventing, using the law, 116–19; responding to, with realism and grace, 126–30; similarity to homosexuality issue in the RCA, 114–15; TC report on, 127–29
documents, keeping and reading historical, 85–98; written, and faithfulness, 3
Doeschot, Phil and Stephanie, note about Russell Gasero, 172
Doll, George, 142
Dongan, Thomas, 87, 88
Dordrecht. See Dort.
Doremus, Sara, 170
Dort, Articles of, committee on, 93–94
Dort, Church Order of, 71–72
Dutch American Historical Commission. See DAHC.
Dutch Cousins of Kentucky, note about Russell Gasero, 172
Dutch to English language, 135–50; in Albany, 140–41; in Brooklyn, 142–43; in communities, 148–50; in Kingston, 142; in New Jersey, 138–40, 143–44; in record keeping, 147–48; in worship, 145–48

E

Ecclesiastical Office and Ministry, Committee on, 79–81
Eerdmans, Sr., William B., 35, 37, 38, 40

Elijah's Promise, 11
Eltinge, William, 143
Estes, Elizabeth Colmant, 168
Explanatory Articles of 1782, 71–72, 93

F

Feket, Julius, 19
Fillette, Barbara, 165
Fletcher, Benjamin, 88, 90
Foering, Christian Frederick, 140
Froeligh, Solomon, 139
future, and God's time, 2

G

Gasero, Carol, 153
Gasero, Maria, xxi; dedication to, v
Gasero, Matthew, xi, 167
Gasero, Russell, biography of, xix–xxi; career of, 152–56
Gasero, Virginia, 153
Genesis, as core archive, 4
Gnade Fellowship, 163–64
Gnade, Hazel B., 164
Gnade, Jerry, 164
Gnade, Ken, 164
Goetschius, John Henry, 135–36
Gosman, John, 142
Granberg-Michaelson, Wesley, 14

H

Hageman, Howard, ix
Hands, Hearts, and Voices: Women Who Followed God's Call, 160, 162
Hardenbergh, Jacob Rutsen, 138, 140
Hardenbergh, John J., 50

Harris, Wendy, 63
Heemstra, J.F., 120
Historical Series of the Reformed Church in America, 156; work by women, 160
history, engagement in by God, 1–2
homosexuality, issue of, in the RCA, 114; similarity to divorce issue in the RCA, 114–15
House, Renée S., 162; chapter by, 47–67; note about, xiv
How, Samuel, 19
Hyma, Albert, 35, 36, 40

I

Interfaith Dialogue Center, 10
Ippel, Henry, 44

J

Jackson, Anna M., 168, 169
Jackson, Karen, 168
Jackson, Wilhelmus, 138
James Murphy, life of, 47–67
Jamison, David, 53
Janssen, Allan J., 81, 83, 101
Japinga, Lynn, 168; chapter by, 113–33; note about, xiv
Johnson, Elizabeth, 168
Johnson, John, 150
Johnston, David, 51, 63; owner of Jane Cox and James Murphy, 52–54
Johnston, Elizabeth Jamison, 53
Johnston, John, 51, 53
Johnston, Jr., John, 53
Johnston, Magdalen Walton, 53
Justin Martyr, First Apology of, 6

K

Kansfield, Mary L., chapter by, 151–70; note about, xiv
Kansfield, Norman J., 101, 105, 152, 155
Kennedy, Cornelia B.("Nella"), note about Russell Gasero, 172
Kennedy, Earl Wm.("Bill"), note about Russell Gasero, 172
Kennedy, John F., 95
Kramer-Mills, Hartmut, chapter by, 9–20; note about, xiv
Kramer-Mills, Susan, 15
Kruhly Architects, 13

L

Laidlie, Archibald, and preaching in English, 136
Lansing, Abram, 149
Law of God first written, 3–4
Leonard, Carolyn, note about Russell Gasero, 173
Lessing, G.E., 10
Letters to Hazel, 157, 163, 164
LGBTQ+ people. See homosexuality.
Linn, William, 97, 141
literacy, relation of to worship, 5–6
Livingston, Henrietta Ulrica, 26
Livingston, John Henry, 94, 97, 99, 100, 105; papers of, 25–26
Lubbers, Irwin, 35, 38

M

Marcus, Beth, 158, 160, 170
Mast, Gregg, 100, 101
May, John R., 44

Subject Index 201

McCreary, Micah L., chapter by, 99–111; note about, xiv
Meeter, Daniel, chapter by, 1–8; note about, xiv
membership, ecclesial, of Reformed church ministers, 69–84; local church, how it happens, 76; local church, what it means, 76; nature of, 81–83
membership of minister, 1916 constitutional revision on, 75–76; 1958-59 constitutional revision on, 77; 1980 theology report on, 78–79; Cascades, classis of, 1978 overture on, 77–79; ecclesiastical office and ministry report on, 79–81; Grand River, classis of, 1906 overture on, 73–75
Meyer, Hermanus, 105
Michaelius, Jonas, ix, 86
Michigan Historical Commission, 37
Milledoler, Phillip, 97
Miller, Rabbi Bennett, 10
minister, 1916 constitutional revision on membership, 75–76; 1958-59 consitutional revision on membership, 77; 1980 theology report on membership, 78–79; accountability of, 70; as members of churches, 73–81; Cascades, classis of, 1978 overture on membership, 77–79; early church membership of, 71–73; ecclesiastical office and ministry report on membership, 79–81; Grand River, classis of, 1906 overture on membership, 73–75; serving in non-ecclesiastical settings, 79–81
Ministerial Formation Coordinating Agency, 28
Min, Lynn, 167, 168
missionary correspondence and the New Testament, 6–7
Mosterman, Andrea, 64
Mouw, Dirk, chapter by, 135–50; note about, xv
Murphy, James, and affects of slavery, 52; case against based on parentage, 50–52; early life of, 48–50; elected president of synod, 50; manumission of, 53; ownership of slaves, 65; publication of *The Bible and Geology Consistent*, 50; *The Memorial* seeking discipline for, 47, 56–61; unfolding of case against, 55–61
mustard seed, 20

N

Nathan the Wise, 10
National Department of Women's Work, 158
National Women's Assembly. first at Buck Hill Falls, PA, 160
Na, Young, 168
Netherland Information Service, 37
Netherlands Museum, 37
New Brunsick, NJ, Suydam Street Reformed Church, 15

New Brunswick, NJ, Anshe Emeth Memorial Temple, 10, 16
New Brunswick, NJ, First Reformed, Community Development Corporation, 13–14; description of, 9–11. *See also* Town Clock Community Development Corporation.
New Jersey Historic Trust, 11, 21
New Netherland. See New York, NY.
New Testament as an archive, 6–7
New York Manumission Society, 63
New York, NY. Bethany Reformed Church conflict with Collegiate church, 85–86
New York, NY. Collegiate church, archives, 25–26; charter granted to, 89–91; conflict with Bethany, 85–86; conflict with synod over charter and elections, 95–97; origins of, 86–88
New York, NY. Trinity Church, charter granted to, 89
New York School of Printing, 153
"Nine Partners", 53
Notes on the Constitution, 95

O
omniscience of God, 1–2
Open Doors, Open Mind Program, 10
Ostrander, Elisha, 50

P
Pater-Ennis, Pamela, 168
Patterns and Portraits, 162
Peace Islands Institute, 10, 16
Peale, Norman Vincent, 95
Peninsular Club, 35
Pickman, Arnold, 63
Pierce, Monica Schaap, 167
Pierce, Stephen D., foreword by, xix; note about, xv
Pieters, Albertus, 126; on divorce and biblical interpretation, 122–23
"Plan of Union", 93, 105
privilege and power in society, 66–67
Proctor, Cathy, xi
professorate, founding of in RCA, 105
professorial certificates, 25–32. *See also* Tesitmories, Form for.
Professor, General Synod, accountability of, 70 office of, in the RCA, 99–111; role of, 100
Professors Task Force, General Synod, 105–109

R
Ratmeyer, Roland, note about Russell Gasero, 173
Ratmeyer, Una, 160
RCA Women's Project, 163
record, reading it as worship, 5–6
Reese, Jennifer, 167
Reformed Church Women, 158
Reformed Church Women's Ministries, 158, 165–66
Reid, Claudette, 166
remembrance and hope, 8
remembrance, nature of human, 2–3
resurrection and God's remembering, 2

Subject Index   203

Riggs, Arad M., 96-97
Rindge, Warren L., 37
Rissseeuw, P. J., 38
Roberts, Emma, 154
Robert Wood Johnson University Hospital Community Health Promotion Program, 11
Romeyn, John, 150
Romeyn, Thomas, 140

S

Scholte, Hendrikus, homestead of, 38
Schoonmaker, Henricus, 142-143
Schoonmaker, Jacob, 135
Schoonmaker, Martinus, 142
Schuyler, Brant, 88
Scudder, Ida, 167
Sealy, Patricia, 168
Second Vatican Council, 152
Selens, Henricus, 88, 91, 92, 97
Sharpe, George, 148
slavery, and church membership, 63-64; and racist attitudes in the church, 64-65; and the case of James Murphy, 47-67; in New York, overview of, 61-65; view of in Dutch church, 62
Spoelhof, William, 41
sponsors, xvii-xviii
Standing Seminar on RCA History, 160-63
Stedge, Joyce, 159, 170
Stryker, Elsie, 154
subscription pledges, and decision making, 139-40
Sykman, Gordon, 44

T

Ten Eyck, Conrad, 72
ten Harmsel, Larry, 37
ten Zythoff, Gerrit, 41-42, 44, 45
TerLouw, John, 120
Tesschenmaecker, Petrus, 137
Testa, Elizabeth, 167, 168
Testimonies, Form for, 26-28; transition to professorial certificate, 28
testimoniorum formula, 29-30; translation of, 30-32
Theological Education Agency, 28, 161
Torah, expansion of covenant, 4
Town Clock Community Development Corporation, 13-14
Transformed and Transforming, 167
Travelers' Club, 162
Tutu, Desmond, 19

V

Van Cortlandt, Jacob, 88
Van Cortlandt, Stephanus, 88
Vander Meer, Albert, note about Russell Gasero, 173
VanEyl, Christina, 158
VanHeest, Eloise, 160
van Maastricht, Mathew J., chapter by, 69-84; note about, xv
Van Pelt, Peter, 150
Van Raalte, Dick, 36
Van Raalte homestead, 35-36; architectural appraisal of, 37-38; demolition of, 41; designated A. C. Van Raalte Campus, 40; deterioration of, 37-39

Van Raalte papers, 36-37; access to by ten Zythoff, 42; donation of to Calvin College, 41;
Van Raalte Room, at Eerdmans offices, 40
Venezia, Jeff, 14

W

Waanders, David, 23
Waldorf, Arlene Walters, 159
Walker, Diana Paulsen, 158
Washington, George, 150
Wellwood, Anita, 158
Westbrook, Derrick, 50, 55
Westbrook, Rachel Hoornbeck, 47, 55; urging investigation into Murphy, 50-52
Westerlo, Eilardus, 140-41
Westfield Architects, 12
Westfield, Margaret, 12
White, Robert, 161
Whittaker, Damaris, 168
Wichers, Willard C., 37, 43, 44
William B. Eerdmans Publishing Company, 34
William III, 89
William of Orange, 89
Williams, Irma, 168
Witherington, Ben, 17, 20
Woman's Board of Foreign Missions, 157
women, at 1969 General Synod, 159; commission for, 166; commission for, establishment of, 159; office for, 166; ordination of, 159; transition of, in groups, 156-59
Women, Ecumenical Decade: Churches in Solidarity with, 159-60
Women's Board of Domestic Missions, 157
women's transformation and leadership, coordinator for, 167; ministries, coordinator for, 166; stories, saving, 151-70; triennial, last, 169
Women's Stories Day, 167-169
Woods, Lynn, 52
Woodson, Clara, 167